Smuggler's
End

Smuggler's
End

The **Life** and
Death of
Barry Seal

Del Hahn

Edited by Tom Aswell

PELICAN PUBLISHING COMPANY
Gretna 2016

The word "Pelican" and the depiction of a pelican are
trademarks of Pelican Publishing Company, Inc., and are
registered in the U.S. Patent and Trademark Office.

ISBN: 9781455621002
E-book ISBN: 9781455621019

Photo credit Musemeche/Flashpix

Printed in the United States of America
Published by Pelican Publishing Company, Inc.
1000 Burmaster Street, Gretna, Louisiana 70053

Contents

Introduction

*The world is made up for the most part of fools and
knaves, both irreconcilable foes to truth.*

The Dramatic Works
George Villiers,
Second Duke of Buckingham

President Ronald Reagan declared war on drugs in 1982 and federal drug task forces began to spring up all over the country. I was the FBI agent assigned to the task force that mobilized in February 1983, in Baton Rouge, the home of the Middle District of Louisiana. Baton Rouge was also home for Adler Berriman Seal, one of the largest cocaine smugglers in the US.

I'm a Clevelander — born there in 1934 and grew up in what was once billed as "the best location in the nation." My crowd didn't smoke marijuana. We didn't huff, shoot-up, or snort. The only pills we took were aspirin. Cocaine was a word I heard in Cole Porter's song, "I Get a Kick Out of You."

WW II started and I was seven. My mom went to work building electric motors for the Navy. My dad was a photoengraver employed by the morning paper, the *Plain Dealer*. He was too old to be drafted. I read Ernie Pyle's stories from the front. Blue Star flags hung in the windows of many houses in my neighborhood. We knew that meant a member of the family was in the war. Some homes displayed Gold Star flags. That meant someone was killed in action. We were quiet and respectful when we walked past.

I graduated from Cleveland Heights High in 1952. The Korean War was on. I had friends in the fight. That fall I started my freshman year at Ohio University — the Bobcats, not the Buckeyes. I made my grades but I was bored.

On June 25, 1953, I enlisted in the US Marine Corps. I was

nineteen, with a year of Army ROTC under my belt. I was itching to get to Korea to get in the fighting. Never gave a thought to losing an arm or leg — or worse.

On April 1, 1954 I walked ashore at Inchon. I was in the Land of the Morning Calm but too late. The armistice was signed July 25, 1953. I was a scout observer/intelligence clerk in the S-2 Section, 3rd Battalion, 1st Marines.

We were in positions on the DMZ. There was no shooting but we carried our M-1 rifles and two clips of ammo wherever we went. From time to time a Condition Red would signal that North Koreans were running a column of tanks toward the DMZ. We'd grab our flak jackets and head for our fighting positions.

Korea was good duty. Few inspections, two cases of beer a week, a waterproof tent, Coleman lanterns, and a swim in the Imjin River during the summer. In the winter, Mickey Mouse boots and fleece lined parkas.

The 1st Marine Division was pulled out of Korea in April 1955 and I returned to Camp Pendleton. I was a corporal, still with the Thundering Third.

I was discharged in September 1956 and went back to Ohio U on the GI Bill. I met Carolyn Ann Schoulin in 1958. She was a junior at Bowling Green State University. We got engaged and set the wedding date for June 1959.

In January 1959, I applied to the CIA. I had a clandestine meeting — I thought — in a hotel in Lakewood, Ohio. Turned out the CIA guy was from Lakewood and it was a chance to visit his parents.

The CIA offered me a job as intelligence analyst, Grade 5, $4,040 a year. Carolyn and I talked it over and decided we did not want to move to Washington, DC. We married. I had a job as a parts expediter at the Euclid Division of General Motors — we built those huge lime-green dump trucks and bulldozers.

I left General Motors and went with the IRS as revenue officer. We moved to Toledo, Ohio where I collected delinquent taxes for three-and-a-half years while attending Toledo University Law School nights. I wanted to be an FBI agent.

I met an FBI agent in the law school and learned I didn't have to have a law degree. I had twenty-nine law school credit hours when I applied to the FBI.

In February 1963, I received a letter from J. Edgar Hoover. I was appointed a special agent and told to report to FBI headquarters — if I still wanted the job. He had to be kidding.

I was one of twenty-two white males in New Agent Class 7. On February 25, 1963 we raised our hands and swore to uphold the constitution of the United States. Carolyn sold our home. She joined me in Alexandria, Virginia with Jannean, our two-year-old daughter, and our Boxer dog.

My first office was Jacksonville, Florida. We got there in May 1963 and stayed eighteen months. Our son, David, was born in Jacksonville. I worked on a general criminal squad but most of our work was on a string of bombings of railroad trains. The Florida East Coast Railroad was on strike and the union got very angry and started dynamiting trains.

Our next move was to New Orleans. I was on a criminal squad for five years. Then I went to the security squad where we worked mostly on civil rights complaints, the Ku Klux Klan, Black Panthers, Cointel and Students for a Democratic Society (SDS).

In 1972 I asked to be transferred to Baton Rouge RA, in FBI-speak, a resident agency. When you're in an RA you work everything. And I did — including about a month on Brilab, involving bribery, labor officials and public officials.

I loved being an FBI agent. I had been at it for twenty years when the war on drugs was launched. I was assigned to the Baton Rouge drug task force.

I accepted my new assignment and eagerly, though somewhat naively, entered the war on drugs. I had no experience in drug investigations and was not knowledgeable of the statutes. I couldn't pronounce the names of most of the drugs I was supposed to be at war against.

I thought "keys" were for doors. I had never encountered marijuana — at least not that I was aware of. I didn't know what it smelled like. I heard it looked like oregano.

My experience with drug investigations was limited to what I heard from four friends, Jack Compton, Roger Coston, Jim Hunter and Jim Bland. In 1964 they staffed the New Orleans office of what was then the Federal Bureau of Narcotics. I had heard some of their war stories.

I saw my first cocaine in New Orleans in 1967. Two plastic bags of white powder about the size of bricks were found during the search of the apartment of a bank robbery suspect. I was busy looking for the loot and a sawed-off shotgun. I wasn't that interested in the cocaine—although everyone else was excited about the find.

I spent the last two years of my career working on this drug task force.

Our target from day one was Barry Seal.

I retired February 25, 1985. A year later, almost to the day, Seal was murdered.

The congressional hearings that followed in the wake of the Iran-Contra affair generated a lot of headlines. The CIA's Contra resupply effort was accused of being funded by profits from drug trafficking. Barry Seal's name began to be tossed around, mostly by people who didn't know anything about him or his career as a convicted drug smuggler-turned-DEA informant.

Jim Dahl, an investigator for the House Subcommittee on Crime, called me in 1988. He was trying to establish a connection between Barry Seal and future president Bill Clinton, and the CIA's Contra resupply operations. Dahl wanted to know if our Baton Rouge task force investigation had uncovered any evidence of such a connection.

Around this same time Bill McCoy, a private investigator working for the Christic Institute, contacted me looking for the same information. He was trying to corroborate information from a pilot named Billy Joe Tolliver.

I'd never heard of Tolliver. I told McCoy and Dahl that we obtained no evidence of any connection between Seal and an alleged CIA drugs-up-guns-down operation to fund the Contras. Many believed the CIA was shipping arms and ammunition to the Contras in Nicaragua and bringing cocaine back to the US. The hub was rumored to be at the Mena airport in rural west Arkansas. It's surrounded by the Ouachita National Forest, closer to Texas than Hot Springs or Little Rock.

In 1991 Dennis Hopper starred in *Doublecrossed*, a movie that portrayed Barry Seal as a kind of soldier-of-fortune who was victimized by the government. The public got a distorted view of a legitimate criminal investigation and Seal's well-deserved prosecution.

I started to write a book to set the record straight. I wasn't really motivated and only worked on it intermittently.

Author John Cummings came to Baton Rouge while he was working on his book about Seal. When we met on December 5,

1993, I answered his questions and we discussed the investigation and what I knew about Seal. I let him borrow a very detailed Chronology of Events that I had written in anticipation of a book or maybe a movie script. Cummings told me he had an "informant" that knew some damaging things about the FBI agent in Arkansas who worked the Seal case. He said he wasn't going to name him in his book to prevent a defamation suit but it would not be difficult to figure out who he was. I was more than skeptical.

When *Compromised: Clinton, Bush and the CIA* was published in 1994, I was astounded. The CIA was supposed to be involved in drug trafficking. Gun-running in Mena, Arkansas and Seal, Bill Clinton and Oliver North were implicated. The source of this information was Terry Kent Reed, who was Cummings's informant and co-author.

I think Terry Reed is an intelligent and clever guy with a "near-photographic memory." Based on everything I knew about Barry Seal and the research and interviews I did for this book, I don't believe Reed ever met Barry Seal or Oliver North. I believe he did some research and latched onto public information, half-truths and rumors about Seal and Mena. And then he spun it all into a self-serving but largely fictional story.

Daniel Hopsicker, a producer, writer, investigator, and promoter from Venice, Florida, contacted me in 1997. He was writing a book about Barry Seal and wanted to talk with me. We met and he asked me to help with his book. I agreed and interviewed Eddie Duffard, Barry's flight instructor, and sent the interview to Hopsicker. After several meetings it was obvious that Hopsicker wasn't interested in telling Barry's true story. I ended my dealings with him and said I'd continue working on my own book.

He told me his book would come out long before mine would. On that score he was right. He self-published *Barry and the Boys* in 2001 and included some of my interview with Duffard. I found his book to be full of flawed logic, innuendos and made-up facts.

William Bottoms was Seal's former brother-in-law and his principal drug pilot from June 1980 until early 1984. In 1997 I found him on the Internet refuting the myths and lies about Barry Seal. I knew he was the guy who flew Seal's cocaine. We began exchanging e-mail. We both learned some things about Seal that we hadn't known. We both wanted the truth to be told. He helped me tell it.

I live in Oak Hills in south Baton Rouge near where Barry Seal lived. On April 17, 1985, I saw him in his Cadillac as he was about to pull away from a convenience store located near our homes. He saw me and waved me down. I had nothing to lose so I stopped.

We parked and got out of our cars and started talking. He began by asking me if I was following him. I wasn't sure if he was serious. I had been retired from the FBI for almost two months.

I wasn't following him and I told him so. I thought I ought to yank his chain a little so I asked him if he was still using pay phones.

He laughed then asked what pay phones we had tapped.

I told him I wouldn't discuss any aspects of our investigation.

It wasn't any secret, he said. "Lewis" [Unglesby] told him we did. He said he had no hard feelings and knew I was doing my job.

Seal asked what kind of planes we used to tail him.

Again, I told him I wouldn't discuss the investigation.

He said he knew we used a Cessna because he had once spotted one flying low and circling his subdivision.

I asked him if he had waved a bath towel at the plane.

He said he sure did. He asked, "Was that you up there?"

I told him yes. He asked where I had learned to fly.

I told him I wasn't flying the plane—I was a passenger.

He said the government was wasting money trying to stop drug smuggling. He said it couldn't be done while it was so profitable. The way to decrease profitability was to start jailing the users— which would lower the demand. Another way was to shoot down the drug smuggling planes. Seal said he had told Congress the same thing. He said he would bet that more people died from throat cancer from cigarettes than from cocaine overdoses.

He asked me what I was doing.

When I told him I was a private investigator, he asked for one of my business cards. "You never know, I might want to hire you."

I laughed and told him I doubted that day would ever come.

I gave him a business card and then asked him if he was retired.

"Of course," he answered. He said he had to go and stuck out his hand and we shook. He told me to take care of myself.

I told him to do the same.

Barry could be very likeable. We had a cordial conversation.

Barry Seal moved his smuggling planes from the Cajun community of Opelousas, Louisiana to the little-known Mena Intermountain Airport in rural, mountainous west Arkansas in early 1982. At that time the town of Mena had a population of about 5,200 — about 96 percent white. Some town notables were Herbert A. Littleton, winner of the Congressional Medal of Honor for actions during the Korean War, Mike Simpson, a defensive back for the San Francisco 49ers and Dennis Montgomery. A software designer, Montgomery conned the government out of $20 million in contracts for software he claimed, among other things, could spot terrorist plots hidden in the broadcasts of Al Jazeera and detect noise from hostile submarines.

Mena served as the air base for the planes Seal used to smuggle cocaine and not as a transshipment point for cocaine. His pilot William Bottoms continued to airdrop cocaine at various rural locations in the vicinity of Baton Rouge, the capital city on the Mississippi River and Seal's hometown.

The CIA had a presence at the Mena airport. I found no credible evidence that Seal was involved or that he had ever been an "asset" or an employee of the CIA.

I am not a disinformation specialist sponsored by the CIA — as some are certain to believe. It's too late for that. And, if I were, this book would have been published years ago.

What I have written is based on facts, not rumors, untruths and wishful thinking.

— Del Hahn, October 2015
Baton Rouge

Acknowledgments

Many thanks to my task force pals, Jerry Bize, Charlie Bremer, our first-rate lawyer, Brad Myers and the late Jerry Phipps who replaced me on the task force when I retired.

I'm grateful to Ed Grimsley, the FBI senior supervisory resident agent in Baton Rouge for assigning me to the task force and to our special agent in charge Ed Pistey for his support and sense of humor.

Thanks to the Special Operations Group (SOG) team of Bob Tucker, John Fleming, Dale Farmer, Joe Slaughter, Ed Lee, Bill Thees, Bob Dunbar and Jerry Smolinski for their handling of the challenging though sometimes boring surveillances. Most of them are retired but they could remember. I wish I could remember the names of the many DEA agents and FBI agents who worked the Title III wiretap, for they certainly deserve thanks. Lloyd East needs special recognition for keeping the lid on things at the "plant" which allowed all of us to survive Operation Coinroll.

Thanks to FBI agent Freddie Cleveland who brought me up to date on the case he worked against Fred Compton and others. Thanks to Jeff Santini and Cliff Cormier, who made the undercover buy from William Earle, Sr. Thanks to FBI Investigative Assistant Rebecca Cossey for her help. Thanks to Dick Gustafson, Stan Howard and Butch Milan who were willing to jog their memories.

I am especially appreciative of Rut Whittington's help. The "Colonel," who I've known for 40 years, read the manuscript for me. Thanks to attorney Tommy Benton, Army Lt. Col. John W. McInnis, (Retired), Dr. Philip Smith and to the late Eddie Duffard.

Sadly, another lawyer who helped me tell the story is no longer with us. Al Winters, "The Dancing Bear," died in June 2013. Thanks to Arkansas Judge J. Michael Fitzhugh and former Little Rock FBI supervisor Ron Kelly for their help.

Retired FBI agents Buzz Barlow, O. T. Eubank, Oliver "Buck" Revell, Francis "Bud" Mullin, Rudy Ferguson, Jack Lawn, Anne E. Buttimer, and Tom Ross were all supportive and assisted me in this effort. Thanks to Jim B. Brown and the late Clint Hebert, both retired from the US Marshals Service, and to Bob Seville, former chief US probation officer for the Middle District of Louisiana, now retired.

I'm particularly appreciative of Russell Welch who spent a lot of time searching his records and answering my e-mail. Thanks to Bill Duncan for doing the same. Reporter Richard Behar was extremely helpful and provided me with a wealth of information from Reed's lawsuit against him and *Time* magazine.

Red Hall died in December 2013—I want to acknowledge his willingness to talk with me and to answer my questions. Thanks to attorney Nicole Seligman for taking my phone call and encouraging me to send my questions to her client.

And thank you Colonel Oliver North for answering those "powder puff" questions.

Thanks to attorney Thomas R. Spencer, Jr., who represented Major General John Singlaub in the Christic Institute suit and gave me a copy of Dr. Susan Hauck's book. Thanks to Scott Wheeler for reading the manuscript, giving me encouragement and once putting me on the airways.

Federal Judge James L. King was kind enough to spend considerable time on the phone with me and I want to express my thanks.

Investigative journalist Mara Leveritt deserves credit. Because of her tenacity, the FBI responded to her Freedom of Information (FOIA) request and released documents from the Barry Seal investigative file. She posted them on her Web site for anyone to use. Thanks to Pam Rotella who was kind enough to search her inventory of Mena airport photographs.

The University of Arkansas, University Libraries, Special Collections Division has much of the material generated by the Arkansas Committee during their investigation of Mena. Anne Prichard of the Research Department was very helpful in providing the documents I requested from Special Collections.

Thanks to Matt Ehling of Public Record Media who provided me with background information given to him by Gene Wheaton. I am appreciative of the efforts of Projects Editor Sonny Albarado, of the *Arkansas Democrat-Gazette* and Head Librarian Michelle Goad, in finding the photo of Seal's C-123. I'm very appreciative of the efforts of Alyson Hoge, deputy managing editor of the *Arkansas Democrat-Gazette* in making the C-123 photo available.

I am grateful for the efforts of my agent and editor Tom Aswell. Without his interest in the story of Barry Seal, I wouldn't be thanking anyone.

Once my book was accepted for publication, Pelican Publishing assigned the task of final editing to Mark Mathes. He did a masterful job and never chastised me for a constant flow of my stets and revisions.

This was a family project. My son, David, Chairman of the Department of Mechanical Aerospace Engineering at the University of Florida, encouraged me but reminded me that he published first with *Heat Introduction*. His wife, Allison, spent hours on the phone editing. My daughter, Jannean, and her husband, Kevin, saw to it that I got regular breaks from the computer and went to the casino.

Finally, thank you Carolyn, my soul mate. Your patience during my eruptions, your support and encouragement in the face of rejection slips too numerous to count kept me going for years. Your insistence that we meet every afternoon for happy hour enabled me to complete the project. You helped immeasurably.

Barry Seal. Photo by the Advocate, *Oct. 16, 2015, Capital City Press/Georges Media Group, Baton Rouge, LA. Used with permission.*

ഇൽ

Chapter 1

Friendly Skies

Shortly after midnight on Thanksgiving in 1982, a few residents of the tiny community of Port Vincent, Louisiana, were roused from their sleep by the sound of engines from a low-flying aircraft. No one bothered to get up and look because there was a private landing strip nearby and a plane at night wasn't unusual.

Landing lights flared. A twin-engine Piper Navajo skimmed over the trees, dipped down and touched gently onto the grass of the three thousand-foot landing strip. The plane slowed and braked to a halt near the end of the runway as a Ford pickup, headlights ablaze, sped up to the plane and stopped. Rossi, the young driver, trotted toward the plane whose engines were still idling.

The cargo hatch opened. The pilot jumped down, dressed in a khaki flight suit. At two hundred and forty pounds and standing only five feet nine inches, Barry Seal was porky-looking. The sweat-stained flight suit was stretched to its limits around his pear-shaped body.

"Stay clear of those props," he growled at Rossi.

Co-pilot Emile Harold Camp, Jr., remained aboard and began to shove military-style duffel bags through the open hatch. Seal watched and glanced nervously at his wristwatch, as Rossi grabbed the bags and slung them into the back of the pickup. When the last of six duffel bags was loaded Rossi pulled a tarp over the cargo. Seal shot him a thumbs-up, climbed into the plane and pulled the cargo hatch shut as Rossi carefully backed the pickup away from the plane until it was clear.

The twin engines accelerated to a roar and the plane turned and began to roll. The pickup was speeding down the gravel road that ran parallel to the landing strip just as the Navajo was clearing the trees at the end of the strip. The plane had been on the ground less than six minutes.

Twenty minutes later the Navajo landed at Baton Rouge

Metropolitan Airport, also known as Ryan Field when P-47 fighter pilots trained there in World War II. As the lone airport employee refueled the plane, Seal was talking on a pay phone. He trusted coin phones when he was doing business. By the time he hung up, refueling was completed. He paid the attendant from a wad of bills and climbed into the cockpit. The plane lifted off at approximately the same time Rossi was pulling the pickup into the parking lot of the Holiday Inn on Siegen Lane in southeast Baton Rouge.

Rossi drove the pickup to the rear of the hotel and stopped behind a midnight-blue Mercury Grand Marquis four-door bearing Florida license plates. He got out, glanced around then walked quickly to the front of the parked car. He bent down and retrieved a set of keys from the top of the left front tire, then unlocked the trunk lid. He tossed two duffel bags into the trunk and slammed the lid. He returned the keys to the top of the left front tire, climbed in the pickup and drove away.

Ten minutes later Rossi pulled into the parking lot of Our Lady of the Lake Hospital on Essen Lane. He cruised slowly among the rows of cars until he came to a second midnight-blue Mercury Grand Marquis. Like the first Marquis, this one had a Florida plate. Following the same routine at the Holiday Inn, Rossi tossed two duffel bags into the trunk, slammed the lid shut and placed the keys on top of the left front tire.

Rossi pulled out of the hospital parking lot and drove about three miles to the parking lot of the Sheraton Hotel. Again, he cruised the lot until he spotted a third midnight-blue Grand Marquis—also bearing a Florida plate. He tossed the remaining two duffel bags into the trunk of the vehicle, closed the lid and returned the keys to the top of the left front tire. Rossi stopped at a nearby gas station pay phone where called the three drivers who were awaiting word. He didn't know who they were so he addressed them by their code numbers. The cars were ready. After the last call, Rossi drove away.

The year 1982 was before mobile phones. Maybe some car phones—and this crew was not likely to use them anyway.

Usually Seal's cocaine was airdropped. When an airdrop was scheduled, Rossi and a guy who went by the name of "Ace" would recover the goods. Seal would send them to some remote location in the Atchafalaya Basin swamp, populated by mosquitos, snakes, and gators west of Baton Rouge. Sometimes it would be a dirt road in the middle of a sugar cane field near New Roads west of the Mississippi.

Wherever Seal sent them, the routine was the same. They would wait for the sound of the plane. Then Ace would use the radio provided by Seal to contact the pilot, and give him the "all clear."

After pilot Billy Bottoms acknowledged, they would switch on a low density light to mark their position. They had used a strobe light but Bottoms didn't like it because it was too conspicuous. Bottoms would spot the light and then fly low and slow over them and drop the duffel bags. Rossi didn't know a lot about flying but he had heard Seal talk about the Very Low Frequency (VLF) and GPS navigation systems Bottoms used to arrive at the designated drop.

He and Ace would haul the bags to a prearranged location where they were picked up by a helicopter flown by a pilot named Ramie. He would fly to another location where the bags were loaded into the three identical Mercury sedans for the trip to Florida.

Rossi didn't like airdrops. He always faced the risk of getting busted. Sometimes there was a screw-up. A couple of months earlier, one duffel bag had been dropped off-target. He and Ace had mucked around in the muddy swamp for two hours among the snakes and mosquitoes looking for the damn cocaine. Luckily, they had found it. They both got a royal ass-chewing from Seal — even though it was the pilot's fault for dropping too early.

Tonight, Seal flew the plane. He said Bottoms refused to fly because he wanted to spend Thanksgiving with his family. Rossi handled the delivery himself. He hoped to get paid something more than the usual $1,000 he usually got for a night's work. He was doing very well for a twenty-four-year-old high school dropout.

Because it was a federal holiday, no DEA or US Customs agents had been spotted snooping around Port Vincent or the airstrip. Seal said the feds were too lazy to work holidays and, as usual, he was right. "GS pukes" Seal called them — GS for government service. The delivery went smoothly. Rossi was glad that he didn't have to go "duck hunting," as Barry said when he called to tell him a load was due and to stand by.

Two hours and fifteen minutes after Seal departed from Baton Rouge, he landed at Mena Intermountain Regional Airport in Mena, Arkansas. Mena is surrounded by the Ouachita National Forest, close to nowhere. He taxied into his hangar adjacent to Rich Mountain Aviation. Seal shut down the engines and climbed out, leaving Camp to drape a blanket over the cockpit controls to conceal the array of elaborate avionics. As Camp tended to his chore, Seal

peeled the strips of black tape that had been used to transform the
"3" in the N numbers into an "8" on the fuselage. When the two
men finished, they pulled shut the large sliding doors and clicked
the padlock.

Mena Intermountain Airport at a Glance

History: The airport began modestly for pilots and hobby flyers
in the 1930s. In 1942, Hartzell Geyer built the first hangar and a
small flying school. The airport gained status in 1946 when the
federal government designated it as an emergency landing strip
for commercial planes. It was approximately 100 miles midway
between Fort Smith and Texarkana. Today, it's a city-owned
general aviation airport on 1,079 acres.
Airport identifier: MEZ
Location: Two miles from Mena, Polk County, Arkansas.
Services: Maintenance, repair and overhaul of small to mid-size
commercial planes. Including: aircraft painting services, engine
repair or rebuilding, airframe repair, upholstery, or avionics repair.
How it's known: The airport's strategic location, albeit rural, has
been popular for aircraft servicing for aviators and smugglers. The
movie *Mena* was being filmed about the Barry Seal story in 2015,
starring Tom Cruise.

Over the next few days Seal's trusted friend, Joseph Nevil
Evans, an FAA-certified aircraft mechanic, would service the
Navajo. It would remain in the hangar until the next mission. Most
importantly, the plane would be concealed from the prying eyes of
Polk County Sheriff A. L. Hadaway, the local GS pukes and Russell
Welch, the Arkansas State Police investigator who was assigned to
the Mena area.

Seal's arrival at Mena had not gone unnoticed. His friend, Fred
Hampton, the owner of Rich Mountain Aviation, had warned him.
Hadaway and Welch had been snooping around the airport—and
his hangar in particular. Hampton said one night when he stepped
out of his hangar he caught FBI agent Tom Ross and an Arkansas
State Police narc dressed in camouflage.

Although Seal didn't know it, a month earlier Sheriff Hadaway
and the Little Rock FBI SWAT team had set up a surveillance at
his hangar. FBI agent Rudy Ferguson, now retired, remembered

the surveillance. He had just arrived in Little Rock without cold weather clothes. Hadaway took him to his home and got him some warm clothing. "It was freezing cold and we hunkered down until about 2 am. Then we heard the hangar doors open and a big King Air was rolled out on to the runway. The sheriff said, 'that's him, that's Seal.' Then the King Air fired up and took off heading south. There wasn't much else we could so we went back to Little Rock."

Seal climbed aboard his plane and barely managed to squeeze his bulk into the left seat. He was dog-tired. Camp, who had slept part of the way back from Colombia, would fly back to Baton Rouge while Seal snoozed. Seal congratulated himself as he prepared for the take-off. He had just logged another successful drug smuggling flight. Three hundred kilos of cocaine were en route to Miami. There the coke would be turned over to the wholesale distributor who was running 500 kilos of cocaine a week through a car dealership front.

Once again Seal had outsmarted the feds and evaded all of their interdiction efforts in the Gulf of Mexico.

By observation and experience, Seal knew when DEA or US Customs planes were in the air. Their pilots liked to talk and they flew predictable patrol routes. He had carefully plotted out several flight paths to confuse their radar. By flying low and slow he blended in with the hundreds of oil drilling platforms and slow-flying service helicopters that were always present in the offshore oil patch. It was a simple strategy that kept his drug flights relatively safe from capture. The Louisiana Gulf Coast was perfect for his needs. He hadn't been caught yet.

In Seal's judgment, the government's recently launched "war on drugs" was a phony war. It was nothing but a joke. He'd often thought if the government really wanted to win the drug war all they had to do was order the US Navy, the Coast Guard and the US Air Force to patrol the coastline and shoot down all suspected smuggling planes. Forget about the *posse comitatus* law. One Sidewinder missile was all it would take to win the war on drugs. Seal knew he wouldn't be up there any more after the first plane-load of dope got shot out of the sky by an F-14 Tomcat.

He had long since rationalized what he was doing. After all, cocaine and marijuana weren't much different than cigarettes and booze. They were consumer products of choice. A hell of a lot of people in the United States drank and smoked. Sure, people died from smoking cigarettes and drinking liquor yet they were readily available—and legal. The government made billions in taxes by permitting them to be sold. He found it hypocritical that the same government that sanctioned cigarettes would outlaw marijuana, which wasn't a hell of lot different than plain old tobacco. As for cocaine, it was like booze and no one was forced to use it. It was a personal choice and none of his business.

Anyway, he figured there were probably more people dying of cirrhosis of the liver than there were dying from cocaine overdoses. Seal did not see himself as a drug dealer because he wasn't pushing the stuff on streets. He merely provided a transportation service that was second to none.

The wholesale price of one kilo of pure cocaine was presently in 1982 around $46,000 on the street in Miami. This made the 300 kilo load he had just delivered worth close to $14 million.

The wholesaler would cut the coke to fifty percent purity, making the load worth about $28 million. And then he would sell it to a distributor.

The distributor usually cut the cocaine to twenty percent purity and sold ounces to the coke retailers at around $2,000 an ounce.

One kilo of fifty percent pure cocaine cut twenty percent yielded 176 ounces worth $352,000.

Do the numbers and it was obvious the Colombian traffickers he hauled for could pay his fees easily.

It was risky business flying the stuff into the United States so Seal was entitled to be paid well for his services. Therefore, the $5,000 per kilo fee he charged to haul cocaine was fair considering the value of the "product," the precarious nature of the work and the expenses involved. Airplanes, vehicles and fuel weren't cheap and he had to pay the pilot, the co-pilot, the ground crew, the drivers and many other expenses.

Seal's problems started with finding people he could trust, covering up the purchase of vast amounts of aviation fuel and moving large amounts of cash. The logistics were mind-boggling and the challenges were far greater than most business operators encounter in a lifetime.

He didn't look at what he was doing as a business but was certainly more exciting than sitting behind a desk pushing paper, and the dough was rolling in. He was forty-two years old and well on his way to becoming a multi-millionaire. Doing what he loved. Flying and taking risks.

Chapter 2
The Natural

Books, blogs, myths, and a movie have ignored or embellished facts about the life of Barry Seal.

His full name was Adler Berriman Seal. Everyone called him Barry. Adler means "eagle" in German — the name fit. At fifteen and still in high school, Seal got his student pilot license.

The late Eddie G. Duffard, his flight instructor, said he was a natural pilot and was so good that he let him solo after only eight hours of instruction. He remembered that Seal's mother came to him several times and begged him not to teach her son to fly because she was afraid of the dangers. Duffard told her that even if he didn't teach him, someone else would. The lessons continued.

Seal's favorite haunt was the old downtown airport in his hometown of Baton Rouge where he would hang around talking to pilots and hoping to bum a plane ride and get some flying time. Seal was a licensed pilot at age sixteen. Several years later he had a commercial pilot license and was checked out to fly helicopters.

Duffard, an expert pilot, thought Seal was wild and didn't have enough sense to be afraid. He was likable but irresponsible, a man who was always operating on the fringes of the law. "Barry was the 'black sheep' of the family and he did what he wanted to do with little regard for the consequences," said Duffard.

He once saw Seal taxiing a plane preparing to take off. The passenger door opened suddenly and he saw that the passenger was trying to get out. "Seal had hold of the kid by the neck and was struggling to keep him in the plane."

Duffard found Seal to be amiable and talkative. He seemed always to be trying to prove something, perhaps to compensate for his five-foot-nine-inch height. Duffard recalled that Seal started a flying business, towing advertising banners across the skies of Baton Rouge. He also flew a helicopter and would occasionally fly so low over Tiger Stadium during LSU football games that play would be interrupted.

Duffard didn't know anything about Seal's later career as a smuggler but said he did once see him at the airport with a twin-engine Beechcraft. The plane had a large cargo door and he remarked to Seal that the door was just the right size to load a bale of marijuana.

Seal just laughed.

Seal was a good pilot, but he wasn't bulletproof. He was flying in a Piper Tri-Pacer on August 10, 1958, when he crashed on the grounds of Pike Burden Plantation on Essen Lane in Baton Rouge. He had

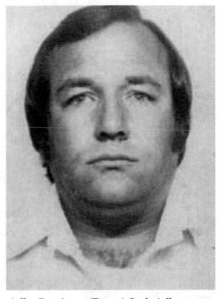

Adler Berriman (Barry) Seal. Adler means "eagle" in German – the name fit.

rented the plane from Dr. Philip West, an LSU chemistry professor. According to Eddie Duffard, Seal stalled the plane and crash-landed on a grass field.

Dr. West knew differently. He said Seal was showing off to his passengers. Seal cut the engine, could not re-start it and crashed the plane.

The Baton Rouge *Advocate* reported at the time that the plane developed engine trouble and Seal landed in a field on the Pike Burden Plantation. While on the ground, the engine began to run smoothly so Seal took off again. The plane climbed to about one hundred feet. The engine quit. Skimming across the treetops, Seal brought the plane down in a soybean field, gouging a path about thirty feet long and six feet wide. The plane was so mangled that the only a section of the wing and the tail assembly could be salvaged.

Seal spent a week in the hospital. His jaw was wired shut for over a month. He was eventually fitted with a plate and five false teeth. His passengers were uninjured.

A year later, Barry's father filed a civil suit against Dr. Philip West and the Royal Indemnity Co. He sought to recover $115,855 in damages on behalf of his son, who was still a minor under Louisiana law. According to the petition, the engine quit running because non-aviation fuel had been used by someone a day or so before Seal rented the plane. The suit itemized Seal's injuries as consisting of five anterior teeth knocked out, fractures to the crown of several lower teeth, a deep gash to his lower chin that left a noticeable scar, fractures of the lower jaw, left elbow, left wrist and a fracture of the left ankle.

In addition to physical injuries, Barry claimed a loss of prestige and a damaged reputation as a competent professional pilot because of the unfavorable publicity resulting from the crash. It was a claim that was somewhat exaggerated inasmuch as Barry eventually flew as a command pilot for TWA.

Barry and his father were represented by Baton Rouge attorney Thomas Benton. Two hours before the trial was scheduled to begin Benton was in his office preparing Seal's only witness for the testimony he was supposed to give. Benton said he began to sense a great reluctance on the part of the witness to give his testimony. Benton, an experienced and savvy lawyer, suspected the witness was lying. Benton confronted him about the story of the wrong type of fuel. The witness finally admitted he was lying and had been told by Seal to tell the story of improper fuel usage.

In no uncertain terms, Benton told Seal to get himself another lawyer because he would not put a witness on the stand who was going to commit perjury. The suit against Dr. West was dismissed in April 1960.

In addition to being an attorney, Benton was a pilot and distributor for Mooney aircraft. Benton had sold a Mooney plane to a client in Jackson, Mississippi and was flying the plane there and bringing back the trade-in, which was a Bellanca. Barry was still in high school and hanging around the downtown airport. Seal asked if he could go along and Benton said okay.

The Bellanca was old and so was its compass. On the way back, Benton let Seal take the controls. Benton gave him a compass heading and told him to maintain it. He saw that Barry had an "incredible touch" at the controls. The compass did not waver one degree off the heading. Benton had never seen anyone else who could fly so well. Seal was a natural pilot who could "fly the pants off an airplane" but he had "not one scintilla of conscience or morals," said Benton.

Seal graduated from Baton Rouge High in 1957. Perhaps somewhat prophetically, his high school yearbook photo contained the inscription "full of fun, full of folly." He enrolled in Louisiana State University but stayed less than a year.

Seal's military service is a part of the myths. Was he a Green Beret? Did he serve in Vietnam?

Here are the facts from his military records.

On August 31, 1961, he enlisted in the Louisiana Army National Guard for six years. The terms of his enlistment were six months active duty followed by five and a half years of inactive duty. He was assigned to Company B, 21st Special Forces (Airborne). Six months of active duty began in July 3, 1962 when he received basic combat training with Company C, 2nd Battalion, 3rd Training Regiment Engineers at Fort Leonard Wood, Missouri. After completing basic combat training, Seal was reassigned on September 14, 1962 to Company B, 1st Battalion, 1st Training Regiment, Engineers at Fort Leonard Wood. There he was trained as a radio telephone operator.

On November 11, 1962 he was transferred to Fort Benning, Georgia where he was assigned to Headquarters and Service Company, (Airborne) 4th Student Training Battalion. There he took parachute jump training. His active duty time ended around January 3, 1963 and he was promoted to private first class and was assigned to Company D, 2nd Operation Detachment, 20th Special Forces (Airborne).

Lt. Colonel John W. McInnis US Army (Retired), was formerly the commanding officer of Operating Detachment D, 20th Special Forces. He explained that the Special Forces unit Seal joined was a Louisiana Army National Guard unit and remained so until 1971 when Special Forces reorganized. Seal was eligible to wear the celebrated Green Beret. Seal would have been required to complete the Special Forces qualification training program before he could be deployed into the field to serve with the Green Berets.

For the last part of his remaining non-active duty time in the military, he was assigned to the 245th Engineer Battalion, Louisiana National Guard at Baton Rouge, where he served with a military occupational specialty of radio telephone operator.

This experience would help his next career as a drug smuggler.

Seal served in the Army National Guard and Army Reserve from August 21, 1961 to July 31, 1967, when he was honorably discharged. He was awarded the expert rifle badge, the expert carbine badge and the parachutist badge. In July of 1964 Seal enlisted in the Louisiana National Guard for an additional three years. Sometime in September of 1965 Seal received his annual National Guard training in St. Louis, Missouri. On July 31, 1967, Seal completed his three-year enlistment.

In fact, Seal did not receive Special Forces qualification training, he never served in Vietnam, and this is supported by his military records. Furthermore, there is no evidence that Seal ever claimed to have served as a Green Beret with US Army ground forces in Vietnam. The Vietnam service as a Green Beret is another of the myths that surrounded Barry Seal.

Seal married Barbara Bottoms in March 1963. A son and a daughter were born to them. Their marriage eventually unraveled and ended in a messy divorce.

In the summer of 1967 Seal joined Trans World Airlines. Starting out as a flight engineer, he rapidly worked his way up to command pilot. He was assigned to the Boeing 707 and began flying a regular European route.

In November 1968 Barry filed for divorce alleging that Barbara had abandoned him. There was a reconciliation until March 1970 when Barbara filed her petition for divorce. She alleged that Barry beat her up and threw her out of the house. She called the police. Their divorce was finalized on October 1, 1971, with Barry obligated to pay $703 per month child support.

One of the myths that grew out of Seal's employment with TWA was that he was the youngest Boeing 747 command pilot there. TWA officials would later advise that Seal was never a regular command pilot assigned to the 747. He was one of the youngest— if not the youngest—command pilot in the fleet assigned to the Boeing 707. Barry and Barbara lived on Long Island for a while. He did make one flight to Europe as command pilot of a Boeing 747. He took Barbara with him.

Seal had no military service in Vietnam but he did contribute to the US war effort there. While he was flying for TWA, he volunteered to make several military supply flights into Vietnam. He was paid slightly more than his regular salary and, again, it was something he said he did for excitement.

Seal was a bit of an entrepreneur. He acquired a Texaco service station called B.C. Seal Texaco. located at the corner of Acadian Thruway and Government Street. When he wasn't flying, he helped his father and brothers run the station.

In February 1969 he incorporated a company he named Helicopter Airways, Inc. In August 1970 he and a partner incorporated

National Searchlight Company, Inc. A Baton Rouge doctor loaned Seal $24,000 to start the business. Seal bought four 16-kilowatt searchlights that he rented out for advertising purposes. The business didn't do very well and eventually the doctor would file a suit against him to collect the loan.

Seal also formed a companion company called Rent-A-Sign, which, as its name implied, rented portable signs. Both companies struggled and failed. The City of Baton Rouge would eventually sue Seal, claiming that Rent-A-Sign hadn't filed tax returns and didn't have any books or figures.

In 1977 he formed Creole Sign Company.

On October 23, 1971, he married Linda McGarrh Ross. On their marriage license Linda indicated she was employed as a secretary by National Searchlight Company. Seal showed his employment as a pilot for TWA and said he had four years of college.

Linda would subsequently file for divorce November 17, 1972, alleging that she was abandoned by Barry.

Seal's third marriage was in November 1974 to Deborah Ann DuBois, a young woman from Ascension Parish near Baton Rouge. She had been working in a fast-food restaurant when Seal met her. They were married by a justice of the peace. On the marriage license application she showed her employment as being a secretary at National Searchlight Company.

He and Debbie had three children, Aaron, Dean and Christina at the time of his death in 1986.

Chapter 3
First Arrest: Origin of the CIA Myth

Barry Seal's career on the wrong side of the law began officially on July 1, 1972. He and seven others were arrested by US Customs agents for their involvement in a plot to smuggle a planeload of explosives out of the United States.

Seal and Murray Morris Kessler of Brooklyn, New York, were arrested in a suburban Kenner motel room where they were awaiting the arrival of a plane that Seal was to fly. At the time of the arrests, Seal was a command pilot for TWA. He was on a medical leave of absence.

Seal was moonlighting.

This arrest and the subsequent trial mark the origin of myth that Seal was a long-time CIA operative.

The DC-4 Seal was scheduled to fly was seized at the airport in Shreveport, Louisiana where it sat loaded with 1,350 pounds of plastic explosives, seven thousand feet of prima cord and 2,600 electric blasting caps. The explosives were supposed to be flown first to Mexico, and then allegedly on to Cuba, although the federal prosecutors were never to name Cuba as the final destination.

Outwardly, the entire scenario reeked of CIA involvement.

Those arrested at Eagle Pass, Texas were Richmond C. Harper, Sr., the owner of the DC-4 and a well-known banker and rancher, and Marion Hagler, who was identified as a former inspector with Immigration and Naturalization Service.

James M. Miller, Jr., a pilot, and Joseph Mazzuka, both of Baton Rouge, were arrested at Shreveport.

Arthur Henry Lussler of Ft. Lauderdale and Antonio Maldonado and Juan Martinez of Vera Cruz, Mexico were also arrested.

Newspaper stories reported that an arrest warrant was issued for one Francisco "Paco" Flores of Piedras Negras, Mexico who had not been arrested and was said to be a fugitive.

And Barry Seal.

C-123 cargo plane at Mena airport. (Photo Courtesy of the Arkansas Democrat-Gazette.)

Seal was arraigned before US Magistrate Morey Sear on July 11, 1972 and was released on a $50,000 bond.

The CIA legend began to grow.

Seal subsequently filed motions seeking more latitude in the travel restrictions set on him at the time he made bond. He was confined to the New Orleans Eastern District of Louisiana. In 1972, the Baton Rouge Middle District of Louisiana had not been established and Baton Rouge was in the Eastern District with New Orleans and southeast Louisiana.

His motion was denied, but he was permitted to travel to New York to attempt to get a letter from TWA saying that he would be permitted to resume his flying status. He did not receive the letter because he had been dismissed by TWA shortly after his arrest.

The complaint that triggered the arrests was filed with a US Magistrate in New Orleans by a US Customs agent. The Customs agent alleged in the document that Murray Morris Kessler planned to sell explosives to a man identified as Carlos Diaz who claimed to be a Mexican citizen. Kessler was said to have links to Manny Gambino, who had connections to the Gambino organized crime family.

Michael Pollack, a Brooklyn federal strike force attorney, was quoted in newspaper articles as saying the government was tipped off. It was a scheme to sell weapons valued at about $1.2

million, consisting of M-1, M-16 and AR-15 rifles and Thompson submachine guns. Pollack refused to comment on whether or not the Mafia was involved and made no statements indicating it was in any way associated with a CIA operation.

One of the US Customs agents involved in the investigation was Dick Gustafson. He arrested Seal and said the entire case was a Customs sting operation. Gustafson subsequently transferred to the DEA and was assigned to the Baton Rouge DEA office at the time the Middle District drug task force began investigating Seal. As he remembered the story, Manny Gambino, the nephew of New York Mafia boss, Carlo Gambino had been kidnapped for ransom. Murray Kessler had acted as the go-between and delivered the ransom on behalf of the Gambino family.

The case went to trial in New Orleans before US Judge Herbert Christenberry beginning on June 25, 1974. Witness Alfonso Cortina Rodriguez, an administrative officer with the Mexican Treasury Department, testified. He said that he had been approached in February 1972 by Jamie Fernandez who asked him if he knew of anyone interested in buying weapons, including 10,000 M-1 rifles that were available in the United States. Rodriguez reported the conversation to Mexican Customs agents and then continued to work with Mexican and US Customs undercover agents. Rodriguez said Fernandez put him in contact with Francisco "Paco" Flores. Through Flores he met Hagler and then Harper.

Rodriguez testified that Hagler told him he and his associates had everything they needed, including M-1 rifles, M-15 submachine guns, and ammunition. Rodriguez was paid approximately $4,000 by Customs for his undercover work. He did manage to purchase an AR-180 automatic rifle from Fernandez. The government introduced the rifle into evidence and kept it in plain view of the jury during the trial.

Under cross-examination Rodriguez said that Fernandez had agreed to cooperate with the US government in an effort to free a friend who was being held in jail in the United States. Fernandez was named as an unindicted co-conspirator.

Carlos Diaz, the person to whom Kessler planned to sell the explosives, was actually Cesario Diosdado, a twenty-two-year veteran of the US Customs Service. Diosdado testified that he began to work undercover in Mexico in late May 1972 after a Mexican agent received information concerning arms and munitions being

offered for sale. He met "Paco" Flores in Mexico and then met
Hagler and Harper in Eagle Pass, Texas. Hagler and Harper told
him they had access to almost unlimited supplies of automatic
weapons and ammunition. It was Harper who then put him in
contact with Murray Kessler.

The Customs undercover agent described taking a tour through
a Port Newark, New Jersey, steel plant that Kessler claimed to
own and where he said he manufactured arms and spare parts
for weapons. He said that Kessler regularly referred to Harper
as his partner. The guns, although continuously promised, never
materialized. The first shipment agreed on by Kessler was supposed
to include 2,000 M-16 rifles. They were never delivered and never
shown to Diosdado for his inspection.

Diosdado testified that he met with Barry Seal, and traveled with
him to examine an airfield located about 200 miles from Vera Cruz
where the DC-4 was to take the munitions.[1]

The agent's testimony directly contradicted what Seal told
members of the press two years earlier. "I haven't done a thing.
That's what you're going to find out," Seal proclaimed after being
released on bond following his arrest.

Seal was represented by Baton Rouge attorney Ralph Brewer
who at first contended that an export license had been issued to
export the C-4 explosives.

The government countered and put Clyde G. Bryant, Jr., on the
stand. Bryant, an intelligence assistant in the Office of Munitions
Control, US State Department, testified that no such license had
been requested or issued.

During trial testimony, there was a brief reference to the
possibility of a Cuban revolution in connection with the gun deal.
Kessler was representing himself. He asked Diosdado if they had
a conversation in New York in which Kessler told him he would
introduce him to a US general who knew how to make revolutions
and would help him. Diosdado insisted that the only mention he
made of Cuba while undercover was that his wife had two sons in
Cuba. Diosdado testified that he never told Kessler he had an army
in training in the Yucatan Peninsula in Mexico for an invasion of
Cuba. He also testified that never in his discussions with Harper
or Hagler did he ever use the words "revolution" or "plastic
explosives." Kessler was trying to put words in Diasdado's mouth.

Flores and Fernandez were named in the indictment as co-

conspirators but only Flores was indicted on a substantive count. Fernandez refused to come to New Orleans to testify. Flores who was actually an informant for US Customs but was not publicly identified as such at the time, remained in fugitive status during the trial. During the trial the prosecution had referred to both Flores and Fernandez extensively and both had roles in introducing Diosdado to Hagler and Harper. Customs officials delayed, stalled and ultimately refused to produce their informant. Gustafson said that in 1972, US Customs adhered to an inflexible policy: they would not identify their informants.

On Friday, June 29, 1974, the fifth day of the trial, Brewer moved for a mistrial on the grounds that the defense had no opportunity to cross-examine Fernandez and Flores, both of whom were key principals in the alleged smuggling plot.

Judge Christenberry, after hearing Brewer's arguments, granted the motion for a mistrial. He reasoned that without a chance to question Flores and Fernandez it would be impossible for the defendants to get a fair trial. The judge was also critical of the government's use of the AR-180 rifle as a trial exhibit. Judge Christenberry commented that since no other weapons had been found, a jury would be more likely to find it was a scheme to defraud people who had money.

There may well have been a scheme to defraud afoot. Diosdado testified that at a meeting with Kessler held late the night before the arrests, he was told he would have to produce $100,000 in cash as a down payment.

A request for cash up-front or a good-faith down payment is sometimes an indicator that a rip-off is planned. Whatever may have been the case, Diosdado did not make the down payment because up until then he had not seen any of the rifles that had been continuously promised.

The government appealed the decision to the Fifth Circuit Court of Appeals. The appellate court was also critical of the prosecutor's performance with regard to producing witnesses and viewed the introduction of the AR-180 automatic rifle as intentional misconduct. Judge Christenberry's decision to grant a mistrial was upheld.

Although Seal was not convicted, the 1972 arrest cost him his job with TWA. Years later, Seal testified that he was brought into the deal by his friend, Joseph Mazzuka, who was a childhood acquaintance of Murray Kessler.

Although it was Mazzuka who got him involved, Seal focused his blame on the government and federal agents. The arrest embittered him. The dismissal of charges gave Seal the opportunity to blame the entire matter on sinister "government misconduct" without explaining what it was. The misconduct was to display the AR-180 rifle during the trial. The judge eventually ruled it was a prejudicial act.

Some would later claim that Seal thought he was being patriotic and doing a good deed that would help free Cuba from Castro's oppression.

However, there may have been a more plausible motive for his involvement than patriotism. Seal eventually testified that he, Mazzuka, and the co-pilot expected to divvy up $300,000 or $400,000.

Stories that Seal had an affiliation with the CIA stem from his 1972 arrest and the trial that followed. They did so primarily because of Cesario Diosdado's involvement in the case and some vague references to Cuba during the trial.

Investigative journalist Gaeton Fonzi, a former investigator for the House Select Committee on Assassinations, mentioned Cesar Diosdato (sic) in his book, *The Last Investigation*. He wrote that a confidential US Customs source told him that Diosdato was working for the CIA in Key West in 1963 soon after the Kennedy assassination.

The Custom agent's brief affiliation with the CIA was confirmed to Fonzi by another source close to the head of the local US Customs office. According to the source, the CIA was reimbursing Customs for Diosdado's salary.

When Diosdado's past but temporary association with the CIA became known, it gave birth to the rumor that the CIA was involved in the affair. Dick Gustafson confirmed that he heard about Diosdado's CIA connection at the time of the New Orleans trial.

The CIA rumor persisted and spread, sometimes, with Seal's help, until it eventually became generally accepted as a "fact" that the affair was a CIA operation—and Seal had been working for the CIA.

Seal was not working for the CIA in 1972 and there was no evidence that the CIA had anything at all to do with what was, in fact, a US Customs sting operation.

Yet, more than thirty years after Seal's death, there are writers, reporters, and so-called investigators who continue to claim that Seal was a longtime CIA operative. They often cite the 1972 case as proof. For example in 1996, Roger Morris, writing in *Partners in Power*, implied that some shadowy government agency, perhaps the CIA, had interceded on behalf of Seal when he described the 1972 case as being "quietly dropped on the pretext of national security." That statement is hardly accurate in view of the fact that Seal and the other defendants were indicted by the US Attorney for the Eastern District of Louisiana. They underwent the ordeal of a public trial that lasted for five days and was reported daily in the *New Orleans Times-Picayune* newspaper and elsewhere. Obviously the case wasn't quietly dropped for national security purposes.

There is further evidence that the CIA story was nothing more than a rumor. Consider the fact that during the trial neither Seal nor his attorney ever claimed that the CIA was involved in the activity that resulted in the indictment. Likewise, there were no assertions and no evidence produced by any of Seal's co-defendants to show they were working on a CIA project. If a "black operation" had been underway, the CIA would have intervened as soon as US Customs agents became involved. There wouldn't have been any indictments.

Moreover, it is doubtful that the CIA would have stood by and done nothing while Seal, their alleged asset, was dismissed by TWA.

In the long run, his 1972 arrest did become a boon of sorts to Seal. From then on, he was able to humbug people into thinking he was a CIA operative whenever it suited him.

Money was tight. The trial had cost Seal significant attorney fees. He was making several hundred dollars in monthly child support payments for two children from his first marriage to Barbara.

He had been earning a relatively high salary as a TWA pilot. The arrest and indictment had cost him his job and there was little chance he'd be hired by another airline.

He no longer had a steady flow of income. Seal still had his flying skills.

The timing couldn't have been better.

Americans were developing a taste for cocaine. South American drug barons wanted the new markets. And there was a growing demand for pilots willing to take risks.

Barry Seal was a risk taker.

Chapter 4
The War on Drugs

President Richard Nixon told Congress in 1971 that drugs were "America's public enemy number one" as more and more cocaine flowed into the country.

No war was declared.

In 1974 US Customs Service seized a total of 907 pounds of cocaine, a little over 400 kilos.

By 1980, cocaine seized by the Drug Enforcement Administration totaled 2,590 pounds or about 1,175 kilos. Because of the success of smugglers like Barry Seal, by the early 1980s drugs had become so prevalent across America that public outcry forced the government to take action.

Maybe it was time for a war.

On January 30, 1982, President Ronald Reagan declared "war on drugs" and ordered the creation the South Florida Drug Task Force. It was established to coordinate the efforts of the various federal agencies engaged in skirmishing with drug smugglers. Some agencies had varying degrees of success — or failure.

Earlier in the month the White House accepted the resignation of DEA Administrator Peter Bensinger, and gave the Federal Bureau of Investigation concurrent jurisdiction with the DEA to handle drug investigations.

President Reagan selected Francis "Bud" Mullen, Jr. who had once been special agent in charge of the New Orleans FBI office, to replace Bensinger at DEA. Mullen brought FBI supervisor Jack Lawn with him as his deputy. The appointment of Bud Mullen as DEA administrator immediately set off rumors within the DEA and the FBI that a merger of the two agencies was imminent.

Some staff quit. Some FBI agents retired rather than become involved in the nasty business of narcotics. DEA agents who didn't want to trade their permanent pressed designer jeans for suits and ties, sought employment elsewhere. The rumor proved to be false. The two agencies have never merged.

The enemy in the new war was the Medellin Cartel. It was a consortium of Colombian cocaine wholesalers named after Medellin, Colombia's second largest city, where some members resided. The most conspicuous organization in the cartel was the Ochoa family. They were sometimes innocently described as an old established Catholic family of cattle breeders and landowners. The Ochoas resided on a hillside estate near Medellin. From their lofty aerie, they made billions of dollars in a single year and ordered the deaths of hundreds of people.

Fabio Ochoa, the family patriarch, and his wife had three sons and three daughters. The oldest son was Juan David and the youngest son was Fabio. Jorge Luis, the middle son, had the most active involvement in the cartel. The second and third principal members of the Medellin Cartel were Pablo Escobar Gaviria and Carlos Enrique Lehder Rivas.

There is no certain date to mark the beginning of the Medellin Cartel. Some investigators traced it to November 1981 when a leftist revolutionary group known as M-19 kidnapped Fabio Ochoa's daughter, Marta, and demanded a ransom to be used to finance their revolution. Reportedly, dozens of M-19 members were killed or kidnapped. Marta Ochoa was released unharmed in February 1982.[1]

By another account, Jorge Ochoa formed an organization of 225 businessmen. Their purpose was to unite and make it clear to guerrilla groups, who hoped to finance their revolutions, that kidnappings would no longer be tolerated. Each member contributed two million pesos to create an armed force. Hardly the Rotary Club of Medellin, the group was appropriately named "Death to Kidnappers."[2]

By 1982, the business of the Medellin Cartel was high-tech and specialized. The Escobars managed production, the Ochoas handled transportation and Carlos Lehder ramrodded distribution.

The success of the Medellin traffickers was phenomenal. By 1988, despite the efforts of the South Florida task force, their annual income was estimated at eight billion dollars. Pablo Escobar was listed in *Forbes*, July 1988 issue as sixty-ninth among the world's one hundred twenty-five non-US billionaires.

President Reagan wanted to ensure that his South Florida Drug Task Force would succeed and not be lost in a bureaucratic tap dance. He designated Vice President George H. W. Bush to lead the war on drugs.

Stanley Marcus, the newly appointed US Attorney in Miami, was placed in command of the task force. He brought with him an established track record in the area of organized crime. Vice President Bush saw to it that a credible force was available to Marcus.

How Federal Agencies Mobilized in the Drug War

The various government agencies, some with reluctance, responded to the task force approach and made their personnel and resources available.

The DEA hired twenty new agents for their Miami office and transferred in another forty, along with ten supervisors and three intelligence analysts.

The FBI added forty-three new agents.

US Customs added 145 investigators and some Army Cobra helicopters to aid in the interception of drug smuggling planes.

The Bureau of Alcohol Tax and Firearms transferred forty-five agents to Miami.

The US Marshals Service transferred in eleven more deputies.

The Treasury Department added twenty new analysts to its Financial Law Enforcement Center who were to devote their talents exclusively to the investigation of money laundering.[3]

The US Navy, after some nudging by the Senate Armed Services Committee, agreed to use their Grumman E2C Hawkeye surveillance aircraft. They would be allowed to track suspected drug planes and ships in the southern Florida region.[4]

Eventually, "aerostat" radar balloons costing $12 million apiece would be deployed.

Politically, the viewpoint was that the government had finally recognized what a huge problem drugs had become and was attempting to do something about it. In March 1982 Vice President Bush was in Miami where he declared that major steps had been taken to stop the torrential flow of cocaine, marijuana and counterfeit pills that had been drowning the residents of Florida.[5]

Within six months the results were sufficiently impressive to allow President Reagan to visit South Florida. He was photographed standing in front of tons of seized marijuana, hundreds of kilos of cocaine, and an arsenal of assorted weapons. From this heady stage he proclaimed the task force to be a "brilliant example of working federalism." Not surprisingly, one of the raids that produced the goodies on display was delayed to coincide with the presidential visit.[6]

The war on drugs started out with what appeared to be some pretty good numbers. In the first year of the task force the Miami US Attorney and his assistants prosecuted 664 drug-related cases, an increase of sixty-four percent over the previous year. Six tons of cocaine were seized in South Florida in 1983. A lot of publicity was generated. South Florida newspapers like the *Miami Herald* and *Sun-Sentinel* regularly featured photographs of federal agents decked out in their respective agency raid jackets, heavily armed in front of large piles of cash, cocaine and marijuana. Headlines proclaimed the seized drugs to be worth millions of dollars in "street values."

In 1985, the seizure figure was twenty tons. In 1986, cocaine seizures in the South Florida region were in excess of 30 tons.[7]

The increase in the tonnage of cocaine seizures would seem to demonstrate that the task force was enjoying unprecedented success.

Conversely, other statistics pointed to an opposite and disturbing conclusion.

When the South Florida Drug Task Force entered the war on drugs, the purity of cocaine on the streets averaged 12.5 percent. This indicated that one kilo of cocaine assumed to be one hundred per cent pure, was being cut or "stepped on" approximately eight times.

In 1987, the average purity on the streets of Miami was 33 percent, meaning a kilo of cocaine was being cut only three times.[8]

These percentages were significant because they revealed that one kilo of cocaine that had been cut to provide eight kilos was now being cut to provide three kilos. This pointed to the fact that despite the increase in the tonnage seized, there was a glut of cocaine on the market.

Another indicator that the drug war was not going so well was the price per kilo of cocaine. Cocaine is a commodity like corn, wheat, or pork bellies. Like any other commodity, the price of a kilo of cocaine follows the economic laws of supply and demand. An increase in the available amount of cocaine, the supply, results in a decrease in the price.

The cocaine glut in 1987 can be demonstrated by a comparison of the price of a kilo of cocaine. In 1982 in Miami, a kilo went for between $47,000 and $60,000. By late 1987 the cost of a Miami kilo of cocaine was between $9,000 and $14,000.[9]

The numbers provided some statistical evidence that the South Florida Drug Task Force's war on drugs was not doing as well as was being proclaimed by the politicians. This viewpoint was held by many in law enforcement who felt that the task force had failed because it was fighting on the wrong front, using a flawed strategy. The feeling was that the powers in Washington who were calling the shots lacked an understanding of the problem. They did not have the political will to win.[10]

Some said that many officials in the federal law enforcement community never took George Bush's anti-drug projects seriously and suspected that they existed mainly to add a few lines to Bush's political resume.[11]

Another explanation offered for why the plan was failing was that the government's attack plan was flawed. It was weakened by ignorance, bad planning, insufficient commitment, turf wars between investigating agencies and a lack of understanding of the smuggler.[12]

The National Narcotics Border Interdiction System (NNBIS) and the General Accounting Office (GAO) suggested that the claims were used by the Reagan-Bush team for political advantage in the 1984 presidential campaign.

In 1984, DEA administrator Francis Mullen, Jr. said the drug-fighting program headed by Vice President Bush made grandiose claims of success it couldn't support. Mullen said the program would become the administration's "Achilles' heel" for drug enforcement and, in a report to the attorney general, recommended it be abolished.[13]

This was not what the administration wanted to hear. Mullen soon retired.

There were other examples of flaws in the drug war. In 1986 US Customs opened and operated a marine surveillance center as a specialty force within the task force. Named "Blue Lightning," twenty-seven federal, state and local agencies were linked together by a radio network to a fleet of more than one hundred boats. The heart and soul of this armada were some catamarans operated by US Customs. These boats were very, very fast and flashy and were probably a real kick for their crews to operate.

Bearing such exhilarating names as *Blue Thunder* and capable of speeds of as much as sixty miles an hour, these boats were a match for most anything the smugglers could put in the water. However, a September 1986 GAO investigation found that the Customs Service did not have enough crews to keep the boats in service for twenty-four hours a day, seven days a week. Furthermore, the GAO investigation reported that smugglers had obtained the crew work schedules. Consequently they knew when they could do their smuggling with relative safety.[14]

It was simply a matter of scheduling deliveries to coincide with the downtime of the boats.

The increase in the weight of seizures over a six-year period was approximately 250 percent. This was properly viewed as significant. The statistical evidence indicated that the task force approach that was intended to halt the dangerous trend in Florida wasn't working as planned or as the politicians were claiming. The importation of cocaine was plainly on the increase notwithstanding the presence of the sizable task force that had been deployed to combat it. Estimates were that sixty to eighty tons of cocaine were smuggled into the United States yearly.[15]

On October 14, 1982, less than a year after establishing the first drug task force and before the dismal figures were in, President Reagan delivered a speech to the Department of Justice. He declared the South Florida Task Drug Force to have been highly successful in slowing the flow of illegal drugs into the United States. In fact, the results were so good that the president announced the formation of twelve additional Organized Crime Drug Task Forces to serve in key areas of the US. The units began to spring up in judicial districts across the nation.

A drug task force opened for business in the Middle District of Louisiana, centered in Baton Rouge, in February 1983, in compliance with the wishes of President Reagan and the Department of Justice. The commander of the task force was US Attorney Stanford O. "Stan" Bardwell, a Reagan appointee who had been on the job for several years. He placed the day-to-day operations of the task force in the capable hands of Bradley C. Myers, a young and talented assistant US attorney. The task force was quartered in the same commercial office building occupied by the US attorney. There, task force agents shared a large table in Myers's office and conference room.

The task force participants included DEA Special Agent Charles Bremer, who had twelve years of experience. And Special Agent

Jerry Bize from the IRS Criminal Investigation Division, who had fourteen years of experience. And the author, who had been an FBI agent for twenty years. Myers's secretary, Carol Long, soon to be dubbed "Task Force Tootsie," became another important member of the task force. Local participation included Captain Stan Howard, the regional head of Narcotics for the Louisiana State Police and Greg Phares, an experienced sergeant from the Baton Rouge Police Department who would eventually became its chief.

Howard Whitworth, the resident agent in charge of the Baton Rouge DEA office, although nearing retirement, was available to lend his expertise and keep things on an even keel. His successor, Mike Long, did the same.

FBI agents did not work narcotics violations while J. Edgar Hoover was the director because he feared there was too great a risk of corruption. Following Hoover's death in May 1972 and for the next ten years, the succession of directors managed to keep the FBI out of drug investigations.

The FBI's isolation from the drug scene ended in 1982. Then-Attorney General William French Smith ordered the FBI into the narcotics investigation business. Regrettably, within two years, Hoover's fears were realized when news of the first prosecution of an FBI agent for bribery hit the newspapers. Not surprisingly, it was a Florida agent named Dan Mitrione, Jr.

A ten-year veteran, Mitrione, was assigned to an undercover drug investigation and was teamed up with an informant who was an active narcotics trafficker. In March 1983, Mitrione was sent to Memphis, Tennessee, to seize 235 kilos of cocaine. When he returned with only 193 kilos, a red flag went up. Fellow agents in the Miami office grew suspicious.

A special team of FBI agents from around the country were sent to Miami to investigate one of their own. They found evidence that he had been corrupted by the informant he was working with. In March 1984, Mitrione pleaded guilty to possessing and distributing more than ninety pounds of cocaine and taking $856,000 in bribes and payoffs from the people he was supposed to be investigating.

The FBI reacted with training. A handful of Louisiana FBI agents were sent to a three-day school in New Orleans put on by the DEA. The goal was to familiarize the new FBI recruits with the intricacies of narcotics investigations and possibly as a deterrent against more Mitrione-like incidents.

The school was informative as well as interesting. The DEA educated noses as well as brains. One morning the DEA instructor fired up several small pills that began to emit smoke. Students were invited to take a whiff and were told that the smell was just like marijuana. Some in attendance argued that a puff on a real "joint" might be a more realistic introduction to the drug scene but the DEA instructor nixed the idea. At the end of three days the new recruits were schooled and ready to join their fellow agents in the war on drugs.

A sporty, gray two-door 1982 Pontiac Trans-Am was assigned to this writer for task force work. On the down side, he had to surrender his 1982 Buick Le Sabre four-door which was truly a great ride and one of only two in the New Orleans division. Later, it was learned that the Trans-Am had been used for undercover work and had been partially sunk in some sort of driving mishap. FBI agents being who they are, it was never possible to find out the exact details of the sinking.

It made no difference. The car ran well, carried Texas plates front and back and didn't look like an FBI car. It was a neat ride and proof that the FBI in Louisiana was supporting the task force concept.

Vice President George H. W. Bush came to New Orleans in April 1983 to celebrate the start-up of the Louisiana drug task forces. A contingent of representatives from the Middle District of Louisiana traveled to New Orleans to take part in a photo op along with fifty or so. They included DEA, FBI, Customs, Marshals Service, IRS, Coast Guard, and the Louisiana State Police, as well as some assistant US attorneys. The vice president made a brief address. Everyone queued up to shake his hand while a Coast Guard photographer took pictures.

The newly-assigned drug warriors of the Baton Rouge Middle District drug task force soon learned that kicking down doors was not part of their mandate. They were not going to be allowed to direct their efforts against ordinary street pushers. Instead, they were ordered to go after the major traffickers in their respective territories — and they did.

Chapter 5
The Target and Little Rock

Barry Seal knew what Jean and Pierre Lafitte and the Barataria pirates knew. And rum runners knew during Prohibition. The Louisiana coast is perfect for smuggling just about anything.

The Gulf of Mexico creates approximately 3,900 miles of US coastline extending in an arc from Mexico in the west to Florida in the east. About 1,630 miles of this coastline are in the United States. And approximately 500 of those miles make up the coast of Louisiana.

By the time the government's drug task force concept was extended to Louisiana, Seal had already concluded that the coast of his native state was a natural for smuggling drugs into the country. He was firmly established in the business. He had become the scourge of local DEA agents and the Louisiana State Police narcs.

At the first task force meeting Seal was nominated by the DEA to be the target and unanimously approved. His name was sent to the Department of Justice for the required approval, and it was soon granted.

DEA informant reports documented some of Seal's earlier flights and left no doubt that he was a drug smuggler and a worthy target.

On December 16, 1976, Seal flew to La Ceiba, Honduras in a twin-engine Piper Navajo and it was there that he met Joe Cooper who was employed as an air traffic controller at Golozon National Airport. La Ceiba is a port city on the edge of the Caribbean coast.

They became fast friends. Seal would take Cooper on flights for his off days.

In early 1978 Cooper and Seal met to start smuggling marijuana. They flew to Honduras in Seal's Beechcraft D-18 and began looking for farmland which they could convert to a landing strip. The plan was subsequently abandoned. They decided to use the Golozon airport because Cooper knew all the air controllers and other employees.

Cooper came to the United States in April 1978 and took a job working on offshore drilling rigs. He eventually quit and went to work for Seal at National Searchlight Co. He took flying lessons and eventually got his license.

In April 1978 Barry flew to Santa Marta, Colombia and met with Jose and Enrique Lacutir to arrange a marijuana deal. Seal and Cooper flew in a Piper Seneca on August 26, 1978, to a remote airstrip about eighty miles from Santa Maria, Colombia where they picked up 600 pounds of marijuana.

They refueled at La Ceiba and flew to Louisiana and unloaded the marijuana at Seal's private landing strip at Port Vincent in Ascension Parish. They flew to LaCeiba and parked the plane at Golozon airport. They returned to the United States on a commercial flight. This is how Seal covered his tracks.

Seal and Cooper made another flight to the airstrip near Santa Marta on October 30, 1978. They picked up 170,000 barbiturate tablets, 100 pounds of marijuana and two kilos of cocaine. They brought the drugs to Barry's private landing strip.

The two flew on a third trip to Colombia on December 18, 1978. They flew to the same airstrip near Santa Maria and picked up 100 kilos of cocaine from Jose and Enrique Lacutir. They brought the cocaine to Seal's private landing strip where it was loaded into a pickup truck by two men.

DEA informant reports left little doubt that Barry Seal was into the smuggling business big time. His notoriety had spread. Information provided by a Dallas FBI informant identified "Barry" as a cocaine smuggler who owned a long-range Panther aircraft, red, white and blue in colors, N7409L which was kept hidden at Opelousas Airport in southwest Louisiana.

Seal began building his smuggling fleet. He usually paid cash. In March 1979 an individual named William Jarvois Earle, Sr. purchased a surplus DC-3 from the Honduras Air Force. In March, 1979 Cooper and Seal flew to La Ceiba with $500,000 cash to buy a surplus aircraft from the Peruvian Air Force. On July 13, 1979, Cooper and Seal meet in La Ceiba with William Earle who was there to set up a front operation so the Peruvian Air Force surplus planes could be rebuilt in Honduras and used in the smuggling operation.

Seal was arrested a second time in December 1979 when he and Stephen Burnham Plata were on a drug smuggling flight and landed in Guayaquil, Ecuador. They had a passenger with them, Abbes LeBarr. He left the plane carrying seventeen-and-one-half kilos of cocaine in an army duffel bag.

Seal's next stop was scheduled to be the Golozon airport. Honduran narcotics officials had been tipped off. They were there to greet him when he landed on December 15, 1979. Honduran officials did not find cocaine when they searched the plane—but they did find an M-1 rifle. Seal was arrested and jailed.

The authorities soon tracked down LeBarr and arrested him. In subsequent interviews with DEA agents, LeBarr admitted to being recruited in Miami by Barry Seal to join his cocaine smuggling operation.

While Seal was in jail in Honduras he met a pilot from Hammond, Louisiana, named Emile Harold Camp, Jr. Camp had been arrested in December 1977 in Tegucigalpa, Honduras with 24 kilos of cocaine. Camp was interviewed by a DEA agent at the time of his arrest. Camp admitted that he worked for a man named Ellis McKenzie and had flown drug shipments which he airdropped to waiting boats at predetermined locations.

McKenzie was in the same jail and the three became friends and eventually joined forces in the smuggling business. Camp became one of Seal's pilots, usually flying as a co-pilot with William Bottoms.

In later debriefings, Seal said he developed a close and caring relationship with Camp as a result of their prison experience. Seale thought of him as almost like a brother.

The relationship extended further after Seal's death. Camp's wife, Carole, was initially named administrix of the succession of Seal's estate after his murder. She was relieved of her appointment in October 1986 when Deborah Seal was appointed.

Ellis McKenzie lived in La Ceiba but grew up on Roatan Island and owned land on the Mosquito Coast that abutted Nicaragua. Seal was interested in the land because it could be used as a landing strip for aircraft up to the size of a DC-6.

According to Bottoms, McKenzie was a small-time operator who was not capable of running an organization—though he did know many of the smuggling players. He was adopted into the Seal organization mostly as a "gofer" until Seal started purchasing boats. Then Seal trained McKenzie to run them. The boats were bigger with better equipment but they were never placed into actual smuggling operations. Had the boats been used, Ellis would have played an integral role as a boat captain. Instead he was used in various roles but never significantly.

While Seal and Camp were stuck in the Honduran jail, they likely had visitors. US Customs reports reveal that Seal's secretary, who at that time was Dandra Graves, and Camp's wife, Carole Camp, made several trips to Honduras.

Retired US Customs officer Terry Hoxworth was assigned to New Orleans International Airport, now Louis Armstrong International Airport during the time Seal was in custody in Honduras. He searched Dandra Graves and Seal's brother, Wendell Seal, on several occasions when they were returning from visits to Honduras. He recalled that Wendell was always recalcitrant and difficult to deal with.

Dandra was loyal and Seal trusted her. Wendell was very close to Barry. They may have been carrying cash to Seal but it would have been in amounts less than $10,000. Amounts over $10,000 would have to have been reported to Customs and Barry Seal would not have wanted that.

Seal remained in prison until he was released on July 21, 1980, allegedly after bribing a Honduran judge.

Seal seemed to have a knack for finding people in jail or traveling who might join his enterprise. He managed to meet another person who would join him. Seal said that on his flight home he met William Roger Reaves who would join with him in the smuggling business.

Hoxworth was on duty at the airport when Seal returned from Honduras. He recalled that Seal was very cooperative and cordial and went so far as to offer his apologies for the conduct of brother Wendell.

Not surprisingly, a stretch in a Honduran prison didn't stop Seal from smuggling. He would eventually find himself caught in the middle of a war in which he would become the target.

Stan Bardwell and Barry Seal were not strangers. They attended Baton Rouge High School around the same time. Seal graduated one year ahead of the man who was heading the drug task force that made him its target.

Seal was a colorful character. Bardwell recalled that one night some of Seal's classmates had lined their cars up in a vacant field and turned their headlights on so Seal could land a plane with his date then attend a school dance.

Several years before Seal became the task force target, he got caught up in a DEA undercover operation code named Operation Screamer. In April 1981, an informant introduced Seal to Miami DEA Special Agent Randy Beasley. Beasley was working undercover. Over several months he was able to negotiate a deal with Seal that involved 1,200 pounds of counterfeit methaqualone tablets. They were made from chalk.

In a meeting on September 16, 1981, Seal told Beasley that the tablets he was selling him would be delivered packed in boxes and left in the trunk of a Ford Thunderbird. The car would be parked in the parking garage of the Ramada Inn with the keys left on the front left tire. It was a familiar hiding place.

Between April and November 1981, agent Beasley learned all about Seal's drug smuggling operation and the air route he had perfected. He told Beasley he had been using the route successfully for nearly five years.

Seal boasted to Beasley how he flew his plane low and slow along Louisiana's Gulf Coast to blend in with the many drilling rigs and numerous helicopters that were picked up by radar. By doing so he could avoid interdiction by US Customs and the Coast Guard. They talked during several face-to-face meetings and in numerous conversations on pay telephones.

Once back in the United States, Seal could deliver the drugs a couple of ways.

Seal could unload the drugs at his private airstrip near Baton Rouge. From there he could send them south by car.

Or, Seal could refuel and fly a normal 5,000 foot altitude course from north to south into Florida. Seal said US Customs agents were so lax and naive that they would never suspect a plane coming from the north because they spent all their time watching for flights coming into the US from the south—the Caribbean, Central America and South America.

As a result of Seal's penchant for boasting, by November 1981 the DEA knew all about his smuggling operation.

The US Attorney in Miami did not get around to prosecuting Seal until 1983. Apparently there was no urgency because Seal was only one of eighty or more defendants who had been caught by Operation Screamer.

A federal grand jury in the Miami Southern District of Florida returned two indictments against Seal on March 17, 1983. One indictment, assigned docket number 83-6038, charged Seal, alone, with two counts of conspiracy to distribute methaqualone and possession with intent to distribute Quaaludes, the powerful sedative and hypnotic medication that was abused as a recreational drug. This indictment was allotted to US District Judge Norman C. Roettger, Jr.

A second indictment, docket number 83-6034, charged Seal, Gary Seville, John Vredenburg and Calvin L. Briggs with multiple counts of possession and distribution of meperidine hydrochloride (a painkiller), phenobarbital (a sedative) and methaqualone and the use of a telephone in commission of a felony. The second indictment was allotted to US District Judge Jose A. Gonzalez, Jr.

On March 18, 1983, one of Seal's cronies rented a suite at the Boca Raton Club in the name of Mr. K'Lean. Seal went into hiding.

On March 22, 1983, DEA agents went to Seal's residence in south Baton Rouge at 7:30 am to make the arrest on the Florida indictments. They learned that he was in Florida. While there, the agents noticed a lot of sophisticated electronic and radio gear and a paper shredder.

Seal was still in Florida on March 25 when DEA agents returned to his Baton Rouge residence with search warrants. The paper shredder and the electronic gear were gone but they seized a Carribank, NA bank statement bearing the name of a seafood company. There was a balance of $98,000 in the account.

Emile Camp, Jr. was arrested at the New Orleans airport on April 15, 1983. He carried a .25 caliber Beretta, $35,000 cash, and a one-way ticket to Miami. He was uncooperative when interviewed by federal agents.

Seal was still in hiding and the agents assumed that Camp was on his way to meet him.

Charlie Bremer and the author traveled to Miami on April 19, 1983, to meet with a DEA squad supervisor to discuss the Barry Seal case. There was some concern among Louisiana task force personnel that their investigation might interfere with the prosecution in Florida. The issue needed to be resolved.

Of major concern was the fact that the Baton Rouge agents were considering the use of wiretaps. Seal was under indictment and there was a possibility that Brady Rule material might be intercepted on the wiretap.

The Brady Rule is named for a federal case titled *Brady v. Maryland*. It requires prosecutors to disclose to the defense all materially exculpatory evidence in the government's possession.

Brady material includes any evidence favorable to the accused and evidence that goes towards negating a defendant's guilt, that would reduce a defendant's potential sentence, or evidence going to the credibility of a witness.

Assistant US Attorney Brad Myers would be reviewing all interceptions and DEA and FBI agents assigned to monitoring duties were to be instructed to be alert for Brady material. Thus, the Miami DEA expressed no opposition to the use of wiretaps in Louisiana.

The Miami DEA supervisor was asked if there were any objections to Barry Seal being targeted by the Baton Rouge Middle District of Louisiana—or if the investigation would hamper the pending cases against him in the Miami Southern District of Florida. The supervisor was of the opinion that the Louisiana investigation would not jeopardize prosecutions in Florida and he expressed his assurance that their undercover case would stand up in court.

During their visit, the Baton Rouge agents learned that Seal had offered to cooperate.

Seal had been turned down by the assistant US attorney handling the prosecution in Miami.

Seal remained a fugitive until April 26, 1983 when he surrendered to federal authorities in Ft. Lauderdale. During the bond hearing, he said his 1982 income was $250,000. He described his occupation as being an oil and shrimp broker. He was released on a $1.25 million surety bond.

Of course, his income at the time was in the millions. He may have eaten shrimp but he was not a shrimp dealer.

Seal turned to another friend from high school who loved flying.

Several months before Seal was indicted in Florida, he sent James Kenneth Webb to Miami to run various errands. Ken Webb grew up in Baton Rouge and was well acquainted with Seal. They were good friends who had attended Baton Rouge High at the same time—along with prosecutor Stan Bardwell, who was targeting them. They both took flying lessons from Eddie Duffard.

After the Operation Screamer indictments were returned, Webb was still in Florida. Fearing he would be arrested and prosecuted, Webb fled to his home in Missouri. From there he called Lt. Russell Milan, who commanded the Louisiana State Police Southeastern Regional Narcotics Task Force headquartered in Baton Rouge.

"Butch" Milan was an experienced investigator. Webb had been providing him with information. Milan and Sgt. Jack Crittenden of the Louisiana State Police had been investigating Seal so they were always interested in hearing what Webb had to say about the smuggler. Both officers were well-practiced in dealing with informants and were not was so naive as to think Webb was always telling the whole story. Milan was sharing Webb's information with the Baton Rouge DEA agents.

In mid-April 1983, Charlie Bremer, Lt. Milan and Baton Rouge DEA agent Jack Redford traveled to Shreveport where they spent several days in a motel room listening as Ken Webb talked about the cocaine smuggling operation of his former employer.

Webb first became associated with Seal's smuggling operation in the fall 1978. Seal sent him to Florida with a suitcase full of "pills" which he loaded into a twin-engine plane at an airport in Marathon, Florida. Later on the same trip he was sent to a residence in Miami. There he picked up the same suitcase. This time it was full of cash. Webb delivered the cash to Seal in Baton Rouge. Webb was afraid he'd be arrested so he quit working for him and went home.

The next contact Webb had with Seal came in December 1979 when Seal telephoned to ask him to come to Baton Rouge and discuss going to work for him again.

Webb came to Baton Rouge and spent several days with Seal. During the visit, Seal told Webb he was involved in importing illegal drugs and was working for some "big people" and was making tons of money. Seal told Webb that he was flying to South America on weekends and was gone two or three days at a time. He offered Webb $3,000 a weekend to fly co-pilot with him on the drug flights.

Webb was staying at a Holiday Inn at the time of Seal's second offer of employment. Again he worried about going to prison. He decided to call the FBI and tell them of his involvement.

Webb made the mistake of telling the motel clerk to call the FBI and ask them to come to the motel and talk to him.

As Webb later explained it, shortly after he talked to the motel clerk, Seal came to his room and told him to check out because he was sending him home. Webb did as ordered. Seal drove him to the Greyhound station and put him on a bus. Webb wasn't cut out for the kind of business Seal was in.

In March 1982, Webb returned to Baton Rouge after Seal called him and told him he could have another chance to work for him.

Seal had strict rules about how Webb could call anyone. This time he was instructed to have his wife obtain ten pay telephone numbers in his hometown and to assign a code name to each phone. The coded pay phones were the only way Webb was permitted to contact his wife once he began working. Seal briefed him thoroughly on what was expected and told him to contact him only by pay phone or pager.

After agreeing to work for Seal for the third time, Webb drove with Seal to the Roselawn Cemetery in Baton Rouge. Seal took him to the grave of Clarence J. Babin, Jr. Webb did not know who Babin was. Seal didn't tell him anything about how Babin had died. Seal only said he "loved him like a brother." Babin was dead because he "talked too much."

Taking Webb to the cemetery might have been mere showmanship to scare Webb into keeping his mouth shut. Webb didn't see it that way. To him it was a clear message that he could expect to be killed if he said anything to anybody about Seal and his drug smuggling operation.

Webb would later testify under oath during a deposition that Seal was a "psychopathic liar" who had threatened his life and the lives of his children.[1]

Webb's curious story about Babin was verified in part by a visit to the Roselawn Cemetery where his grave was viewed. Further investigation by the author revealed the unusual details surrounding his death.

On October 24, 1976, Lafourche Parish Sheriff's deputies found an abandoned boat floating in Lake Salvadore. The lake is situated in Lafourche Parish about twenty-five miles south of New Orleans. It is a popular fishing area. An abandoned fishing boat would not necessarily be a notable event.

This boat was of particular interest because of what it carried: an AR-15 semi-automatic rifle, with a loaded clip, and an Alpha-100 369P Aircraft Radio Transceiver. The abandoned boat was registered to Barry's brother, Wendell Seal.

Barry Seal and his attorney arrived at the Lafourche Parish Sheriff's office by helicopter on November 19, 1976. Seal exhibited a bill of sale and said the aircraft radio was his.

The body surfaced the next day. So did the questions.

On November 20, the body of Clarence J. Babin, Jr. was found floating near the location where the boat was found. The autopsy performed on Babin failed to reveal any evidence of foul play. However, the circumstances of his death suggested that he might have been the victim of an accidental drowning while involved in an airdrop of drugs.

The story takes another twist.

Babin and Wendell Seal were former Baton Rouge Police officers.

On Sept. 5, 1974, Baton Rouge police served a search warrant at the residence the two officers shared. Some marijuana was found. Both officers were dismissed.

Wendell Seal went to trial May 25, 1975, and was found not guilty. He appealed his dismissal from the police force and was reinstated. He later resigned.

Former Police Chief Wayne Rogillio, now retired, worked in Internal Affairs at the time of the Babin-Seal incident. He investigated the case and made the arrest of the two officers.

Rogillio said the search warrant was ruled defective as it applied to Seal. That's because Babin was renting a room from Seal and the marijuana was found under Babin's bed.

For his first assignment after the cemetery visit, Seal sent Webb to Houston to arrange the purchase of a pickup truck that was advertised for sale in the paper by a private owner. Webb remembered his name was Arthur Hedge. [Real name concealed by author by request.] Using the alias Mr. West, Webb told Hedge to bring the pickup truck to the Hilton Airport Hotel in Houston so Seal could examine it. Seal met with Hedge and after looking at the truck, paid him $8,000 cash.

In April 1982 Seal sent Webb to a motel in Lufkin, Texas. While there two Latinos arrived in a red Mercury Marquis bearing Florida plates. They gave him a nylon bag weighing about 20 pounds. Webb delivered the bag to a man in a restaurant in Lafayette, Louisiana. He thought the bag contained cash but he didn't look.

One task Seal sent Webb to Florida to perform was to monitor the overhaul of two motor vessels, the *Captain Wonderful* and the *Lauren Lee*. He told Webb he was going to use the boats in his smuggling operation. Both vessels were in Miami being refurbished, including electronics and navigational devices that would enable them to rendezvous with aircraft at sea.

Captain Wonderful was afloat and docked. It was large enough to be equipped with a helicopter landing pad. *Lauren Lee* was dry-docked.

Webb told of a meeting with Seal and William Earle, Sr. in the

Omni Hotel on January 28, 1983. Seal gave him $50,000 cash to pay for the work being done to the *Lauren Lee* and he had delivered the cash to the shipyard owner.

One reason the author and Charlie Bremer visited Florida was to corroborate as much of the information provided by Ken Webb as was possible. As with most informants and especially Webb, their information is always suspect and needs to be verified.

The *Captain Wonderful* was observed by the author tied up at the dock where Webb said it would be. It did have a helicopter landing pad topside. *Lauren Lee* was seen in dry dock.

The owner of the shipyard where *Lauren Lee* was being overhauled was interviewed and provided details of Seal's involvement with the vessel. He confirmed that several cash payments for the work he performed had been delivered by an associate of Seal's. He did not know the name of the man who delivered the cash to him but he provided a description which matched that of Ken Webb.

Just what kind of drugs would Barry Seal smuggle? Almost anything that paid. According to Ken Webb, Barry's longtime friend, Seal would handle any kind of illegal drug that would make money.

Seal measured success in terms of how much money he could accumulate. His philosophy was that money could solve all problems. And he believed everyone had their price.

Webb told of being in room 2107 at the Omni Hotel in Miami on March 20, 1983. He watched Seal use a Japanese-made Glory currency counting machine to count more than $700,000 in cash. When Webb expressed his amazement, Seal told him that he hadn't seen anything yet.

Webb noted that Seal got a big kick out of flaunting cash. For example, leaving a $20 tip to a waitress for a $4 hamburger. This attribute was confirmed by some additional investigation. An East Baton Rouge Parish Family Court divorce record revealed that Seal remembered his oldest son's fifteenth birthday by giving him a gift of $10,000 cash in a paper bag—all in $20 bills.

The president of Baton Rouge Aircraft told task force agents that Seal had brought him $160,000 cash in payment for a Piper Seneca. The cash was packed in a fruit box.

DEA agent Dick Gustafson was in Ruby Red's when he saw Seal repay the doctor who loaned Seal the money to start his searchlight business: $24,000 cash in a paper bag.

Webb said Seal liked to have people think he was associated with the CIA. He often heard Seal talk to people about working for "the company" — and many thought he was referring to the CIA. Seal was aware of this and used the term with that in mind. These vague hints of a CIA connection also kept people from asking the smuggler a lot of questions he didn't want to answer. Webb was quite certain that Seal did not work for the CIA.

The second time Webb went to work for Seal, he gave him a copy of the book, *Snowblind*. Seal told him to read it because "this is what I do."

Snowblind, written by Robert Sabbag, is the true story of Zachary Swan, a cocaine smuggler who operated in the early 1970s.

An informant provides timely information about current or impending criminal activity. They're usually in the middle of it. Their information is of present intelligence value or it can be acted on to stop criminal activity or to nab the bad guys in the act.

Webb was never an informant. He was a confidential source. He provided some useful information about Seal, his associates and his smuggling activities but it was history about past activity. He never said, "Hey, I'm with Barry and here is what's going to happen."

Webb never knew where or when a load of cocaine was going to be delivered. Seal was smart enough not to tell Webb because he didn't trust him.

They may have been high school pals but their on-again-off-again relationship and their visit to Babin's grave was evidence Seal didn't trust Webb.

Lt. Milan said Webb never provided any useful information that could be acted on. He played both sides — or tried to do so. He was in a constant state of vacillation about the nature and degree of his cooperation with LSP. He had a weighty conflict of loyalties due to his "love-hate" relationship with Seal. Webb often mentioned how Seal had "helped" his family. "I questioned his motive for coming to us in the first place, which was never clear," said Milan.

Webb never met the requirements for informant status with LSP and he was closed out.

"Little Rock" was the code name given to Webb to help conceal his identity — but that doesn't always work.

Webb was a hometown boy and so was Seal. They had mutual friends. And Webb liked to talk. It was only a matter of time until Webb talked to the wrong person.

Anyone in law enforcement knows informants can be difficult to control, and tough to deal with—sometimes exasperating. The same thing is true of confidential sources.

Seal knew that Webb's information he shared with the State Police and DEA was accurate and damaging. Seal attempted to neutralize him. He eventually persuaded Webb to give an affidavit in which he claimed the things he told the task force agents about Seal's smuggling business were not true and had been coerced. Webb was talked into falsely claiming that Howard Whitworth and State Police detectives had tried to get him to plant dope on Seal. Clearly, Seal was very much interested in compromising Ken Webb to save himself.

There were those who would later complain that Baton Rouge task force agents had no reason to believe anything Ken Webb told them. He was said to be a perjurer.

Webb did tell investigators the truth about Seal's money counter. The notice of federal tax lien filed by IRS in the East Baton Rouge Parish courthouse in February, 1986 listed items seized from Seal's residence. Included on the itemized list is one "Glory electric money counter."

Most of what Ken Webb told task force agents about Seal and his smuggling operation was corroborated by independent investigation because no one wanted to rely solely on what Webb said.

For example, a Houston FBI agent was able to locate and interview the seller of the pickup truck. He confirmed that he sold his truck for $8,000 cash to Barry Seal. The sale took place in a room at the Hilton Airport Hotel.

A Texas FBI agent had interviewed the former owner of the *Lauren Lee* in November 1982. He told the agent that Barry Seal bought the boat and paid for it with a cashier's check for $129,931.50 and $80,000 in cash. This corroborated what Webb told Bremer, Redford, and Milan during the Shreveport interviews.

Kenneth Webb was a controversial figure but he wasn't coerced into cooperating with the Louisiana State Police or the DEA in the investigation of Barry Seal.

It was Webb who fled from Florida when Seal was indicted and contacted Lt. Milan and provided information. Webb continued to cooperate with task force agents throughout the course of the investigation. He eventually testified before the federal grand jury for about six hours.

Not only did Ken Webb have a great deal of personal knowledge about Seal, he knew the smuggling operation. And Webb had an excellent memory. In a series of in-depth personal interviews and numerous long distance phone conversations, Webb named most of the people involved in Seal's smuggling operations and explained the role played by each.

Webb's insider knowledge of Seal's operation got the task force off to a running start. It would have been foolish for agents not to take advantage of his willingness to cooperate. In criminal investigations, you take your informants as well as confidential sources as you find them, warts and all.

Critics wondered why the Baton Rouge Middle District task force would target Seal for a major investigation when he was already being prosecuted in the Southern District of Florida in Miami. To do so would seem to be a duplication of investigation and prosecution efforts and a waste of government resources. On the other hand, there were valid reasons for targeting him in both states.

First of all, Seal's Florida indictments did not guarantee convictions. They were merely accusations that needed to be proven at a trial, probably several years away.

Secondly, in the Florida cases, an informant had introduced Seal to the undercover DEA agent Randy Beasley. Prosecutions based on undercover buys arranged by an informant can be iffy prosecutions because juries are generally unsympathetic toward the government's use of informants. Some jurors will not convict a defendant whose misfortune is due to the work of a snitch. Moreover, an undercover case is often countered by a claim of entrapment. It is a defense tactic that occasionally outweighs the evidence and proves to be a successful.

Thirdly, there were a dozen or so other men and women associated with Seal's smuggling operation and they were included in the Baton Rouge task force investigation — but not in Florida.

All of these factors were considered.

The deciding factor was that the Florida charges involved fake methaqualone tablets made of chalk. And there was reliable information that Seal had escalated from smuggling pills and marijuana to smuggling tons of cocaine worth vastly more per load.

Chapter 6
Cocaine Airline

By his own admission, Seal began smuggling small quantities of marijuana by air beginning in early 1976. During those fledgling years as a drug smuggler he based his smuggling plane at a small airport located about fifty miles west of Baton Rouge near the Cajun community of Opelousas, Louisiana.

An FAA-certified aircraft mechanic named Joseph Nevil Evans lived in a trailer at this airport and managed it. Evans was from Mena, Arkansas and was reportedly a first-rate mechanic who had once been employed by Louisiana Aircraft at Ryan Airport in Baton Rouge. While there he serviced Seal's plane. The two became friends.

Seal often made professional friends through shared experiences — high school, prison and love of planes and flying.

Evans was working for an Opelousas company that owned a plane and it was his job to maintain the aircraft. Unfortunately, a mid-air collision killed the company pilot. Suddenly, Evans was out of a job so he moved back to Mena, Arkansas, and went to work for Fred Hampton, the owner of Rich Mountain Aviation.

Barry Seal started smuggling marijuana. He eventually escalated to cocaine because, as he later explained, pound-for-pound, it was more profitable to carry "coke than weed." Marijuana was a bulkier product that took up more room in the plane. Marijuana made a smelly cargo that was easily detected by US Customs agents and their drug-sniffing dogs.

Seal smuggled his first significant load of cocaine on December 17, 1978, when he landed at the airstrip near Santa Marta and picked up 100 kilos from the two Lacutir brothers, Jose and Enrique. He delivered the cocaine to his private strip near Port Vincent, Louisiana, where the load was turned over to several of his underlings to be transported to Florida in a car. Seal left the plane parked on his private strip and returned to his home in Baton Rouge.

Barry Seal's grass landing airstrip in Ascension Parish. His warning sign carried contact information.

In April 1979 he and one of his Baton Rouge pals, flew from La Ceiba. Somewhere over Ascension Parish south of Baton Rouge in the vicinity of the Sunshine Bridge, his passenger bailed out wearing a backpack containing several kilos of cocaine. On the way down, the skydiver started to drift toward the nearby Texaco refinery. He lost the backpack while jerking the shrouds to avoid certain disaster.

Seal sent him back the same night with orders to find the backpack. He found it.

Some of Barry Seal's Favorite Rural Smuggling Strips

Opelousas airport: Barry Seal's drug shipments were usually brought into the Opelousas airport, also known as St. Landry Parish Airport or Ahart Field.

Occasionally Seal used several other landing strips that were located within fifty miles of Baton Rouge.

White Castle: Seal also used a private strip near White Castle, a town of about 1,900 and named after the White Castle Plantation in Iberville Parish, amid sugar cane and chemical plants.

New Roads: A small public airport across the river from Baton Rouge in Pointe Coupee Parish near New Roads,. It's a community of about 4,800 built on Mississippi floodplain near False River.

Melville: Seal used another private strip near Melville, a small community of about 1,376 in St. Landry Parish near Opelousas.

Ascension Parish: Seal had his own grass strip in Ascension Parish. Seal's private strip was about three thousand feet long. It had been carved out of a semi-remote wooded area about twenty miles southeast of Baton Rouge near the tiny town of Port Vincent. It was situated in a rural area that could be reached only by a gravel road. Far from being clandestine, the airstrip was in a remarkably accessible location with several families residing within viewing distance of the landing field.

Seal's private strip was a poorly-kept secret. Almost everyone in local and federal law enforcement knew where it was. Seal had erected a large sign at the end of the runway that read, "Posted. Private Property" and proclaimed that aircraft operations took place twenty-four hours a day. Trespassers were warned that tampering with an aircraft was a federal offense. Seal's name, address and phone number was on the sign.

The delivery technique that Barry Seal finally settled on required the pilot to airdrop the cocaine at predetermined locations, usually somewhere in the Atchafalaya Basin, the swamp between Baton Rouge and Lafayette.

The cocaine, usually 300 kilos per flight, was packed into six military duffel bags. The bags were dropped from the plane, recovered by the ground crew, loaded into a helicopter and then flown to another secure location where they were transferred to cars for the trip to Florida.

When the Baton Rouge task force began operating, the duffel bags were being transported in the trunks of three identical dark-blue, 1979 Mercury Grand Marquis four-door sedans, each bearing Florida license plates. Seal would later explain to agents that he used the Grand Marquis because it had a deep trunk.

On the return trip, one or more of the cars would usually be carrying a suitcase full of cash in payment of the delivery fee. The three cars were kept parked at various locations around Baton Rouge when they weren't hauling cocaine or cash. Occasionally Seal would loan the cars to friends.

"Air Seal" became a first-class smuggling operation: sophisticated, well organized and well equipped. Seal maintained a shortwave radio station near Baton Rouge. He or an assistant would monitor the flight and stay in radio contact with the plane. Seal paid the assistant $10,000 per flight. They used a numeric code to communicate with the pilot who would be flying a predetermined route from Colombia to Louisiana. His pilots were provided with Baird night vision goggles costing over $5,000 each.

When a flight was scheduled, one of Seal's people would be stationed as a lookout at the location on the Louisiana Gulf Coast. The lookout's job was to make certain that a US Customs or a DEA plane was not following the plane. If the plane was being tailed, the pre-planned scenario called for the mission to be aborted. Seal's plane would fly back to the Gold Button Ranch in Belize.

The preferred smuggling plane for Air Seal was a twin-engine Piper Navajo that he had fitted with a Panther conversion consisting of more powerful modified engines, four-blade propellers and vertical winglets. Seal used two Navajos, each fitted with state-of-the-art electronic gear and navigation equipment that he bought through his friend and avionics guru, Homer "Red" Hall, who at one time resided in Baton Rouge.

Hall, now deceased, lived in Baton Rouge when he first met Seal. They became friends. Like Seal, Hall had learned to fly under the tutelage of Eddie Duffard. Hall left Baton Rouge and went to Columbus, Ohio, where he went to work as a salesman for ElectroSonics. The company specialized in the sale and installation of avionics equipment. Seal eventually bought approximately $750,000 in avionics gear for his planes from ElectroSonics.

Although Seal was cautious and his operation was sophisticated, he could not expect to always operate in a risk-free environment. One time he gave Red Hall a paper bag full of cash in part payment of an equipment bill for his Piper Seneca. When Hall brought the cash to ElectroSonics one of the company executives got suspicious and contacted the US Customs Service. From then on, Customs agents in Columbus were able to keep tabs on every Seal plane brought to ElectroSonics.

Seal's principal pilot became his former brother-in-law, William Larry "Billy" Bottoms. Following his graduation from Northeast Louisiana University in Monroe in 1974, Bottoms was commissioned in the US Navy then pilot training at Pensacola Naval Air Station where he graduated second in his class.

As mission commander and plane commander, he flew an anti-submarine warfare P-3, the Navy version of the Lockheed Electra, with Patrol Squadron VP-47, the Golden Swordsmen. He made six-month deployments to Misawa, Japan and to Okinawa. He was also assigned to La Réunion off the coast of Madagascar to fly surveillance on the first Soviet aircraft carrier task force to sail into the Pacific. He was a lieutenant at the time of his release from active duty in June 1980 — shortly before Seal got out of the Honduran prison. Bottoms was a skilled Navy-trained multi-engine pilot who had extensive experience navigating and flying lengthy flights on precise routes.

Billy Bottoms was exactly the pilot Seal needed.

Bottoms said he began making drug flights for Seal soon after he left Navy active duty. He began in the summer of 1980. And after a few "training flights" with Seal, Bottoms flew all of the smuggling flights, about twenty-five, between Colombia and Louisiana. Usually Emile Camp was his copilot.

Bottoms would always fly up the Yucatan Peninsula to Tizimin then across the Gulf of Mexico. He would drop very low among the hundreds of offshore oil and gas platforms to enter Louisiana between Houma and New Iberia.

After Bottoms came aboard as pilot, Seal continued to set up the flights, handle the logistics, oversee the recovery of the cocaine and arrange for it to be transported to Florida and elsewhere.

Bottoms isn't proud of what he did but he doesn't alibi or claim to have been seduced into smuggling by his former brother-in-law.

Seal was intelligent, creative and a stickler for detail. Every flight was carefully scripted and meticulously carried out. He relied on Joe Evans to keep his planes in tip-top flying condition. He had no tolerance for screw-ups. Mistakes were few and far between but they did strike on occasion.

Bottoms recalled that on one flight he was supposed to make the drop near the end of the runway in Opelousas, but he could not make radio contact with the ground crew. He made two passes over the runway. Silence. On the third approach, he was finally able to raise the ground crew and the helicopter pilot who was waiting to pick up the cocaine. Bottoms radioed to the ground crew and told them to open the hangar doors and stay in the office trailer. He radioed to the chopper pilot and told him to leave. Bottoms landed and taxied into the hangar and shut the doors.

As the helicopter was lifting off, a sheriff's deputy drove up with his emergency lights flashing. Bottoms sent one of the ground crew out to talk. The deputy wanted to know why the helicopter took off so fast without running lights. The deputy was told that the oil field service helicopter had landed for fuel — and the pilot was just another of those crazy former Vietnam chopper pilots. Satisfied with the explanation for the suspicious take-off, the deputy drove away. He had no idea that a Piper Navajo loaded with three-hundred kilos of cocaine was sitting in the hangar not twenty feet away.

On another occasion Bottoms could not raise anyone at the drop site so he flew on to Opelousas, landed and parked the plane in the hangar. He was thoroughly "pissed." He loaded the cocaine into Joe Evans's pickup truck then drove it to Baton Rouge. He called someone to pick him up at the 7-Eleven store near Seal's house. Then Bottoms drove the truck through the drainage ditch in Seal's front yard and parked it on his front lawn. He then called Seal and told him where the load was. Seal was watching TV at the time. He panicked when Bottoms told him that 300 kilos of cocaine were sitting in his front yard.

How Air Seal Fleet Grew

Smuggling by air became Barry Seal's full-time occupation.

By 1982, his fleet of planes had grown to a mini-air force. He started with the single Beechcraft D-18 he acquired in 1972—the one with the oversize cargo door seen by Eddie Duffard.

Two Piper Navajos served as the workhorse of the fleet hauling cocaine from Colombia to Louisiana.

His personal plane was a Piper Seneca, which made several drug flights and was sometimes flown as a decoy when a drug flight was scheduled.

He had a Grumman Albatross, a Convair C-131, and a Lear jet that was used for "executive transportation."

Two leased Beech King Air planes were used for hauling cash and running errands.

A Hughes helicopter was used to transport the cocaine from the drop zone to another location where it could be safely loaded into the three Mercury sedans. Eventually, he would acquire a C-123 cargo plane.

In mid-1982 Seal moved his flight operations from Opelousas to Mena Intermountain Regional Airport in Mena, Arkansas. Hall later confirmed to task force agents that Seal moved his planes to the airport at Mena in 1982 and rented a hangar from Fred Hampton.

The location was perfect for Seal because of the presence of Rich Mountain Aviation with its aircraft modification and repair services and Joe Evans, his trusted mechanic. Seal soon had his own hangar built at a cost of about $70,000.

An added plus was the fact that Mena was far enough from Baton Rouge and Opelousas. This afforded Seal some needed relief from Lt. "Butch" Milan and Sgt. Jack Crittenden.

Milan said he was well aware of Barry's smuggling operation. He didn't have the budget or the planes to keep up with Seal. Because Crittenden spent a lot of time at the Baton Rouge airport and often saw Seal, he asked Crittenden to arrange a meeting with Seal. Crittenden was able to do so. The meeting took place at Ruth's Chris Steakhouse in early 1982.

At the meeting Milan told Seal he knew that he was smuggling drugs. He suggested that Seal might help himself by working for the Louisiana State Police and the DEA. Seal wanted to think about it. He called Milan a few days later and said he was not interested. Milan told Seal that he was not going to let him operate in Louisiana and he was going to put his detectives on him round the clock until they caught him.

He said Seal responded with something like, "What if I move out of the state?"

Milan told him that would be fine—do it soon. Not very long after the steakhouse meeting, he learned that Seal had moved his planes to Mena.

The Ruth's Chris Steakhouse sit-down with Lt. Milan and Sergeant Crittenden was not the first dealings Seal had with Louisiana State Police officers.

Sometime in 1980 or 1981, Seal suspected that the Alcohol, Tax and Firearms (ATF) agents were on him for something. He didn't know what, but he was still edgy from being caught up in the 1972 Customs sting that resulted in his trial in New Orleans.

Seal contacted the State Police and told them he had information he wanted to provide to Colonel Grover "Bo" Garrison who was then state police superintendent.

The matter was assigned to William "Rut" Whittington and Charles S. Koon. Whittington held the rank of corporal and was a detective. Koon was a CPA and special financial analyst, and both men were assigned to the LSP Intelligence Unit. Charlie Koon retired and has since died. Rut Whittington, eventually became the superintendent of the Louisiana State Police and is now retired.

Whittington said that Seal made several visits to the intelligence unit's office. It looked like Seal's only purpose was to establish some credibility as an informant in the event he had another run-in with federal agents.

Seal claimed to have information about explosives but he never produced it.

What he wanted was a letter from LSP attesting to his cooperation. He didn't get it.

Rut Whittington and Charlie Koon found their short-lived association with Barry Seal to be an amusing interlude. They told him they knew he was just playing them for "insurance."

When they quizzed him about his searchlight business and asked how he made his money, he would just laugh. Although Barry Seal never provided any information of value, he was signed up as a confidential "source" of the Louisiana State Police.

The period between June 1980 and February 1984 was Barry Seal's most prolific smuggling years. Aerial delivery of cocaine by Air Seal was a routine activity. He began by flying between five and ten smuggling trips himself. He planned another twenty-five that were flown by William Bottoms.

US Customs or DEA never interdicted any of the drug flights that Barry Seal flew or planned. Both agencies certainly had substantial and reliable information that he was a drug smuggler.

One of the reasons for Seal's "achievement" was the inability of either agency to concentrate their efforts on him. They did not have sufficient personnel to devote full-time to one smuggler. This was a shortcoming that the task force concept was designed to surmount.

Baton Rouge task force agents were able to devote almost 100 percent of their time to the investigation of Barry Seal, his associates, and the smuggling operation.

Chapter 7
Title III Wiretap

With Barry Seal's bona fides as a drug smuggler firmly established, and with reliable information on how he was making the deliveries, the Baton Rouge task force made a plan.

They would to try to nab the ground crew and pilots during the delivery of a load of cocaine. That's a great plan if you know when and where the delivery is going to take place.

The task force didn't have that kind of information. The government doesn't issue crystal balls and no one knew how to work a Ouija board — so then why not try a Title III?

A Title III is a wiretap and is so named because the law authorizing the interception of telephone communications is contained in Title III of Public Law 90-351. Somewhat complex in function, this law gives authority to the FBI and the DEA to intercept telephone calls to combat criminal activity.

The four pay phones at this Baton Rouge convenience were monitored by the FBI when smuggler Barry Seal made calls beginning in May 1983 and ending a few months later.

Agents knew Seal planned much of his drug dealings and flights over public pay telephones. He had dealt with Randy Beasley almost exclusively over pay phones. DEA agents had spotted Seal on numerous occasions using pay phones at various locations throughout Baton Rouge.

When Seal was out on the street, he carried a pager and a camera case loaded with rolls of quarters. When he got a page, he headed for a pay phone.

Agents would try for a Title III wiretap. Wiretap cases are commonly given a code name. FBI headquarters approved "Coinroll" as the official code name for the investigation of Seal in the Baton Rouge Middle District of Louisiana.

FBI critics and "big brother" conspiracy advocates believe that government agents run around the country tapping phones based on nothing more than whimsy. This is simply not true.

There are procedures and safeguards written into the Title III law that make it difficult for the government to tap a telephone. One safeguard is that a federal judge, not the FBI, must sign an order authorizing the interception of telephone calls.

The FBI cannot unilaterally decide to tap a phone and then go out and do it. In fact, an FBI agent cannot apply to a federal judge for a wiretap order on his or her own authority. Specific written permission from the US attorney general or from a specially-named assistant attorney general who has been designated to give the required authority is required before an FBI agent can go to a judge to seek an order. Moreover, FBI procedure does not allow an agent to apply to the Department of Justice for wiretap authority without first getting the approval from several levels of high-ranking FBI officials including, at times, the director. These checks and balances prevent the FBI from indiscriminately using wiretaps to solve criminal cases.

There are effective deterrents keeping FBI agents from illegally tapping phones. When they get caught doing so, not only will they lose their job, they can end up paying a $10,000 fine and spending up to five years in the federal penitentiary, or both.

Use of a wiretap is restricted to investigations involving any offense punishable by death and certain specific criminal violations that are named in the statute. A partial listing of the specific violations for which wiretaps are authorized includes kidnapping, obstruction of criminal investigations, gambling, bribery of public officials, racketeering investigations, and of course the activity in which Barry Seal was involved: offenses involving importation, receiving, buying, selling, or concealing or otherwise dealing in narcotic drugs, marijuana, or other dangerous drugs.

The application for the order authorizing the interception of telephone calls must be in the form of a sworn affidavit stating the authority of the applicant. Among these requirements is the need for a complete statement of the facts and circumstances. The agent must justify the order. The agent must describe whether or not other investigative procedures have been tried and failed and why they reasonably appear to be unlikely to succeed if attempted. Specific details of the particular offense that is being, or about to be, committed must be included, along with a particular description of the types of communications sought to be intercepted and the identity, if known, of the person or persons who might commit a crime. Several levels of FBI hierarchy must be convinced that a wiretap is necessary.

The affidavit for the wiretap had to be a factual account of what the government agents knew about Barry Seal's smuggling activities. After top managers and attorneys in the FBI approved the affidavit, it would be sent to the Department of Justice. There more lawyers would go over it. After the affidavit and the probable cause it contained had run the gamut of intense legal scrutiny, it be presented to a judge. That judge could still find fault and reject the application as lacking sufficient probable cause.

The FBI doesn't employ a staff of writers to do affidavits. That task is traditionally handled by the case agent.

This writer was to be the "investigative officer" who would write the affidavit and swear to the truth of its contents. It would be a document that would be studied by a lot of experts before the judge would ever see it. It had to be legally unblemished because no one working on the investigation wanted to give Seal's lawyers any opportunity to attack the affidavit. The attorney could get it quashed because of some technicality or lack of probable cause. The GS pukes that Seal despised did not intend to give him any reason to gloat.

The process of writing the affidavit began early in May 1983 with the review of reams of reports prepared by DEA, US Customs, Louisiana State Police and several foreign government agencies. Howard Whitworth and Charlie Bremer had gathered the investigative reports and other documents together at the DEA.

Based on information provided by several informants, and from Randy Beasley's personal experience in dealing with Seal, it was reasonable to conclude that Seal was delivering the drugs, either to his own private grass strip in Ascension Parish or to isolated waterways such as Lake Salvadore. The investigative reports indicated that Seal had been for some time and still was a major player in the drug smuggling business.

Task force agents looked into the possibility of renting property near Seal's private grass landing strip from where they could watch a plane landing. With the help of Murphy Painter, then the chief deputy of the Ascension Parish Sheriff's Office, one prospective location was found. The rent was high and agents would have to live in the place.

The plan was abandoned because the bosses were reluctant to commit the manpower. They considered using sophisticated listening devices and cameras, but agents never pursued finding a source for the equipment or researching whether it was legal.

The wiretap was going to involve pay telephones. A lot of them. Since it would be physically and technically impossible to intercept and monitor calls from every phone Seal was using, the choices had to be narrowed to a realistic number. This required extensive surveillance of the smuggler. This ushered in the next phase of Operation Coinroll.

Most FBI field divisions have a Special Operations Group (SOG) to handle surveillance work and Bob Tucker supervised the New Orleans group. His crew consisted of Ed Lee, John Fleming, Joe Slaughter, Joe Leake, Bill Thees, and Dale Farmer.

They had an assortment of undercover vehicles, namely a van, some Dodge two-doors and a rented Mercury — though not a Grand Marquis like Seal favored.

Agents even had an air force and two pilots, Bob Dunbar and Jerry Smolinski. Admittedly, the undercover air force was not as large and sophisticated as was Seal's because they didn't have the budget he had. What they did have was a crew of experienced agents who knew what they were doing. Their mission was simply to follow Seal day and night to identify the pay phones he was using most frequently, then get the phone numbers. It was an uncomplicated request that sounded easy. It was not. It was an assignment that would take a lot of hours, lots of patience, and ingenuity. The group accomplished their mission in an exemplary manner.

Beginning on May 2, 1983, the team took to the streets of Baton

Rouge. There were usually three or four agents using an assortment of vehicles at any one time. When the weather permitted, the air force was brought in to assist in the surveillance. Because some of the New Orleans SOG agents were on another assignment for the first few days of the surveillance, Tucker arranged to borrow a couple of cars and agents from the Atlanta FBI office.

Surveillance activity entails long periods of tedium interspersed with sporadic outbreaks of panic.

Agents on surveillance can quickly become convinced that the target of the surveillance has spotted them. Sometimes it does happen. It is called getting "burned." Agents don't like to get burned. Getting burned was especially risky with Barry Seal.

To illustrate, on the morning of their first day on the job Seal led the Atlanta FBI team up a church driveway that ended in a cul-de-sac. He then blocked the exit with his Cadillac. There was a brief staring contest between the fox and the hounds. Seal finally gave them a finger-wave, shook his head in disgust and drove off. The incident involving the Atlanta agents was ample proof that Seal would be very difficult to follow, and was characteristic of his contempt for GS pukes.

More evidence that Seal was a formidable adversary is a photo of him in his helicopter following a landing in his Baton Rouge back yard. Agents shot the photo and presented it to the author as a constant reminder.

Because of his own paranoia, Seal was suspicious of virtually every stranger he encountered — and anyone else who he thought was showing too much interest in him.

He drove his car erratically. Sometimes he stopped suddenly to get out and stare at a car that he thought had been behind him for too long a time. Usually, the "suspect car" was occupied by an innocent civilian who had no idea why they were getting the evil eye from Seal. They probably thought he was a nut case.

Seal frequently drove his electric golf cart up and down the dead-end street of his subdivision. The fact that he lived on a dead-end street made surveillance even more difficult. The surveillance cars couldn't loiter on his street or on the two-way road connection. Neighborhood Watch programs, heavy traffic, and a four-foot deep drainage ditch on each side of the main road made surveillance duty in a car rather hazardous. Agents were able to deal successfully with the obstacles and avoided serious mishaps.

The team worked from April into October 1983 following Seal as he drove around Baton Rouge on his errands. He was seen using pay phones throughout the capital city, sometimes as many as five different pay phones in a one-hour period. He traveled in any one of four different vehicles, sometimes accompanied by a companion who would act as a lookout while he was on a pay phone.

Radio traffic among task force vehicles was carried on guardedly over a scrambled VHF frequency using code words. Even though the team was using what was supposed to be a secure VHF frequency, Bob Tucker suspected that Seal was able to monitor their radio transmissions so he put out some bait to find out if that were the case. He had learned about radio telephones in his Army career.

On June 8, 1983, the author was aloft as an observer in a Louisiana State Police Cessna flown by a trooper. The SOG air force, a single-engine Cessna, was down for maintenance and the State Police had offered their help. This happened to be the day of the test to determine if Seal was monitoring the task force radio transmissions. Seal was at his home. The state trooper/pilot and his FBI observer were orbiting above the general area of his subdivision at about fifteen hundred feet.

Tucker broadcast a message instructing all agents to proceed at once to the nearby Holiday Inn for an "emergency" meeting. Tucker figured Seal would jump at the chance to catch a bunch of agents and take their license plate numbers — and he was right.

Immediately after the bogus order was aired, Seal bolted from his house, jumped into his Cadillac and sped to the Holiday Inn. He cruised through the parking lot expecting to confront a bevy of FBI agents. He found none. He returned home, without a doubt, fuming over having been snookered by the GS pukes.

With his suspicions confirmed, Tucker broadcast a message to the LSP plane telling the pilot to discontinue observation. Before the pilot had a chance to acknowledge, Seal came waddling out of his house. He stood in his driveway waving up at the plane with what looked like a big white bath towel. His action, although somewhat humiliating, was funny. It certainly wasn't interpreted by the pilot and the author as a sign of surrender.

Occasionally, there were incidents that took the boredom out of Seal-watching for some members of the team. Jerry Smolinski and Bob Dunbar were flying around over Baton Rouge in the FBI plane when Seal suddenly came up on their tail in his helicopter. The agents avoided a dogfight in the skies over Baton Rouge. Their mission was aborted. They barreled back to New Orleans with Seal in hot pursuit part of the way.

Ed Lee recalled an unintentional encounter that took place in a parking lot across from Ruby Red's, one of Seal's favorite Baton Rouge restaurants. Seal was inside dining. Lee was sitting in his vehicle in the parking lot. When he saw Seal come out of the restaurant, he crouched down on the seat. He heard the sound of Seal's Cadillac, which had a blown muffler. It drew nearer.

Suddenly, a tapping on his car window. Lee looked up. Seal peered down at him and smiled. Seal waved bye-bye and drove away.

The team observed their target as he used pay phones in such places as the Hilton Hotel, at different Baton Rouge restaurants, and several times in a bowling alley. Convenience store and gas station pay phones were his regular haunts. Seal would sometimes be seen using two pay phones at once. Eventually a pattern of coin phone usage began to emerge. He would usually answer his pager by going to the nearest pay phone. He had a fondness for originating and receiving calls from seven pay phones all located a short distance from his residence. By August 1983, SOG had a good handle on the phones Seal was using most frequently.

Four of the phones were on the outside front wall of a 7-Eleven store at Siegen Lane and Perkins Road. Two hung on the outside wall of a drugstore in the shopping center across Perkins Road from the 7-Eleven. The seventh pay phone was on a wall inside the Winn-Dixie store located in the rear of the same shopping center.

Seal's favorite pay phones were well marked. All of them had "Out of Service." stickers covering the coin slots. He had a book of these stickers and he used them to make certain a phone was available when he needed it.

The surveillance was continued because the affidavit had to contain specific dates on which each of the seven target phones was used. The usage had to be ongoing, essentially up to the day the judge would see it.

Once the wiretap started, agents had to be able to physically observe Seal using the phone before they could monitor the call. This requirement would be part of the judge's order. It was a protective measure intended to safeguard against the possibility of intercepting conversations of anyone other than Seal or other named members of his smuggling organization.

The group solved the problem. There were never any intercepted conversations other than Seal's or those of his associates who were named in the order.

Drafting the affidavit, critiquing, and editing it took weeks. Warren Jung did this. He was the FBI agent who served as the attorney and principal legal advisor in the New Orleans office.

The senior editor on the project was a knowledgeable supervisor at FBI headquarters who was experienced in getting affidavits approved by the Department of Justice. Several draft versions were sent to him, talking with him and revising. As the affidavit was being refined, the team continued to watch Seal to provide the required evidence that he was still using the seven phones regularly.

In mid-October, a final draft of the affidavit was sent to FBI headquarters. The FBI supervisors signed off and sent it over to the Department of Justice. On October 22, 1983, Brad Myers was notified by telephone that the affidavit was approved. Deputy Assistant Attorney General Stephen Trott had signed the authorization approving the application for the court order.

The team anticipated that the judge would sign the wiretap order. The main "plant," the confidential location where the monitoring would take place, was ready.

The DEA had donated a couch, some chairs, several desks, and a large TV—Seal couldn't talk all the time and it was football season.

FBI agent Lloyd East of the Baton Rouge office was nominated and had graciously accepted the job of plant manager. He had things well organized and was standing by with a half-dozen or so DEA and FBI agents waiting for the word to begin monitoring.

FBI agent Joe Leake, the technical specialist, was with a security representative of South Central Bell ready to do his thing.

Warren Jung and Brad Myers met with the DEA and FBI agents who would be doing the monitoring to instruct them.

Generally speaking, the wiretap law authorizes the interception of wire communications for the purpose of obtaining evidence of criminal activity. This meant the agents doing the monitoring were required to "minimize" interceptions. Only conversations in which Seal was heard to be planning or discussing criminal activity were to be monitored and recorded. If agents heard conversations that were not pertinent or indicative of criminal activity, they were to immediately stop listening and stop recording. This is the process known as minimization and all DEA and FBI agents who were to participate in the monitoring got minimized.

However, the requirement to minimize is not so rigid that agents are prevented from listening long enough to determine the topic.

Agents were to remain alert for the use of code words as had been used by Seal when dealing with DEA agent Randy Beasley where pills were "Kawasaki parts."

Suspicious conversations were to be monitored and recorded so they could be studied for hidden meaning. The agents were also told to be alert for material that could be considered Brady material.

Late in the afternoon of October 25, 1983, Brad Myers and the writer met with the late US District Judge Frank J. Polozola.

The judge read and studied the sixty-five-page "Affidavit in Support of an Application." for about two hours. As he read, he would ask an occasional question or make a comment. The judge finally decided that there was sufficient probable cause and he signed an order authorizing the interception of calls on the seven pay phones.

Coinroll went online at 8:35 pm that same evening.

There was great excitement among the troops when, at approximately 9 pm SOG agents reported that Seal had left his residence in his Cadillac and was apparently headed for the 7-Eleven. The main plant was alerted. Agents anxiously awaited word from SOG to begin monitoring one of the four pay phones.

The word never came. Seal drove past the 7-Eleven and on to the Holiday Inn. He went inside and used a pay phone.

A revised and updated affidavit was taken to Judge Polozola on December 6 asking for authority to add four new coin phones.

Through surveillance, agents learned that Seal had lost interest in one of the original seven pay phones. He had started using all of four pay phones in another nearby shopping center. Judge Polozola found the necessary probable cause and signed another order adding four new phones. Agents were now monitoring ten pay phones.

DEA and FBI agents were on the watch around the clock, seven days a week, monitoring the numerous calls that Seal was making from the staked out phones. SOG agents were always positioned to be able to observe the pay phones while another crew was available to take Seal under surveillance when he left from his home and was on the move.

There were a few times when agents thought something might be up, based on what they were hearing. As an example, on November 24, 1983, US Customs arranged for an ECM Hawkeye to be aloft over the Louisiana coast for several hours. Nothing materialized.

On another occasion, Baton Rouge agents requested that their Arkansas counterparts observe the Mena airport. The aircraft that was expected never showed up. Foiled again!

The most notable conversation became known as the "duck call." One evening Seal began speaking with a Cajun accent. He was seemingly invited the party on the other end of the conversation to go duck hunting. The FBI agent on duty "minimized" the chat. It was two Cajuns talking about going on a duck hunt.

It wasn't duck season.

Seal was talking to a key member of his ground recovery crew. Agents at the plant were convinced that the smuggler was about to tell the guy the time and place of the next airdrop. The ill-advised minimization prevented agents from learning if they were correct.

The wiretap produced some usable intelligence. A few new associates of Seal were identified. Unfortunately, the agents were not getting conversations naming a specific time or place when a load of cocaine was due.

The operation was burning up lots and lots of DEA and FBI agent staff hours. The respective agency bosses were getting edgy.

By mid-December it became obvious that if things continued the way they were going, the end of the Title III wiretap was drawing near. Judge Polozola was provided with weekly summaries of the activity. He was coming to the same conclusion.

The next phase of the task force investigation was going to be a grand jury inquiry. In an effort to stimulate Seal and his associates into having more informative conversations, subpoenas were served on several key figures known to be involved in Seal's smuggling operation. Several weeks passed, but still there were no significant conversations.

The wiretap operated for eighty-five days, including President's Day, Thanksgiving, Christmas, and New Year's—all federal holidays. This refuted Seal's belief that GS pukes didn't work on holidays.

During the operation, hundreds of conversations were monitored in which Seal and his other associates participated. All of the conversations were recorded and transcribed. The subscribers to originating and terminating phone numbers were identified by a continuous flow of subpoenas to the phone company.

Mena/CIA conspiracy buffs should take note that during the entire time the Title III wiretap was in operation, there were no conversations intercepted between Seal, Terry Kent Reed, Bill

Clinton, Lt. Col. Oliver North, or any representative of the CIA.

Disappointingly, there were no conversations indicating a specific time and place when a load of cocaine was due to arrive.

The wiretap order was allowed to expire. Title III wiretap was shut down at 3:00 pm on January 20, 1984.

The Baton Rouge task force tried another way to arrest Seal. The investigation entered the grand jury phase. Seal's associates began to receive subpoenas.

The function of a grand jury is to gather information and hear testimony from witnesses. A lot of people knew about Seal and his smuggling operation. They were individuals who would be either for or against Seal. Some were likely to take the Fifth Amendment and some were likely to ask for immunity and it was important to see which way they would go.

Witnesses like Ken Webb who did provide testimony under oath would be locked into their testimony and vulnerable to charges of perjury if their story changed.

There was little doubt that Seal would go to trial if he was indicted. The task force was gearing up for a trial.

Upon being notified that the wiretap in Baton Rouge had fizzled out, the Little Rock FBI office arranged for a conference that was held on March 1, 1984 at Hot Springs.

In attendance were DEA and FBI agents and Polk County Sheriff A. J. Hadaway. The Arkansas State Police and the DEA and Customs had been investigating Rich Mountain Aviation, Fred Hampton, and Joe Evans.The investigation was based on information that plane N numbers were being changed and aircraft were being modifying to facilitate drug smuggling.

At the Hot Springs meeting, it was decided that Fred Hampton, Joe Evans, and Rich Mountain Aviation would become targets of a joint FBI-DEA task force investigation.

It was not long after the Hot Springs meeting that Seal made a decisive move that would have a dramatic impact on the outcome of all of the investigations aimed at him.

Chapter 8
Seal Cuts a Deal

When the two Florida indictments were returned in March 1983, Barry Seal knew he was in trouble.

He began looking for help. By his own account, sometime shortly after his surrender and court appearance in Florida, he and his attorneys met with Randy Beasley and Assistant US Attorney Bruce A. Zimet in the office of the US Attorney.

Seal hoped to stir their interest. He told them a little of his involvement with the notorious Ochoa smuggling family.

Much to Seal's amazement, the prosecutor expressed very little interest in what he told them.

Seal was unable to make a deal. This time his Southern charm did not work.

During his presentation to Zimet and Beasley, Seal offered to "flip." He promised big things but wasn't specific.

Beasley said he felt the smuggler exhibited a huge ego and thought he was untouchable. Seal wanted very little control by the DEA and wanted the charges dropped against his two men, Gary Seville and Calvin Briggs. Seal also wanted to cut the deal without telling his attorney, Richard Ben-Veniste.[1]

This was the story investigator Charlie Bremer and the writer heard when they went to Florida in April 1983 to talk to the DEA.

It is undisputed that Seal made an offer to cooperate with the DEA. Seal was rejected.

The government missed its first opportunity to turn Seal into an informant.

Following his arraignment, a discouraged Seal returned to home-town Baton Rouge where he tried to contact Stan Bardwell. They went to Baton Rouge High together. Seal later testified during the Las Vegas trial that he and Bardwell were long-time friends. If anyone would listen to Seal and try to help him work something out, he believed it would be an old friend.

During a debriefing after his guilty plea, Seal told the Baton Rouge agents that he sent an intermediary to Bardwell in the person of a Baton Rouge attorney. Seal paid him $50,000 to arrange a meeting. Seal said his representative made several attempts to set up the meeting. Bardwell kept turning him down and refusing to meet.

Bardwell's explanation for turning down the overture from Seal's attorneys was that he did not think it was "significant" and did not trust the "messenger."

There was nothing improper or illegal about Bardwell's refusal to meet with Seal. All the same, Seal was the target of Bardwell's task force. Some thought Bardwell should have met with him and heard what he had to say. He didn't.

And the government lost a second opportunity to turn Seal into an informant.

On February 14, 1984, Seal, represented by Richard Ben-Veniste, went to trial before Judge Roettger in Florida.

Baton Rouge agents heard very little about the trial. Ben-Veniste was a respected attorney specializing in white collar crimes. He had been an assistant US attorney in the Southern District of New York and the lead attorney on the Watergate Special Prosecution Force.

Randy Beasley, the undercover agent, wasn't going to have an easy time on the stand. But the DEA supervisor had assured this writer and Bremmer that the case would stand up.

He was right. The trial ended on March 17, 1984, when Seal was found guilty. Sentencing was set for May 23, 1984.

Seal was now facing a possible maximum sentence of ten years. Prison loomed. Seal was desperate.

Seal's two prior attempts to talk to government representatives had failed. He decided to go directly to Washington, DC. It was a bold and decisive move. Pure Barry Seal. It worked to his advantage.

Seal flew to Washington in his Lear jet on March 25, 1984. He paid a visit to the office of the Vice President's Drug Task Force.

He identified himself and explained to a secretary who he was and what he had in mind. He was put in contact with US Customs agent Jim Howell who was assigned to the task force. Seal's bona fides as a cocaine smuggler were confirmed by a phone call to the head of the Louisiana State Police. Seal was referred to agents at DEA headquarters.

That's where Seal's offer of cooperation was finally accepted.

Seal was told to contact Robert J. Joura, the DEA Group 7 supervisor in Miami. He did as instructed. Joura assigned DEA agent Ernst Jacobsen to work with him. Seal began to undergo extensive debriefings to establish his credibility.

Typically, the debriefing of a potential informant would require him or her to fully explain their criminal activity. Agents wanted verifiable information of the involvement. The informant would have to provide specific information such as dates, activity, and the names of people involved. The agents need to be convinced the informant can deliver as claimed. Agents would be on the alert for a con job.

Seal had the right credentials.

The DEA was suitably impressed with Seal's potential. On March 28, 1984, Seal signed a letter of agreement with the government.

Later that same day Seal appeared in front of Judge Jose A. Gonzalez, Jr. He entered a guilty plea to the second of the two Florida indictments. His sentencing was postponed. Steve LeClair, assistant US Attorney, authorized the DEA to use him as an informant.

Seal had finally succeeded to make a deal with the government. He was now officially acting as an informant for the DEA in Miami. More accurately, he was a twice-convicted felon facing a ten-year sentence who was cooperating with the DEA in hopes of staying out of prison.

Meanwhile, in Louisiana and Arkansas, Seal would remain under active investigation by the feds. Did they know about the Florida deal? Stay tuned.

Seal's trip to the office of the Vice President's Drug Task Force would eventually become the source of another myth that exists to this day.

The conspiracy crowd claimed that Seal had then-Vice President George H. W. Bush's "private phone number" in his wallet when Seal was murdered in 1986.

This is not true. But for some odd conspiracy theory, it gives the impression that something sinister took place—and makes for a more titillating story.

What Seal had in his wallet was the phone number for the office the Vice President's Drug Task Force. That shouldn't be a surprise since it was the first government agency willing to act on Seal's offer of cooperation.

Seal also had the author's private investigator business card in his wallet at his death — but that's even more ominous and fodder for yet another conspiracy.

Stan Bardwell, Brad Myers, and the task force agents were not told that Seal was cooperating with Miami agents of the DEA. As a result, some hostility developed between the Baton Rouge Middle District task force agents and Miami DEA agents. This came about because the Louisiana agents continued to investigate Seal and his organization. The grand jury investigation was underway. Subpoenas had already been served on several of his associates. More were planned.

The first shot of an internecine conflict was fired by Bob Joura from South Florida. He called Baton Rouge on April 4, 1984, to complain. The subpoenas being served in the Baton Rouge Middle District were messing up a major "deal" that he had going in Miami.

Joura didn't say what the deal was. He made it clear that he wanted the subpoenas withdrawn. This was a very unusual request that called for some kind of explanation. None was offered.

Grand jury subpoenas had been served in Louisiana on Seal's co-pilot Emile Camp and on the owner of an aviation business in New Orleans where Seal had moved his Lear jet. Seal wanted to keep the Baton Rouge feds from tracking its movements.

From the viewpoint of federal agents in Louisiana, it was curious that people who were known to be involved with Barry Seal and had been served with subpoenas were able to get a Miami DEA supervisor to intervene on their behalf. It didn't seem appropriate and made little sense. The subpoenas remained in force.

Joura made a second call several weeks later with another complaint. The subpoenas were messing up his deal. He wanted them withdrawn. That wasn't going to happen because Stan Bardwell and Brad Myers were the only people who could excuse the witnesses. Joura offered no explanation.

The subpoenas were not recalled in Louisiana. Seal was caught in the middle as two federal agencies failed to make their case to each other.

At the time of Joura's second call, subpoenas had been served on Homer "Red" Hall of Columbus, Ohio, and on a helicopter pilot who lived in Baton Rouge. Once again, the Miami DEA had intervened on behalf of two known associates of Barry Seal who were scheduled to appear before the federal grand jury in Baton Rouge.

Task force staff in Baton Rouge did not understand why the DEA in Miami was raising a ruckus about their subpoenas. From their viewpoint, Seal was a convicted drug smuggler facing a ten-year prison sentence.

Seal continued to fly freely in and out of Baton Rouge and to other parts of the country. Agents were convinced Seal was still smuggling loads of cocaine. It was galling to have the Miami DEA complain about the efforts in Baton Rouge to investigate Seal and the other members of his drug organization.

It seemed as though Joura considered the Louisiana agents rank amateurs. Journa had worked cases on major smugglers and dealt with huge planeloads of cocaine and marijuana. Bremer had twelve years of experience as a DEA agent.

Where was their mutual respect?

There weren't any shouting matches. But there was admittedly some rancor. The problem grew because Baton Rouge task force agents did not know Seal's status had changed dramatically. He was now an informer for the federal government. Baton Rouge agents were never given a proper explanation as to why their subpoenas should be withdrawn. In hindsight, perhaps the agents should have figured out what had happened in Washington and Florida—but they did not.

No one in Louisiana had any idea that Seal would flip.

There are theories why this happened.

The late Max Mermelstein had one theory. He was a convicted drug smuggler for the Medellin Cartel who turned US government informant. He observed that federal agencies are jealous of each other. They each play their cards close to the vest. They don't want to share information because it is too hard to come by. And information is too dangerous to give out because of damaging leaks or internal corruption. "Nobody talks to nobody."[2]

The problem could have been avoided had the US Attorney in Miami contacted his counterpart Stan Bardwell and told him that Barry Seal was cooperating with the DEA on a major investigation. The US Attorney could have asked Bardwell to shut down the investigation in the Baton Rouge Middle District—or at least put it on hold.

As an alternative, the US Attorney in Miami could have taken the matter up with the Department of Justice. He could have made the argument that his case—a much more significant one—was being jeopardized by the Louisiana investigation. He would very likely have had the support of the Justice Department in requesting that Bardwell discontinue the investigation.

It would also have been appropriate and helpful for the agent in charge of the Miami DEA to join with the Miami US Attorney in requesting that Bardwell close his investigation — or at least delay it temporarily until Barry was through testifying. Stan Bardwell and Brad Myers are reasonable and professional men and they would have done the right thing.

The situation in Baton Rouge was duplicated in Mena, Arkansas where the other joint DEA/FBI investigation was underway.

Asa Hutchinson, the US Attorney for the Western District of Arkansas, did not know that Seal had flipped to a DEA informant. Nor did DEA and FBI agents working the Rich Mountain Aviation case. Their investigation was originally aimed at Joe Evans and Fred Hampton. It was obviously going to involve Barry Seal because his planes were based at the Mena airport.

To further complicate matters, Albert J. Winters was just starting another grand jury investigation. He was head of the federal Organized Crime Drug Enforcement Task Force in the Eastern District of Louisiana in New Orleans. It was also going to be looking at Barry Seal.

Because of the silence of the DEA in Miami, federal agents from the IRS, DEA, Customs, and the FBI in three separate federal judicial districts were busy investigating an already-convicted drug smuggler who was a DEA informant — and they didn't know it.

It was an absurd situation reminiscent of a Keystone Kops movie, and it never should have been allowed to develop.

As Al Winters put it, Barry Seal had become "the greatest thing since sliced bread" for agents and prosecutors in South Florida.

In Baton Rouge, New Orleans, and Mena, Arkansas, Seal remained the target of an investigation by federal agents of the DEA, FBI, IRS, and US Customs and three federal grand juries as well as the Arkansas and Louisiana state police.

It was a situation relished by Seal, who thought he could play one group of investigators against another.

They were all GS pukes to him.

Chapter 9
The Nicaragua and Las Vegas Missions

DEA Agents Robert Joura and Ernst Jacobsen had to be somewhat skeptical of Barry Seal's claims. Was he trying to con the DEA?

It's not unusual for informants to exaggerate their worth, and the two agents had been in the drug investigation business long enough to know this.

To convince them of his credibility, Seal picked up a phone and called "Lito" Bustamonte and Felix Dixon Bates to set up a meeting.

The two DEA agents were suitably impressed because Bustamonte handled distribution in Miami for the Ochoas. Bates was one of their drug pilots. The brash, overconfident smuggler apparently knew them both.

However, at this point in Seal's smuggling career, it was his associate, William Roger Reaves, not Seal, who handled the South American connections.

Reaves was the smuggler Seal claimed to have met on the plane when he was coming back to the US after being released from the Honduran prison. After they agreed to join forces, it was Reaves who set up Seal's cocaine loads and dealt with the Medellin Cartel leaders.

Seal had never met the notorious Ochoa brothers. Reaves never told Pablo Escobar or Carlos Lehder what Seal's true name was. To the Colombians he was only a pilot called "El Gordo" or "The Fat Man."

In fact, Seal made his call to Bustamonte and introduced himself as El Gordo. He told Bustamonte he was really Ellis McKenzie and he wanted a direct introduction to the cartel because he wanted to start flying a high volume — more than three hundred kilos per flight.

Seal effectively cut Reaves out of the picture. He figured the cartel would not link him to the real Ellis McKenzie — who was a black man.

Seal was five feet, nine inches, about 240 pounds. His hair was blackish-brown, streaked by gray. Thinning at the top and longish sideburns so common in the 1980s.

Barry Seal bought a surplus C-123 cargo plane for smuggling flights.

Seal was Caucasian.

Seal was able pull this off because he had McKenzie's passport altered by adding his own picture. As far as the Colombians were concerned, they were dealing with someone named Ellis McKenzie. Barry Seal was unknown.

It was a fairly effective cover story. It worked for a while.

On April 8, 1984, Seal flew to Colombia accompanied by Felix Dixon Bates. Bates was flying as his co-pilot. He had no idea Seal was working for the DEA.

The two flew to Medellin where they met with Pablo Escobar, Jorge Ochoa, and his brothers, Fabio, Jr. and Juan David. They met to discuss plans for Seal to transport 1,500 kilos of cocaine into the United States. This was a large load of dope even for Miami DEA agents who were used to seeing loads growing all the time.

It was at the April 8 meeting that the first hint of the Medellin drug cartel's connection to Nicaraguan government officials was revealed. Jorge Ochoa told Seal about a 6,000-foot landing strip in Nicaragua he had acquired. Ochoa claimed that the Sandinista government had agreed to enlarge the strip and erect a hangar. They would allow the strip to be used for transshipment of drugs bound for the US. According to one account, Jorge Ochoa told Seal that although the cartel didn't share the Sandinista political philosophy, "they serve our means and we serve theirs."[1]

Seal returned to Florida to brief agents Joura and Jacobsen and to make plans to haul the cocaine. He spent the remainder of April and most of May traveling back and forth between Medellin, Panama and Miami for meetings with Jorge Ochoa and Pablo Escobar to work out the final flight details. Seal was a consummate planner who left nothing to chance. He was a risk taker. He was an egotistical know-it-all. He spoke a bit of Spanish.

On April 18, 1984, Seal, Emile Camp and Felix Bates traveled to Mena, Arkansas, with three or four of Ochoa's people to show them the Lockheed Lodestar, tail number N513V, that was to be used to transport the cocaine.

This Colombian inspection tour was confirmed by Ernst Jacobsen during testimony given on July 28, 1988, before the Subcommittee on Crime of the House Committee on the Judiciary: "After Seal returned from Colombia, the cocaine cartel instructed some of the representatives in Miami to meet with Seal, go to Mena, Arkansas, with Seal and observe the aircraft. Seal met with three or four

Colombians in Miami and then he took them to Mena, Arkansas in a private aircraft."

This appearance of three or four Colombians at the Mena airport drew a lot of attention at the small rural airport. Their visit stirred even more rumors of disturbing activities involving Seal, the CIA, "revolutionaries," and "suspicious Latinos." Actually, the presence of the Colombians didn't have anything to do with the CIA or the Contras. The Ochoas were cautious. They wanted to make certain that Seal could perform so they sent representatives to verify that he was legit and had a plane.

It was during the planning stages for the flight that Seal met Federico Vaughn, a self-proclaimed high-ranking functionary of the Nicaraguan government. US Intelligence sources said he was the senior aide to Tomas Borge, the Nicaraguan Minister of the Interior.[2]

Seal's Florida attorney, Tom Sclafani, later characterized Vaughn as a native Nicaraguan and former lieutenant in the Sandinista Army. He was the intermediary between the Sandinista government and the Ochoa brothers. Sandinistas wanted to set up cocaine processing laboratories that would generate profits to finance their war against the US-backed Contra forces.[3]

In the indictment that was subsequently returned in the Southern District of Florida against the Medellin Cartel, Vaughn was described as an assistant to Tomas Borge, Minister of the Interior of Nicaragua.

Whatever his official role might have been, Federico Vaughn was a semi-big fish because he was the connection between the Sandinistas and the Medellin cocaine producers. Barry had gained Vaughn's confidence.

On May 20, 1984, Seal and Bates flew to Managua where they met with Vaughn. He took them to the Los Brasiles airstrip five miles northeast of Managua. That's where he told Seal he could land and refuel. He also furnished Seal with an identifying code that would be recognized by air-traffic controllers at Sandino International Airport.[4]

Then came the proverbial monkey wrench. The undercover operation was disrupted on May 23, 1984.

That's when Seal appeared before Judge Norman Roettger for sentencing. The judge gave him two consecutive five-year sentences and denied an appeal bond. Seal was immediately taken into custody by US Marshals and locked up.

Did Seal have any idea he might be convicted and jailed?

It was apparent that no one from the DEA or the US Attorney's office had bothered to tell the judge about Seal's cooperation.

The DEA was in a state of panic. The agency was about to lose a highly-connected informant who was in the midst of putting together one of the biggest US cases. This was a big case, whether you measured it in kilos of cocaine or the people involved—and how high they ranked on the smuggling chain.

Seal's attorney filed an emergency motion. Judge Roettger held a closed *en camera* hearing. The judge was informed of Seal's cooperation. DEA representatives and an assistant US attorney persuaded the judge to release Seal on an appeal bond. They wanted Seal to continue cooperating with the DEA—in Florida, at least.

Meanwhile, in Baton Rouge there was rejoicing by task force staff. They had heard only that Seal had been given a ten-year sentence. He was in the custody of US Marshals and presumably was on his way to a federal penitentiary.

The Louisiana task force had it wrong.

Seal and his attorney got the smuggling trip back on track.

Barry Seal with Emile Camp flying co-pilot, flew from Mena, Arkansas on May 28, 1984, in the twin-engine Lockheed Lodestar. With the DEA's blessing, the two were en route to Colombia to pick up a load of 1,500 kilos of cocaine.

Seal landed at a remote landing strip in Colombia where kingpin Carlos Lehder met him. Under Lehder's watchful eye, the aircraft was loaded with 3,500 pounds of coke. Their plane was grossly overloaded. The runway was extremely muddy from rain. Seal did not think it was safe to try a takeoff. Lehder had different plans. He insisted that Seal take off. He was said to have been brandishing a machine gun to emphasize that he meant business.

Seal, against his better judgment, attempted a takeoff in the overloaded plane. The sloppy landing strip prevented the plane from gathering sufficient speed to fly. It crashed and was demolished. Seal and Camp were fortunate—they escaped injury.

The next attempt to haul the cocaine occurred on June 4, 1984, when Jorge Ochoa furnished Seal and Emile Camp with a twin engine Cessna Titan 404, tail number N700FL. Seal and Camp flew the Titan loaded with 660 kilos of cocaine from Colombia to Managua, Nicaragua. They landed at the Los Brasiles air base and refueled under supervision of Vaughn.

Seal took off for the flight to the United States. There had been a breakdown in communications and things didn't go well at all.

Vaughn had not made proper arrangements to clear Seal's flight with Nicaraguan authorities. Shortly after take-off, his plane was fired on by an anti-aircraft battery that guarded the air base and an oil refinery in Managua. The Titan was struck in the left engine. Seal was forced to land.

He and Camp ended up in jail where they spent the night until Federico Vaughn arranged for their release the following day.

This incident brought Barry Seal to the attention of the CIA for the first time. In subsequent testimony before Judge Jose A. Gonzalez, Jr. during Seal's sentencing on the second indictment, DEA agent Jacobsen said that during the time the smuggler was in custody in Nicaragua, the DEA had asked the CIA to find out about him. Was Seal dead or alive?

Being shot out of the sky didn't bother Seal. He told the Ochoas that he would go back to the United States, get a larger plane and return to Nicaragua to pick up the cocaine. He was flown back to the States in an aircraft owned by Pablo Escobar.

Once back in the US, Seal looked for a suitable plane. He came across an ad in *Trade-A-Plane* magazine offering a C-123 cargo plane for sale. The seller was Harry Doan, a wealthy businessman and an aircraft broker residing in Florida. Seal was sure a C-123 would get the job done, so he made arrangements to buy the surplus US Air Force plane that bore tail number N 441OF.

While Seal was getting the C-123 ready for the flight, agents Joura and Jacobsen started working on the details for clearances. Washington DEA agents Ron Caffrey and his boss Dave Westrate began briefing Lt. Col. Oliver North about the details of the upcoming undercover operation. The CIA recognized that Seal's undercover mission presented an opportunity to gather damaging evidence against the Sandinistas. The CIA approached the DEA seeking permission to install cameras on the plane. The DEA consented. On June 23, 1984, at Homestead Air Force Base, two CIA technicians installed two hidden 35mm cameras in the cargo plane.

Seal's crew consisted of co-pilot Emile Camp and flight engineer Peter F. Everson, an aircraft mechanic from England. They took off for Nicaragua on June 26, 1984. They made it to Managua where they landed the C-123 at Los Brasiles air base. There, the plane was loaded with 1,465 pounds of cocaine or about 666 kilos. The smugglers had help from Federico Vaughn, Pablo Escobar, Gonzalo Gacha, and a few Sandinista soldiers.

During the loading, Emile Camp had to operate one of the hidden cameras manually. The remote switch provided by the CIA and concealed inside Seal's trousers failed to function.

Seal flew the cocaine to Homestead AFB on June 27, 1984, where CIA representatives removed the film for developing.

What should the government do with all the cocaine?

DEA could not let the cocaine get into circulation. They staged a fake accident with the Winnebago motor home Seal and Bustamonte had bought to transport the cocaine. The DEA had an agent drive a car into the motor home. The Florida Highway Patrol responded and seized the cocaine.

Jacobsen later testified that the cartel investigated the accident. DEA had taken the precautions to have Seal's prior drug arrests and court records sealed.

It didn't work. The cartel paid an attorney $70,000 to go to Ft. Lauderdale, where he somehow found out that Seal had been arrested, tried convicted and sentenced.

An unwelcome spotlight began to shine on Seal's help to the government to expose the Sandinistas and their apparent connection to drugs.

On June 29, 1984, General Paul Gorman, US Military Commander, Southern Command, made a speech to the American Chamber of Commerce in El Salvador that was broadcast over the radio.

In his speech the general mentioned that the US government had evidence that elements of the Nicaraguan government were involved in drug smuggling. The July 1 edition of the *New York Times* carried a short, two-paragraph article, in which Gorman was quoted as saying that drug traffickers buy off governments and are "conduits for subversion" and "commanders of Nicaragua are deeply involved in these movements in the region."

General Gorman did not name Barry Seal as the source of the information. He made no mention of the undercover flight.

Seal made a second trip in the C-123 on July 7, 1984. The day before the flight, Bustamonte delivered $1.5 million in cash to Seal with instructions to take it to Pablo Escobar. Seal and his crew landed at Los Brasiles. They delivered the cash to Escobar and then learned there would be no return load of drugs even though they observed that there were 700 or 800 kilos of cocaine stored at the airfield.

Escobar told Seal his plans had changed and he wanted him to go on to Peru and fly coca paste to Nicaragua. Escobar explained that he would then send the cocaine manufactured from the paste to the US in a smaller aircraft.

Seal was suspicious. He told Escobar that he would first have to make some repairs to the aircraft before he could make the flight. Seal returned to the States empty. That's when he learned of the leak about his arrest and conviction and General Gorman's speech.

Edmond Jacoby's story outlining Seal's mission to Nicaragua appeared on the front page of the *Washington Times* on July 17, 1984.

From then on there was no longer any doubt about Seal as the DEA informant.

There had been an informal agreement that, after the last cocaine trip, Seal and all the key players would meet to celebrate. They would meet in Panama or Guatemala to celebrate and pass around the money. When they did, the feds would crash the party and arrest them all.

The DEA planned to have Seal gather all of these traffickers together in a jurisdiction where they could be arrested and assured of being extradited to the United States for prosecution. They hoped to arrest Jorge Ochoa, Juan David Ochoa, Fabio Ochoa, Pablo Escobar, Rivas Gacha, Carlos Lehder, and Federico Vaughn.

Had the plan been allowed to go forward, the entire Medellin Cartel could have been bagged.

The US government has maintained that Seal was told of the leak. Always overconfident, he opted to go anyway in hopes that the Colombians had not heard the story.

DEA agents Joura and Jacobsen did not learn of the leak until July 7, 1984. They found out after Seal and his crew were already airborne. They tried to contact Seal and warn him but couldn't make radio contact with the plane.

Peter Everson went on both C-123 trips as flight engineer and is the only living witness to these events. He has said the crew was not informed that their cover had been blown until after they returned to the US.

After Jacoby wrote his article, Seal's days as a DEA informant were over.

Any further opportunities for DEA to develop evidence of the Sandinista government's involvement in cocaine smuggling evaporated as well as the possibility of locking up the entire Medellin Cartel.

Someone had blown the cover of an informant who was

positioned to make one of the most significant criminal drug cases in America's history. They did it while the undercover operation was ongoing.

Seal's further efforts to haul cocaine for the cartel were futile. He had no further use for the C-123, so it was flown to the Mena airport and parked on the apron near his hangar. The plane remained there from July 1984 until June 1985. During the time the plane was at Mena and still owned by Seal, it made three other flights after the two to Nicaragua. It was flown to England to bring Peter Everson's Rolls Royce back to the States. There was an engine test flight. And the third flight was when Seal arranged for a Baton Rouge TV station to film a provocative special investigative report titled *Uncle Sam Wants You.*

On June 15, 1985, Seal sold the C-123 back to Harry Doan for $250,000. William Bottoms flew it to Doan's hangar at the airport at New Smyrna Beach, Florida, near Daytona. Bottoms said Seal was never again associated with that airplane. The plane was subsequently purchased by Southern Air Transport, a known CIA front.

The plane had a tragic ending—just like Seal.

On October 5, 1986, more than seven months after Seal was murdered, the same C-123 was shot down while on a flight over Nicaragua. Pilot William J. Cooper and copilot Wallace Blaine "Buzz" Sawyer were killed. Eugene Hasenfus, a former Marine paratrooper and the air freight specialist working the flight, bailed out. He was captured.

Hasenfus admitted that he worked for "Max Gomez" the "CIA overseer" who was actually Felix Rodriguez, a retired CIA officer.

Rodriguez had been recruited by Oliver North to oversee operations at the Ilopango airfield.

In the wreckage, the Nicaraguans found documents that identified the plane as being owned by Corporate Air Service, a small air fleet that, through several front corporations, was controlled by Richard Secord, the retired US Air Force general who was assisting Oliver North.

What are the links between the CIA and Barry Seal?

Only a camera.

The single event of installing hidden cameras on the C-123 was the only direct involvement the CIA ever had with Barry Seal. His mission was a joint mission only from the standpoint that the CIA was permitted to install the cameras—and then only after getting the approval of the DEA. Francis "Bud" Mullen, then the DEA administrator, confirmed that it was the CIA who approached DEA seeking Seal's help. Mullen allowed it.

Barry Seal was working for the DEA as a documented informant. He was not working for the CIA. A CIA memorandum subsequently reported that on May 3, 1988, Dewey Clarridge was interviewed by two staff members of the House Judiciary Committee's Subcommittee on Crime regarding his knowledge of drug trafficking by the Nicaraguan government or the Contras. Clarridge acknowledged that the CIA had assisted the DEA in the 1984 sting operation.[5]

Despite the fact that his cover was blown after the Nicaraguan flight, Seal was willing to gamble that he could pull off another sting for the DEA. And they agreed to let him try.

The flight was going to be dangerous, and Seal was now in the Witness Protection Program. At that time, he was the only government witness against Pablo Escobar and Jorge Ochoa.

DEA handlers were afraid Seal might not come back if he left the country. Their concern was that he might either skip or be killed. Seal insisted he wanted to develop the case anyway. He told the agents that he knew a pilot who would fly the mission. Seal was cocky and persuasive, and he got his way.

The pilot was William Bottoms, Seal's former brother-in-law. When the DEA agreed to interview Bottoms, Seal called him from Miami and told him what was going on. Bottoms agreed to go to Miami for the interview.

Dick Gregorie, chief of the major narcotics section for the Southern District of Florida, Seal, and DEA agents Bob Joura and Ernst Jacobsen were at the meeting.

Bottoms was asked if he could and would fly the mission. He knew he could. He agreed to make the flight. Bottoms had some conditions. He cautioned Gregorie that he might have to take the Fifth Amendment against self-incrimination on some of the questions he might be asked when the case went to trial. Gregorie said he would send a flyer out to all pertinent state and federal agencies and ask if anyone had a case ongoing that included Bottoms.

Gregorie told Bottoms, "If I get no response back from anyone, I will give you a letter of immunity. You will then have to tell me everything you've ever done. If I find out anything that you didn't tell me, I will prosecute you for everything."

The flyer was circulated and, so far as Bottoms knows, Gregorie received no response.

Bottoms was told to come back to Miami. Gregorie gave him verbal assurance that he would have immunity and a written agreement, at which time Bottoms admitted that he flew all of the drug flights Seal was supposed to have flown. He had flown them with Emile Camp as copilot.

Time was of the essence. Bottoms did not receive his formal letter of immunity signed by US Attorney Leon Kellner and Dick Gregorie until August. The letter, dated August 20, 1985, granted Bottoms "use immunity" meaning he couldn't be prosecuted for any crimes based on his own testimony other than for perjury.

The sting set up by Seal involved a flight from a strip in Bolivia to Las Vegas. Bottoms flew it as a DEA operative. To set up the deal, Seal telephoned the cocaine people in Bolivia and received navigational instructions to the remote landing strip.

Seal relayed mission details to Bottoms, who flew to the area. People on the ground heard the plane and radioed to him that he was right overhead. It was getting dark, and fog had covered half of the strip when Bottoms finally landed. He had flown for six hours from Turks and Caicos islands to Colombia where he refueled. He then flew twelve more hours to the Bolivian strip. Bottoms flew in Seal's Piper Navajo Panther, and it was a long and difficult flight. Several times during the flight, the DEA thought Bottoms wouldn't make it back. In spite of the obstacles and danger, the flight was successful.

It took about six hours to refuel in Bolivia because of primitive equipment. The ground crew had to pour the fuel from fifty-gallon barrels into a bucket and then pour the fuel into the tanks of the airplane. The illegal fuel bladder that was installed in the fuselage held 350 gallons. The crude transfer of fuel to the inside bladder caused spillage all over the inside of the plane. The carpet and everything aft of the pilot seat was soaked with high-octane aviation fuel. Bottoms described the plane as a "flying bomb."

On January 15, 1985, Bottoms took off from Bolivia with about 180 pounds of cocaine. The plane was loaded with extra fuel that brought the weight to more than 11,000 pounds. That was well over the 7,000-pound limit.

He had a copilot who could speak very little English. They had to climb to more than 16,000 feet to clear a pass through the Andes.

They were without bottled oxygen. They would occasionally shine a flashlight on their fingers, looking for the blue tinge to the skin that would signal the onset of hypoxia. At one point the cockpit began filling up with smoke. Bottoms had to shut down everything electrical except the radar and navigational systems. Fortunately, the smoke abated.

He landed at the Colombian airstrip twelve hours later and took on more fuel, then flew twelve more hours to Texas. He refueled and flew at high altitude to Las Vegas but couldn't use the cabin heater because of the danger of fire from the spilled fuel.

It was a trip from hell. They survived.

The case Bottoms helped to make was *United States versus Reyes, Orosco, Ravelo, Rodrigues, Moreno and Montoya*, (85-10 CR). The defendants were indicted in US District Court, District of Nevada. In August 1985, the case went to trial in Las Vegas.

Bottoms testified for the government, and his testimony was reported in great detail in local newspapers. Vaughn Roche, writing for the Las Vegas *Review Journal* identified him as Billy Bob Bottoms in a piece that told about the flight from Bolivia.

Ed Dodrill, writing for the Las Vegas *Sun*, also covered the trial. The newspaper stories about during the Las Vegas trial were the first time William Bottoms was publicly identified as being associated with Barry Seal. During the trial, he testified that, as best he could recall, Bottoms began flying cocaine for Seal in 1981 and continued doing so until the "last load" in early 1984.[6] Bottoms said Seal started "training" him in June 1980 when he got out of the Navy.

The Las Vegas case was successfully prosecuted by assistant US Attorney Donald J. Campbell as a direct result of the work of Barry Seal and William Bottoms, both in gathering the evidence and in testifying when the case went to trial.

The case represented the single largest seizure of cocaine in Nevada and resulted in the conviction of all six defendants.

The DEA was impressed enough with his performance and effectiveness to offer Bottoms employment in other special undercover operations. Bottoms accepted. He worked with DEA and FBI on a variety of undercover assignments until 1990 when he resigned.

After the Las Vegas operation, Seal's career as a DEA informant was ended. He did not participate in any more DEA undercover operations.

He focused on the problems he was facing in Mena and Baton Rouge, which were considerable.

Chapter 10
Continuing Criminal Enterprises

Viewed historically, Seal's luck as a smuggler was dismal. He'd been caught up in a US Customs sting and jailed in Honduras. He was snagged in a DEA undercover operation in Florida and indicted twice. Seal went to trial on one indictment and lost. In one indictment he was charged with using an interstate telephone to facilitate a violation of the drug laws. The drug laws didn't stop him. He kept on smuggling and stayed on the phones.

Seal was willing to take risks.

The number three has different inferences. It can indicate good as in the three musketeers, three wise men or the holy trinity. It can imply trouble as in three on a match, going down for the third time or three strikes and you're out.

Three is also significant in a drug law.

The Comprehensive Drug Abuse Prevention and Control Act of 1970 (CCA) (Title 21, US Code) was signed into law by President Richard Nixon in October 1970. Section 848 of the CCA created the continuing criminal enterprise. The government may charge a defendant who has three, the magic number, prior drug-related convictions with operating a continuing criminal enterprise. The statute has some very tough penalties.

It calls for a minimum sentence of twenty years and a possible maximum sentence of life in prison. Under some circumstances a death penalty can be imposed.

The CCE law is the *bete noire* of drug traffickers. Baton Rouge task force agents were planning to use it on Seal.

Good fortune literally fell on the feds in Louisiana on September 16, 1984. At about seven pm, a man named William Jarvois Earle, Jr., encountered a fuel-flow problem and crash-landed his twin-engine Beechcraft on the beach at Grand Isle, Louisiana.

Grand Isle is the end of the road south of New Orleans where coastal fishing and hunting begins. It could have been the end of the line for a pilot.

Earle did a superb job of bringing the plane down. He was not injured.

Lugging two suitcases, Earle ran from the downed aircraft. He sought refuge in a nearby bar. When the owner told him he had called the law, Earle fled. He hid the suitcases. He headed down the beach, sometimes sandy, sometimes muddy. He was soon spotted and arrested by the Grand Isle Police Chief.

The real problem for Earle aside from tearing up a good airplane, was the 1,500 pounds of marijuana that was aboard the aircraft.

Cops turned Earle over to the feds. Drug smuggling charges were brought against him in New Orleans Eastern District of Louisiana by Al Winters, the chief of the Organized Crime Drug Task Force. Winters was a seasoned and aggressive prosecutor who knew how to deal with defendants as well as their attorneys. In no time, young Earle struck a deal and began to cooperate with the government.

Billy Earle, Jr. had additional inducement to cooperate.

Some trouble in the family.

William Earle, Sr., his father, had tried to sell two kilos of cocaine to Cliff Cormany and Jeff Santini. They were both New Orleans FBI agents who were working undercover. He had offered sixty kilos at $25,000 per kilo. FBI headquarters had provided the two agents with $1.5 million in cash as flash money. The two agents had allowed the elder Earle to view and count the cash.

Santini said Earle first provided two ounces of cocaine as a sample. At a second meeting Earle showed up with two kilos, offered for $100,000. They were meeting in a car near a hotel in the New Orleans suburb of Metairie. Shortly after Earle arrived, two or three vehicles surrounded them.

Fearing a robbery or worse, Santini pulled his gun on Earle and told him he was dealing for 60 kilos—not two—and accused him of trying to set him up to rob him. He told Earle to get out or he'd blow his head off.

The next day Earle Sr. called and said to meet at the Marriott on Airline Highway in Kenner across from the New Orleans airport. The deal would go down. When Earle showed up, Santini and Cormany arrested him. Santini told Earle he knew it was Seal's cocaine and wanted him to cooperate. Earle refused to cooperate and told the agents if he went against Seal and his people, they would kill him and his family.

Earle was very despondent at this point. He wanted the agents to give him a gun and one bullet and let him go into the bathroom alone.

At the time of young Billy's crash at Grand Isle, his father had already been prosecuted. He was in the custody of the US Marshals in New Orleans and on his way to prison.

William Earle, Sr. was interviewed by this writer in the US Attorney's office in New Orleans on October 11, 1984. He refused to cooperate with the Baton Rouge Middle District in any efforts to convict Barry Seal.

It was a different story with son William Earle, Jr. when he was interviewed on October 22, 1984. He was a pleasant young man, very polite and very cooperative. He wanted desperately to help his dad. He was allowed to listen to the tapes of some phone conversations that had been intercepted while the Baton Rouge Middle District Title III wiretap was in operation.

His memory was excellent. He readily identified his own voice and the voice of Barry Seal. He had no difficulty recalling the details and explaining the meaning and purpose of three separate phone conversations between himself and Seal. He agreed to cooperate in the prosecution of Barry Seal by testifying about the phone calls.

With the testimony of Billy Earle, Jr. there were three prosecutable violations of a law prohibiting a drug deal by phone [Title 21, Section 843 (b): use of an interstate telephone to facilitate a drug offense]. They related to a Piper Navajo that Seal was adding to his fleet. Earle admitted that he had flown the plane to Rich Mountain Aviation where it had been prepared for long distance drug flights by having an illegal fuel bladder installed.

Billy Earle Jr.'s admissions linked Rich Mountain Aviation, Fred Hampton and Joe Evans to Seal's smuggling operation because the fuel bladder was installed on December 13, 1983. That was three months before Seal cut his deal to become an informant for the DEA.

Timing was important for Baton Rouge area agents who wanted to nail Seal. Therefore, any claim that the fuel tank installation was made to help Seal in his work as a DEA informant would not stand up.

Government agents had more on Seal than the three phone call violations. Agent Jerry Bize discovered money-laundering activity at several Baton Rouge banks. Bize was developing those cases.

The noose was tightening around Seal. The charges stacked up:
— three counts growing out of young Earle's phone conversations.

—and two Florida convictions already on the books.

—and money laundering violations in the offing.

Baton Rouge agents had hit the magic number—three. There were more than enough violations to support a CCE indictment against Seal.

Billy Earle gave up another choice morsel of information. He acknowledged that Barry Seal had supplied his father with the two kilos of cocaine he had sold to FBI undercover agents Santini and Cormany. He said that Seal had warned his father not to go through with the deal because he thought it might be a set-up. Earle's father had ignored the advice. The son's information placed cocaine into Seal's possession and put him into the distribution business.

Meanwhile, in New Orleans another Eastern District smuggling investigation was coming to fruition. It would eventually involve Seal.

It is a bizarre story about 250 kilos of cocaine belonging the Cali Cartel, another successful and powerful Colombian cocaine smuggling group.

Cocaine belonging to the Cali traffickers was scheduled to be flown into Louisiana by an Oregon pilot named Fred Compton who was to deliver it to a rural pasture in Chalmette, Louisiana. Chalmette resident Claude Griffin, Sr., was handling deliveries on behalf of the Cali Cartel. He made arrangements for the delivery in this small St. Bernard Parish community known for fishing, the port, chemical plants along the Mississippi River and eroding wetlands.

Griffin employed three pilots to fly cocaine: James Edward Eakes, Bobby Ross and Billy Joe Nichols. Griffin in turn was being supervised by a New Orleans resident named Fernando Lopez who handled transportation and payments for the Cali Cartel through a shipping company front in New Orleans.

Ross, Eakes and Compton hatched a plot to steal the cocaine Compton was going to deliver to Louisiana.

Here's how the plan went down. On the night of October 24, 1982, Bobby Ross was flying a Piper Aztec and pretending to be a US Customs plane. Ross faked an air chase with Compton in the skies above greater New Orleans. Compton, chased by Ross, buzzed around over the Chalmette area screaming into his radio such things as:

"It's Customs!"

"I'm afraid I'll be arrested!"

And finally: "I'm diverting!"

Initially, Compton attempted to divert to another clandestine landing strip near Belle Rose, Louisiana.

He found it was a busy night for smugglers. As Compton was preparing to land, the flashing blue lights of numerous law enforcement vehicles converged on the landing strip. He was about to put down in the midst of a DEA and Louisiana State Police bust of a load of marijuana.

Compton diverted once more. He ended up making an unexpected landing on the private airstrip of Robert T. LeBlanc. It was a 3,550-foot sod strip located southeast of White Castle, a small town approximately twenty-five miles south of Baton Rouge along the Mississippi River in Iberville Parish. Compton unloaded the cocaine and made arrangements to stash it.

Compton had flown from the New Orleans Eastern District federal court jurisdiction and landed in Iberville Parish within the jurisdiction of the federal Middle District.

This would make a big difference for Barry Seal.

Compton didn't know it.

Seal didn't know it.

Compton took off and flew to an airstrip in Mexico where he landed. He set the plane on fire.

Next, Compton tried to cover his tracks. He returned to Colombia and spun his cover story to his Cali Cartel bosses, Miguel Rodriguez-Orejuela and his brother, Gilberto Jose. Compton had avoided a bust, he had crash-landed and the plane and the dope were burned up.

The Orejuela brothers weren't stupid. They smelled a rat. They sent a chemist to the Mexican crash scene. The chemist tested for cocaine residue. He found none. He couldn't even find the metal buckles from the duffel bags.

The Orejuela leaders planned to kill Fred Compton.

Fortunately for Fred Compton, New Orleans FBI agents had another Title III in operation on Fernando Lopez. Through the wiretap, FBI agents learned what the Orejuela brothers were planning. FBI agent Fred Cleveland gave Compton a heads-up phone call to warn him of the death threat. The FBI is required to do this in this type of situation.

During the first call, Compton would not admit that he was the same Fred Compton who did business with the Orejuela brothers. FBI agent Fred Cleveland told him he had nothing to worry about since he wasn't the Compton who was going to be murdered.

Cleveland hung up. Compton immediately returned Cleveland's call. Compton admitted he was the right person and began to cooperate with the government.

The sham interdiction brought more problems for the three smugglers.

Ross, Eakes, Compton and LeBlanc found themselves sitting on a load of cocaine they were having difficulty selling.

LeBlanc knew Barry Seal and he finally called him. Although he was not directly involved in the original plot, Seal agreed to buy the load for $10,000 per kilo.

It was a very good price.

Assistant US Attorney Howat "Howie" Peters, who had been prosecuting the phony interdiction cases, was preparing to indict Seal next. Three witnesses were lined up and ready to testify against Seal in New Orleans.

New Orleans had jurisdiction because the plans to get the dope were made over the wiretap in New Orleans and the front man, Fernando Lopez was doing business there.

Robert LeBlanc would subsequently testify that the plane carrying the stolen load of cocaine landed on his property. He said that Ross offered him a million dollars to secure and distribute the load. He helped unload that cocaine, packaged in the customary duffle bags. LeBlanc kept six of the duffle bags, out of which he sold between 15 and 30 kilos of cocaine. He testified that the people involved with this third load eventually gained over $2 million from the transaction.[1]

Federal agents working in New Orleans Eastern District of Louisiana made the case.

The Cali cocaine ended up in the Baton Rouge Middle District. And that gave Stan Bardwell a basis for jurisdiction and another count against Seal.

Bad news for Seal.

The cocaine transaction between Seal and Robert T. LeBlanc allowed the Baton Rouge Middle District grand jury to eventually indict Seal on charges of possession with intent to distribute multi-kilos of cocaine.

The feds could use at least six violations as the foundation of a Continuing Criminal Enterprise (CCE) indictment against Seal. The statute required only three.

Seal was well aware of the dangers of a CCE indictment and he desperately wanted to prevent it from happening. Seal knew there was so much animosity toward him in the Baton Rouge Middle District that it was possible he would get a life sentence if he were to be indicted and convicted.

By the fall 1984, it was clear to Seal that Miami DEA agents were not going to stop the grand jury investigation in the Baton Rouge Middle District of Louisiana.

Baton Rouge area jurors were going to hear the testimony of people who could hurt him badly. Baton Rouge was his home turf. He went to school there. He and his family lived there. He started a couple of legit businesses there. He ate at Ruby Red's often. He might have been the biggest pay phone patron in Baton Rouge.

Seal's agreement with the government did not come with promises that bound the federal judge in Florida. The US Attorney in Florida was only obligated to bring to the attention of the Florida sentencing judges the nature and extent of Seal's cooperation with the government. Seal had high hopes that his ten-year sentence would be significantly reduced as a reward for the good undercover work he had done for the DEA. He couldn't be sure he would have his time completely cut. Bottoms said Seal was deathly afraid of going to prison.

Seal's only deal was with the US Attorney in Miami. His agreement did not include Fred Hampton, Joe Evans or anyone else in his smuggling organization.

The smuggler could be polite, charming and friendly. Seal had managed to ingratiate himself with some DEA agents and prosecutors in Miami and Las Vegas.

It was a different story in Baton Rouge. He was still the target of Bardwell's task force and a Continuing Criminal Enterprise indictment was hanging over his head.

He had no deals in Louisiana or Arkansas. He could not be certain what effect his cooperation would have on prosecutions or sentences in those jurisdictions. Furthermore, he knew there was a federal investigation in progress in Arkansas. And he knew Al Winters was going after him in New Orleans.

The greatest peril Seal faced was a CCE indictment. He knew the federal agents were working to make it happen.

Chapter 11
Counterattacks

Barry Seal was not one to stand idly by while the GS pukes in Baton Rouge tried to put him in prison for the rest of his life. He was desperate to do something to prevent the federal indictment.

Seal and his lawyer launched a vigorous counterattack, and the war on drugs heated up in Baton Rouge Middle District of Louisiana.

Seal used his charm to engineer a favorable local TV news series. He denied he was a drug smuggler.

On September 14, 1984, Lewis Unglesby, Seal's high-profile and knowledgeable Baton Rouge criminal attorney stepped up. He wanted to stop witnesses before the grand jury. He filed a motion for injunctive relief in federal court.

Unglesby's motion was aimed at blocking the testimony from several witnesses who were scheduled to appear in front of the grand jury the following week. Unglesby asked the court to enjoin US Attorney Stanford Bardwell from conducting further grand jury proceedings. The attorney's grounds: that investigative officers were aware that erroneous and misleading evidence had been sworn to before the grand jury.

James Kenneth Webb had testified in front of the grand jury for almost six hours on January 14, 1984, and Unglesby knew it. He singled out Webb, alleging that he had given specific incriminating evidence against Seal which was untrue and which Webb wanted to recant.

Unglesby's motion contained a laundry list of reasons why the grand jury should be blocked from hearing further testimony:

— members of Bardwell's staff had stated publicly that their goal in life was to put Barry Seal in prison,

— that they would do anything to get Barry Seal,

— that certain Louisiana State Police law enforcement officers had instructed Kenneth Webb to lie to the grand jury,

—that investigating agents had spread malicious and unfounded rumors about Seal and his associates,

—and that prosecutors had threatened potential witnesses or defendants with charges if they failed to cooperate to get Barry Seal.

This motion was Seal's first public legal maneuver in an attempt to prevent an indictment in the Middle District. Unglesby's allegations were viewed as a personal attack on agents and prosecutors who were associated with the Seal investigation.

Unglesby was, of course, absolutely correct about the task force goal. They wanted to put Seal in prison. The other allegations were rubbish.

The agents assigned to the task force as well as Brad Myers and Stan Bardwell looked forward to respond to the allegations in open court. Unglesby's motion failed. No hearing ever took place. The grand jury heard the testimony of the witnesses who had been subpoenaed.

On October 9, 1984, more fuel was added to the fire that had been ignited by Unglesby's motion.

Seal had taken a room at a Holiday Inn where he was working on his defense. He was meeting with some of the people who had been summoned to Bardwell's grand jury.

At that time a subpoena had been issued by Al Winters calling for Seal to appear before a New Orleans grand jury.

Agent Charlie Bremer and the writer went to the Holiday Inn and served the subpoena on Seal without incident.

Characteristically, Seal casually announced, "I heard Winters was going to start a grand jury on me."

As the two agents were driving out of the Holiday Inn parking lot, State Police narcotics detective Sgt. Jack Crittenden drove in. He stopped to chat with the agents. And as they talked, Dandra, Barry Seal's secretary, drove in.

Crittenden got out of his car and placed his camera equipped with a telephoto lens on the roof of his car. He aimed it and photographed the secretary as she headed toward Seal's room.

Suddenly Barry Seal came charging out of the room, down the stairs, and across the parking lot. He was big, over 240 pounds, short, and mad. He ran toward Crittenden who was, by then, in his car and starting to pull away. Seal was clearly madder than hell.

The two task force agents had some concern because they didn't know what he might do. The agents stayed in their car, prepared for the worst while hoping for the best.

The tension eased when Seal stopped running and began yammering at Crittenden.

Seal shouted that the truth would soon come out and "you're all going to be taught a lesson." And that there was going to be a "lot of explaining" to do.

Crittenden waved at Seal with the Bible he usually carried in his car and told him that the Good Book was where the truth was.

The incident lasted less than two minutes. Crittenden got in his car and drove away.

As Seal walked past the car occupied by the two agents, he remarked sarcastically, "You all got a lot to do, don't you? Just harassing innocent people."

Seal fired back through his attorney the next day.

Stan Bardwell received a letter from Seal's Florida attorney, Tom Sclafani. The letter was dated October 11, 1984, and was sent by Express Mail.

It read: "Yesterday, Mr. Seal was placed in an apparent life-threatening situation because of actions of your agents. It seems Mr. Seal's secretary was followed to a local hotel and that one of your police officers was pointing an object that, from a distance, looked like a rifle toward the window of my client's hotel room. This is problematical given the fact there is a $350,000 contract on my client's life, which you have been made aware of weeks ago. As a result, my client fears for his life and has hired an armed, licensed Louisiana private investigator to be with him at all times. This letter is to put your agents on notice and to request that you tell them to refrain from harassing my client, especially since either he or his bodyguard could very easily mistake one of your agents for a person seeking to execute the contract on Barry's life. The last thing my client needs is to be involved in a tragic incident."

Sclafani's letter was an obvious warning that task force agents might get shot by mistake by Seal's armed bodyguard. The letter served only to heat up an already contentious situation facing Seal.

Barry Seal's counteroffensive continued on Baton Rouge TV. That's when WBRZ-TV, the Channel 2 ABC affiliate in Baton Rouge, aired a series titled *Uncle Sam Wants You*. The piece was put together by John Camp, the station's investigative reporter. The first segment was broadcast on November 19, 1984. Camp, who is not related to Emile Camp, had been around Baton Rouge for a number of years.

Task force agents learned when the piece was going to be aired. They gathered with their wives at the home of Brad Myers to watch the first segment. This TV "special" was evidently what Seal was referring to during the Holiday Inn confrontation October 9 with this writer and Bremmer.

The premise of *Uncle Sam Wants You* was that the US government targets individuals for little or no reason and then seeks to build a criminal case against them. Agents often employ illegal techniques and use evidence coerced from informants. The star of the show and presumed victim of the government's targeting was, of course, Barry Seal. His co-star was none other than his high-school friend and former employee, James Kenneth Webb, alias "Little Rock."

The series ran for five consecutive nights. During one segment a photograph of Jack Crittenden, who regularly worked drug cases undercover, was shown. It was apparent that Crittenden was being singled out because of the incident at the Holiday Inn a month earlier.

Among the claims made by Webb during the series was that Rand Miller, another assistant US attorney in the Baton Rouge Middle District, had told him to steal an old bilious-green Ford that Seal had been allowing him to use.

In the final segment, Camp and Seal were dramatically posed in the cockpit of Seal's famous C-123 cargo plane.

Camp asked Seal if he was a smuggler.

A stern faced, deadly serious, and appropriately virtuous Seal replied, "I'm no smuggler."

Uncle Sam Wants You was a biased — and deceptive — presentation. Camp and Seal failed to inform their viewers that Seal had signed his plea agreement with Stan Bardwell on the very day the first segment aired.

Admittedly, it is entirely possible that Seal never told reporter Camp he had copped a plea. Nonetheless, the piece was looked upon as a gross distortion of the facts. It epitomized the Seal the task force agents had come to know as a first-rate manipulator with charisma who could get people to do his bidding.

Uncle Sam Wants You was a last gasp effort to strike back and embarrass Stan Bardwell and the GS pukes who had finally succeeded in convicting him.

Jack Crittenden, Russell Milan, and Rand Miller sued John Camp, Channel 2, and Barry Seal. As an undercover narc, Jack Crittenden justifiably believed that airing his photograph on local television and identifying him as a Louisiana State Police detective placed him in some danger.

During the pre-trial work-up of Crittenden's lawsuit, his lawyers took the deposition of James Kenneth Webb who had been portrayed as the coerced informant.

Webb testified that the statements he made in *Uncle Sam Wants You* were all totally false and that John Camp and Barry Seal both knew it. Webb testified that Seal told him that they were going to orchestrate a story that would hopefully prevent any indictments in Baton Rouge.[1]

John Camp eventually gave a deposition in the same suit in which he said Seal contacted him about putting the piece together and provided his transportation to Mena and to Miami in one of his planes.

The suits were eventually dismissed.

The court, guided by the decision in the landmark 1964 case, *New York Times v. Sullivan,* ruled that Miller, Crittenden, and Milan were public figures. They had the burden of proving actual malice or reckless disregard for the truth by Channel 2 and reporter John Camp. Although the malice was likely to have been there, it wasn't provable in court.

The decision with regard to Crittenden still seems somewhat puzzling. Can an undercover cop be a public figure while he's still undercover?

In November 1984, the joint DEA-FBI investigation of Fred Hampton, Joe Evans, and Rich Mountain Aviation got a break.

The FBI recovered a stolen plane in a separate undercover operation. Little Rock FBI agent Tom Ross suggested using the plane in the investigation of Rich Mountain Aviation.

The plan was approved. On November 6, 1984, FBI agent Oscar T. Eubank using the alias Rex Eggleston flew the recovered Cessna 210 to the Mena airport. He landed, taxied the plane to Rich Mountain Aviation, and parked it. Eubank talked to one of Fred Hampton's employees and told him to tint the windows darker and install a fuel bladder tank. He gave the employee his business card and he left.

As investigators had agreed, three days later Sheriff A. L. Hadaway checked with the FBI's National Crime Information Center (NCIC). He determined the plane had been stolen from Pryor, Oklahoma in June 1984.

Hadaway went to the airport to recover the stolen plane. The sheriff found some marijuana in the plane, according to the allegations in the civil suit subsequently filed by Fred Hampton. The story hit the local newspapers.

From 1963 to 1970, before he joined the FBI, O. T. Eubank was a US Air Force pilot. He flew the RF-4C reconnaissance jet while assigned to the 11th Tactical Squadron, 432nd Tactical Fighter Wing at Udorn, Thailand. Eubank wrote the book, *Alone, Unarmed and Unafraid*, a story about his US Air Force experiences.

Eubank is absolutely certain there was no marijuana on the plane when he flew it into the Mena airport.

Fred Hampton was never arrested or charged with a marijuana violation. The marijuana story was "leaked" and was intended to give credibility to "Eggleston." The objective of the joint FBI-DEA undercover operation at Mena was not a drug bust. Investigators wanted to find out if Hampton and Evans were aiding drug smuggling.

Agents suspected them of changing plane registration N numbers, installing illegal fuel bladders and modifying cargo hatches on aircraft being operated by drug smugglers. The hope was that Hampton and Evans would be caught installing an illegal fuel bladder and then they could be convinced to cooperate.

There was a lot at stake if either of these two men agreed to cooperate. They would have been in a position to identify any drug pilots who came seeking fuel bladders or oversize cargo doors and identify the planes they were flying.

It was a good plan against legitimate targets — but it didn't work.

"Rex Eggleston" and his attempted sting enraged Hampton and Seal.

In December 1984 they retaliated by filing a civil damage suit in US District Court in Arkansas. Fred Hampton was the plaintiff. He named as defendants Polk County Sheriff A. L. Hadaway, Polk County Deputy Sheriff Terry Capehart, the Union Bank of Mena, Bill Woods, "Shorty" Williams, Eva Capehart and "Mr. Eggleston, a pseudonym for an undercover agent of the Federal Bureau of Investigation."[2]

In his petition, Hampton alleged that, in March 1984, Barry Seal "a self-styled soldier of fortune who was a paid informant of the Miami, Florida district of the DEA, contacted him."

Fred Hampton's petition was well-crafted. The self-serving narrative read like a synopsis for a low-budget B-movie. The document was more likely intended to absolve Hampton of criminal intent and place him in a favorable light with the authorities and the public than it was intended to remedy alleged tortuous conduct.

The petition raised the flag of national security and set up a defense of "I was cooperating with the DEA and the CIA."

The petition was actually an outline of the defense Hampton and Evans would likely put on if they were indicted on charges of conspiracy to smuggle drugs.

They weren't indicted. Hampton's suit was not pursued and was dismissed not long after Seal was murdered in 1986. Documents subsequently found among Seal's records revealed that he had paid for most of the cost of filing the suit.

Seal may have ingratiated himself with some federal prosecutors and DEA agents in Miami and Las Vegas. There was little they could do to help him with his problems in the Baton Rouge Middle District of Louisiana.

The airing of *Uncle Sam Wants You* and attorney Lewis Unglesby's efforts to block Stan Bardwell's grand jury probe had failed.

Seal faced indictment for a Continuing Criminal Enterprise.

Baton Rouge drug task force members tightened the noose on Seal.

Chapter 12
The Middle District of Louisiana Plea Agreement

US Attorney Stan Bardwell's Baton Rouge task force was on a collision course with the drug task force led by Stanley Marcus, the US Attorney in the Miami Southern District of Florida.

In late October 1984, Dick Gregorie of the Florida drug task force contacted Al Winters. The two federal strike force prosecutors were friends. Gregorie wanted Winters to arrange a meeting with Bardwell to iron out the problem of Barry Seal.

Gregorie's boss, Stanley Marcus, was getting ready put Seal on the stand as the prosecution's key witness in several major drug cases in Florida.

The problem for Marcus was the *Giglio* rule.

In the *Brady v. Maryland*, 373 U.S. 83 (1963), the US Supreme Court ruled that prosecutors must give a defendant on trial any evidence they have that might show the defendant is not guilty.

In *Giglio v. United States* 405 U.S. 150 (1972), the Supreme Court said the prosecution must disclose any information they have that might be used to impeach the character or credibility of their witnesses.

Bardwell was still investigating Seal and calling witnesses to the grand jury. Testimony from Seal's associates could turn up *Giglio* information that could destroy Seal's credibility and effectiveness.

A prime example of problems caused by *Giglio* was Ken Webb, who had given six hours of testimony to Bardwell's grand jury. What he told the jurors is not known because grand jury proceedings are secret.

It is known that in a 1985 sworn deposition he called Seal a "pathological liar."[1]

If he told that to the grand jury, it would be *Giglio* material.

That's juicy material for an attorney trying to impeach Seal.

The same *Giglio* problem existed in the District of Nevada where Seal was to be a key witness in the *Reyes* case he and Bottoms made.

Something had to give.

Winters obliged his fellow prosecutor. A meeting took place in New Orleans. Those attending were Gregorie; his boss, US Attorney Stanley Marcus; Al Winters; Brad Myers; Stan Bardwell; Bob Bryden, head of the New Orleans office of the DEA; and a top-ranking DEA representative from Miami.

Stanley Marcus, now a judge on the Eleventh Circuit Court of Appeals, made no specific demands. The judge wanted a deal worked out with Seal before he testified in the trials of Bustamonte, Escobar, Vaughn, in Miami and in Las Vegas in the *Reyes* case.

Nothing was resolved at the first meeting but groundwork was laid for further negotiations.

A second meeting took place in Miami a month later on Veteran's Day. Al Winters, Brad Myers, and Stan Bardwell met with Seal's attorneys, Lewis Unglesby and Tom Sclafani in the office of the US Attorney.

When the pow-wow ended, the parameters for a plea agreement in the Baton Rouge Middle District of Louisiana were agreed upon.

Later, there would be rumors that the White House had interceded on behalf of Seal.

"They did not tell us what to do, no one did," said Winters.

Neither he nor Brad Myers had knowledge of any mysterious phone calls from the CIA, the Department of Justice, or the White House giving Bardwell orders on what had to be in Seal's plea agreement.

The final plea agreement called for the Middle District grand jury to bring a two-count indictment against Barry Seal.

The first count was a conspiracy to possess with intent to distribute approximately 210 kilos of cocaine. This was the cocaine stored at Robert T. LeBlanc's place.

The critical factor in the first count was the limits on the sentence Seal could get from Judge Polozola.

In legalese the first count said, "defendant will receive a concurrent sentence not to exceed the ultimate sentence he receives in a pending proceeding, No. 83-6038CR-NCR in the Southern District of Florida." This was Judge Roettger's case and he had given Seal a ten-year sentence.

In plain English the first count meant if Judge Roettger in Florida didn't reduce Seal's ten-year sentence then Judge Polozola in Louisiana couldn't sentence him to more than ten years. If Polozola did give Seal a ten-year sentence, he would serve it at the same time he was serving Roettger's ten-year sentence. That's a concurrent sentence, and we're not talking English grammar.

If Roettger did reduce Seal's sentence, let's say to five years, that would be the "ultimate sentence." Polozola couldn't give Seal more than five years.

The second count charged Seal with a violation of Title 18, Section 1001, causing a financial institution not to file a currency transaction report by structuring cash transactions.

Section 1001 basically says you can't falsify, conceal by trick or use a scheme to hide a material fact from any department or agency of the government.

Any bank that handles a cash transaction involving more than $10,000 is required by law to report it on a document called a currency transaction report (CTR). The IRS gets to see the CTRs.

Seal was in the drug smuggling business, where dealing in cash is the norm.

Seal, the solid citizen, wanted to spend $51,000 to pay the IRS his income tax. He didn't want to send cash and he didn't want his name on a CTR. He went to several Baton Rouge banks and used cash to buy cashier's checks in amounts less than $10,000 until he had a total of $51,000. The banks didn't have to file CTRs.

This practice is called structuring. Seal's scheme prevented the IRS from getting CTRs.

Jerry Bize had worked up a structuring violation on Seal.

As will be revealed later, Seal was doing the same thing in Mena, Arkansas.

The agreed-upon sentence on the second count would be a "period of probation to be determined by the court."

Bardwell knew that Seal's attorney was planning to file a motion to ask Judge Roettger to reduce Seal's sentence. That would be his reward for being a productive DEA informant.

Before signing the plea agreement, Bardwell talked to Stanley Marcus to find out whether he would make any recommendation to the judge about a reduction.

Marcus assured Bardwell that he would not make any recommendation to the court and would comment only on the nature and extent of Seal's cooperation with the DEA.

Brad Myers briefed the task force agents on the details of the plea agreement to determine if there were any major complaints. Plea agreements are worked out by US Attorneys, not by IRS, FBI, or DEA agents, so there were no formal objections.

In the final analysis, Seal would stand convicted of two felony counts in the Baton Rouge Middle District and he would be out of the cocaine smuggling business. Stan Bardwell and the task force had achieved their objective.

Seal was the only individual who was included in the plea agreement.

The government did not have to bear the expense of a lengthy trial. An added plus was that Seal was required to cooperate with federal agents and prosecutors in further investigations. Those investigations would be aimed at about a dozen people who helped him smuggle.

All of the cocaine Seal transported was brought into Louisiana. Stan Bardwell, along with everyone on the task force, thought he should spend some time in prison.

No one thought Judge Roettger would cut Seal completely free. They were told that he was a tough sentencing judge who didn't like drug traffickers.

The consensus was that if Roettger reduced Seal's sentence, he might cut his time to somewhere around seven years. If this happened, Seal would still serve three or four years, probably in protective lock-down, at a federal prison such as Sandstone, Minnesota where they specialize in high-risk prisoners.

Everyone was aware the Colombian Cartel leaders wanted Seal dead. The government would have to protect him while he was in custody.

Stan Bardwell, Al Winters, Barry Seal, and Tom Sclafani signed the plea agreement on November 19, 1984. The plea ended the threat of a life sentence for Seal from a continuing criminal enterprise prosecution. The plea agreement required Seal to submit to debriefings by government agents and attorneys. He had to testify before any grand jury and at any trial where his testimony was needed. And, he could not operate in an undercover capacity unless there was a mutual agreement that he could.

Seal also had to forfeit the Piper Navajo that had been used on many of the smuggling runs. The plane, worth $100,000, was turned over to the Louisiana State Police. It was eventually sold as surplus property for about $90,000.

On December 20, 1984, the federal grand jury in Baton Rouge returned the two-count indictment that had been agreed upon.

The following day Seal appeared in federal court for arraignment and was released on a $250,000 personal bond.

The next day Seal appeared before Judge Polozola and pleaded guilty to the indictment.

After the court session, he was interviewed on the courthouse steps by a local TV reporter. He said, "I've reached exactly the type of settlement that I wanted to reach. Whether or not they're happy, you'll have to ask them."

Debriefings of Seal got underway on January 7, 1985, when he met with task force agents for the first time. The meeting took place in the conference room of the US Attorney's office.

It didn't go as expected.

Seal was polite and friendly — the good ole boy. He did a lot of talking and told a few war stories. He spoke in generalities and only confirmed things the agents already knew. It soon became obvious that Seal wasn't going to cooperate to any great degree.

He knew he had made a good deal for himself. He stayed out of the penitentiary. But he wanted to help the people who had worked for him and who were still vulnerable. The best way he could do that was to stall and clam up.

R. T. LeBlanc was interviewed by task force agents on February 12, 1985, in the US attorney's office, where he explained his involvement. What LeBlanc did was fly a Cessna 172 from White Castle to Baytown, Texas. He took $450,000 of Seal's money as partial payment for the cocaine that had been stored at his place after being brought there by Fred Compton.

On April 2, 1986, LeBlanc appeared in federal court in Baton Rouge before Judge John V. Parker. He entered a plea of guilty to a racketeering count charging interstate travel to promote, manage, and facilitate an illegal activity (Title 18, Section 1952).

Parker ordered a three-year sentence. He suspended all but six months and said LeBlanc could serve it in prison or in a treatment center.

Seal had always told William Bottoms that he had nothing to do with the cocaine involved in the count. He told Bottoms he pleaded guilty only because his attorney Lewis Unglesby had told him to take the deal — it was the best he could hope for in the Baton Rouge Middle District.

Bottoms did some checking years later. He got the true story from a source who was directly involved.

The source said he spent three days drying and packaging the cocaine and confirmed that Robert T. LeBlanc called Barry Seal and told him he had the cocaine and wanted to get rid of it. That same night, Seal put $1 million in a suitcase and brought it to LeBlanc.

The last formal debriefing of Seal was in Baton Rouge on December 27, 1985, with Russell Welch and special agent William Duncan, the IRS criminal investigator from Arkansas. Duncan had investigated money laundering — structuring — at Mena.

Attorney Lewis Unglesby was present and told Duncan and Welch that Barry Seal's's case with the United States was concluded. It was their position that he had "completed his job and done what he was to do and had received his sentence."[2]

The government's remedy for reneging on plea agreement was to file a motion to set aside the agreement then go to court and present evidence that Seal was not performing according to the terms of the agreement.

Seal was murdered on orders of Colombian drug lords before that could happen.

The end result was that none of the other people who were culpably involved in Seal's drug smuggling organization were prosecuted.

That was Seal's objective. He did not live to see it.

Chapter 13
Air Max and Air Rik

Barry Seal was once described by his attorney Thomas Sclafani as the "single-most important government witness in the United States." Few can dispute that Seal's deeds and accomplishments on behalf of the DEA were dramatic during the relatively short period of time he cooperated.

It was primarily through Seal's efforts that the DEA was able to begin demolishing the Ochoa cocaine smuggling organization.

Seal was a good informant but there were a couple of other DEA informants who operated during the time period. How did they compare to Seal?

Frederik "Rik" Luytjes was another pilot-turned-cocaine-smuggler-turned-DEA informant. Luytjes put together a company he named Air America that operated from the Wilkes-Barre-Scranton airport in Pennsylvania.

Air America was in the business of modifying airplanes by adding extra fuel tanks, larger cargo doors, and exotic navigational gear like the military. Therefore, it was no surprise that some of Air America's best customers turned out to be drug smugglers. They were interested in loading and unloading quickly and in eliminating as many fuel stops as possible on their flights to and from South America.[1]

The Air America operated by Rik Luytjes is not to be confused with the Air America created by the CIA in the early 1960s to serve as a front for their clandestine air operations in Southeast Asia. Luytjes knew all about the CIA front of the same name. Like Barry Seal, he often dropped hints about being involved in CIA operations.[2]

In 1977, Luytjes bought a dozen surplus planes from the Belgian Air Force. In mid-1978, he sold one of the refurbished Pembroke planes to a Florida drug smuggler. The buyer made a down payment and took delivery of the plane but failed to pay Luytjes

121

the balance owed. He went to Florida to collect the debt. As things turned, out he didn't get cash. Instead, he was persuaded to accept twenty thousand Quaaludes as partial payment.[3]

Several weeks later, two of Luytjes's employees were arrested in New Jersey when they tried to sell the muscle-relaxing pills to a DEA undercover agent. Some of the drugs had been transported in the trunk of Luytjes's Porsche. DEA agents came calling.[4]

Luytjes was persuaded to become a DEA informant in return for the DEA dropping charges against him and giving his car back. He began keeping the DEA and Customs agents informed of the identity of some of his smuggling customers who brought their planes to him for modification.

While establishing his aircraft modification business, Luytjes met Rigoberto "Bobby" Correra who was at the time chief representative in the United States for the Ochoa family, the cocaine kingpins. Correra needed to bring in some cocaine. Luytjes went for the deal.[5]

On Labor Day, September 7, 1980, Luytjes flew his Cessna 310 to the Ochoa's dirt strip at Chonoconta, Colombia where he picked up 100 kilos of cocaine packed in duffel bags.

Luytjes delivered the cocaine to a cow pasture near Lake Okeechobee, in rural South Florida west of Palm Beach. He flew back to Scranton.

A couple months later, in December 1980, he attended the La Natividad festival in Colombia and traveled to Medellin where he met personally with Jorge and Fabio Ochoa and visited their Acandi airstrip.

Luytjes continued to deal personally with Jorge Ochoa and other members of the Medellin Cartel. He regularly hauled their cocaine from Colombia to the United States. Luytjes's performance on behalf of the Ochoa organization was very successful. His Air America became a vital link in their cocaine transportation network.

Luytjes didn't bother to tell the DEA about the trips he was making for the Ochoas—but he did feed them the names of a few of his customers from time to time.[6]

The Ochoas trusted Luytjes.

They told him about their plans for a hit on Barry Seal. At a January 1986 meeting in Bogota, he was told by one of their top leaders that Barry Seal had hurt them very badly. They were paying a crew a half-million dollars to travel to the United States to kill him.[7]

Luytjes knew Barry Seal because he had sold him a Piper Navajo for $400,000 and had arranged for the sale of his Piper Seneca.[8]

Luytjes hired a man named Jim Cooper to help in his smuggling operations. Cooper was an experienced pilot who had made several smuggling flights but not for Luytjes. Cooper was assigned to monitor the high frequency radio kept in Luytjes's basement. His job was to maintain contact with the planes during their cocaine flights. Cooper also traveled to and from Florida to pick up cash payments from the Colombians.

Luytjes became dissatisfied with Cooper whom he regarded as being unreliable. In 1981 Luytjes fired him.[9]

In March 1984, Jim Cooper was flying a twin-engine Piper Seneca loaded with 550 pounds of marijuana. He was headed for a grass landing strip near the town of Madison, Georgia. Cooper was well-acquainted with the landing field, having landed there on previous smuggling trips from Colombia. As he neared the landing strip, Cooper contacted his ground crew. They had a radio and were awaiting his arrival.

Because this was a night operation, standard procedure was to have two cars parked facing each other at each end of the grass strip. The vehicles would turn on their headlights to guide the plane to a landing.

The two drivers were in their vehicles, engines idling, awaiting the plane. The drivers heard Cooper's plane overhead, and both cars turned on their headlights. Cooper came in over the end of the runway and turned on his wing landing lights.

At this point in the operation, one of the cars was to start driving along below and behind the plane to light the runway. Unfortunately, on this particular night, the driver miscalculated and ended up underneath Cooper's plane.

Cooper's plane landed on the roof of the vehicle and crushed it. The impact broke the driver's neck and killed him. The Seneca bounced off the vehicle and then crashed. The ground crew pulled Cooper out of the demolished plane. He was dazed, cut and bruised and had a broken jaw. He was alive.

The smugglers abandoned the marijuana and the dead driver. They took Cooper to an apartment near Atlanta where he could hide and mend.[10]

Sheriff's deputies had been alerted by a local farmer who heard the crash. They came to the scene the following day. The Georgia Bureau of Investigation (GBI) did the investigating. They traced the ownership of the wrecked plane to Jim Cooper. They tracked him to his home in Portland, Maine, where he had fled.

Because the driver was killed during the commission of a crime and, even though the death was accidental, Georgia authorities nailed Cooper. He was charged with felony murder as well as drug smuggling and income tax evasion.[11]

Cooper was in a lot of trouble. He was vulnerable to the government's squeeze. It was an often-repeated scenario in the war on drugs.

Jim Cooper, like Barry Seal and many other criminals faced with the prospects of a lengthy prison sentence, decided it was time to strike a deal. With the assistance of his attorney, Cooper was able to negotiate a very good deal. In exchange for a plea of guilty to a single tax charge, which carried a sentence of five years' probation, Cooper would provide evidence against Air America.

This was a worthwhile trade-off. The government had a good chance of taking out a major cocaine smuggling operation. Jim Cooper would still end up as a convicted felon. The government would not have to bear the expense of a trial and Cooper's imprisonment.[12]

With Jim Cooper on board as cooperating defendant, the Organized Crime Drug Enforcement Task Force that was operating in Harrisburg adopted the Air America case.

Like other drug task forces, it was staffed with agents from DEA, FBI, Customs and IRS.

Air America was a big operation. The ring consisted of four pilots plus radio operators, offloaders, bankers, and assorted minor figures, plus planes and hangars. Cooper knew all about the operation because Luytjes had once employed him. During a period of four years, Air America flew nearly ten tons of pure cocaine into the United States under Luytjes's direction.

Like Barry Seal, Cooper cut a deal with the DEA. Cooper went to work for the Harrisburg office where his handler was DEA agent Keith Miller.[13]

Cooper started cooperating with the government in November 1984, several months after the Reagan administration blew Seal's cover. This gave the DEA another shot at the Ochoa drug dynasty.

Rik Luytjes's first handler was Philadelphian Bob Craven, a US Customs agent since 1977. He was assigned to the Air America Task Force, where his role as Luytjes's former "control" agent made his work a bit awkward at times.

Cooper's input as a knowledgeable informant made it clear that Luytjes had been flying drug runs. This was at the same time he was feeding Craven with selective information—selective from the standpoint that the information was usually about a pilot who was slow paying or had had failed altogether to pay his bill for his aircraft modifications.[14]

Some federal investigators felt Craven had gotten too close to Luytjes. One knowledgeable source said Craven was a good agent and very dedicated but he was "had" by Luytjes. It's a situation that happens at times between agents and their informants. Luytjes would later confirm in court that he had "conned" Craven.[15]

A comparable situation likely occurred in the case of Seal and his handler, Miami DEA agent Ernst Jacobsen. In 1984, largely because of his guile and charisma, Seal talked Jacobsen into taking a weekend vacation in Cancun with their wives. Seal flew everyone down in his Lear jet.

Such a trip can hardly be viewed as a bribe since the agent got nothing out of it but some sun.

But was it a conflict of interest?

The knowledge of this trip could have embarrassed the prosecution had it been brought up during a trial where Jacobsen had to testify. It is a routine defense tactic to attack the character and reliability of government witnesses, particularly the investigators.

Baton Rouge task force agents learned of the Cancun trip and it aroused their suspicions about Seal's relationship with Miami DEA agents.

Bottoms, who learned about the Cancun trip when it happened, is sure that Seal enticed "Jake" to take the trip. Bottoms concedes that it was inexcusable for Jacobsen to bring his wife along.

Seal sent some crawfish to the Miami DEA agents in the spring 1984. Baton Rouge agents were astonished. They became even more suspicious of Seal's relationship with the Miami DEA agents. It looked like the tail was wagging the dog.

Bottoms said he did bring some crawfish to Miami. The Miami DEA agents didn't know they were coming and didn't ask for them. "It was Barry's doing," said Bottoms.

Bottoms never thought Jacobsen was in any way dirty. He had worked with Jacobsen for several years and during all that time Jake never asked for or got a single dime from him. "I liked him and he was dedicated to covering my ass," said Bottoms. "He had no fear, and I was confident that he would do what it took when the time came and he proved that more than once."

By all accounts, Jacobsen was a hard-working and dedicated agent. There was never a hint that he had ever taken a nickel from Barry Seal or anyone else. As Bottoms sees it, task force agents in the Baton Rouge area misinterpreted the two events. They exaggerated the "tail wagging the dog" claim.

Bottoms recalled that there were periods when the DEA clamped down on Seal very tightly.

It became apparent that when they gave him loose reins, he produced.

"There is no such thing as total control over an informant, especially at the levels we were playing." Seal wasn't running Bob Joura or Jake, said Bottoms. "They were playing him like a fiddle."

Cooper's work as an informant resulted in an indictment being brought against Rik Luytjes. Before he could be arrested, he fled the United States and went to St. Eustatius Island in the Netherlands Antilles, on the shoulder of South America. Eventually, the government's efforts to have him returned to the United States were successful. On March 2, 1986, he was arrested at New York after being declared an undesirable alien and being kicked out of St. Eustatius.

In an effort to explain his hasty departure from the United States, Luytjes concocted a story that the CIA had hired him to organize a secret mission to assassinate Muammar Qaddafi. He promised proof from the CIA. No proof of such an assignment was ever produced. The CIA, of course, denied the story.[16]

Luytjes and some of his friends started a public relations campaign in an attempt to portray him as a businessman being harassed by the federal government. It certainly helped that some of his friends were in the media. He attempted to characterize himself as an innocent scapegoat, a swashbuckling adventurer whose exploits rivaled those of Indiana Jones. Barry Seal tried to do the same thing when he got broadcaster John Camp to produce *Uncle Sam Wants You*.

There were even hints that Luytjes was actually a secret CIA agent. The government reacted by increasing the pressure and charging him with a continuing criminal enterprise. Luytjes eventually caved in to the government, worked out a plea agreement and became an informant. This time for real.

In July 1986, Gordon Zubrod, the assistant US attorney in the Middle District of Pennsylvania handling the Air America case was ready to indict. The indictment was brought against the principals of the smuggling operation who were in the US and six of the Colombians including Rigoberto "Bobby" Correa. As charged in the indictment, the defendants were responsible for at least 21 trips involving cocaine and in excess of $25 million in US currency, all of which was smuggled in and out of the United States.

The Air America cocaine transportation ring put together by Rik Luytjes was proclaimed to be responsible for the largest documented amount of cocaine to ever be smuggled into the United States by a single trafficking organization: a record of almost ten tons.

Breaking of the Air America case was a major event. Attorney General Edwin Meese issued a press release congratulating the Department of Justice and acclaiming the case as proof of the effectiveness of federal law enforcement programs aimed at major drug trafficking rings.[17]

Rik Luytjes was a remarkable informant. He had personal contact with Jorge Ochoa and other Ochoa family members and he was engaged in smuggling their cocaine. In 1981 and 1982 alone, he hauled seven loads of cocaine totaling approximately thirty five hundred kilos — or about 3.8 tons.

For anyone keeping score, thus far we have Barry Seal with around 17,000 pounds of cocaine and Rik Luytjes with at least 20,000 pounds.

Now, take a look at Max Mermelstein.

Like Barry Seal and Rik Luytjes, Max Mermelstein arranged for the transportation of cocaine.

Mermelstein was living in Miami in 1978, when he met Rafael Osuna-Rodriguez, alias Rafael "Rafa" Cardona, a native of Medellin. He was coordinating cocaine shipments for the Ochoa family. Mermelstein's friendship with Cardona escalated to full-blown involvement in the transportation of cocaine for the Medellin Cartel.

He met Fabio Ochoa in February 1981 in Ft. Lauderdale. In April 1981, Mermelstein flew to Colombia and met with Jorge Ochoa, Fabio Ochoa, and Carlos Lehder, all members of the Medellin Cartel. Mermelstein, although not a pilot, agreed to move their "merchandise."

Beginning in the early 1980s and continuing through 1985, he smuggled cocaine into the United States. He hired the pilots, acquired the plane and managed the inventory and distribution.

He helped the Ochoa family run their business smoothly. His performance was outstanding. By November 1981, Mermelstein and the six pilots he employed had smuggled 19 tons of cocaine into Florida and another nine tons into California.[18]

In fact, Mermelstein was so trusted by the Ochoa organization that they assigned him the "contract" to kill Barry Seal.

They had learned that Seal was an informant for the DEA.[19]

In June 1985 the government caught up with Mermelstein. An eleven-count indictment was brought against him in the Central District of California. Federal agents arrested him at Ft. Lauderdale. He was charged with multiple counts of cocaine importation, possession and conspiracy as well as the big one, operating a continuing criminal enterprise.

Mermelstein was faced with the possibility of a life sentence plus ninety years. He became another cooperating defendant for the DEA. Over the next six years, he wrote a book about his days with the Medellin Cartel, and served as one of the government's top witnesses against its members.

"I am considered the most valuable witness that the government has ever turned against the cartel," claimed Mermelstein.[20]

According to Al Winters, Air Max transported 112,992 pounds of cocaine into the United States during his career as a cocaine smuggler. That is 56 tons, a record that surpasses the combined totals of Barry Seal and Rik Luytjes.

Unlike Barry Seal, Max Mermelstein went into the Witness Protection Program along with fifteen members of his family. He died at age 65 of cancer — not bullets.

Rik Luytjes, Max Mermelstein and Barry Seal were cocaine transportation specialists. All three hauled tons of cocaine for the Medellin Cartel. They were trusted and able to deal with Ochoa family members on a personal basis. They all gathered quality evidence for the government after they became informants. It was a metamorphosis that did not take place until after each smuggler had been caught and was facing the prospect of substantial jail time and the possibility of a life sentence.

Since they were all involved in smuggling significant amounts of cocaine into the United States and eventually became cooperating defendants, one would expect their sentences to be comparable.

Rik Luytjes didn't fare so well when it came time for him to be sentenced by US Judge Richard Conaboy of Pennsylvania. The judge made it clear to the prosecutor that he was not altogether pleased with the plea agreement Rik Luytjes had entered into with the government. He did not like the limits imposed on his latitude to pronounce sentence.

Conaboy viewed Luytjes's agreement as much too generous and thought the government had paid too high a price for his cooperation. "Just because someone squeals on someone else, why should he be treated better?" Assistant US Attorney Gordon Zubrod attempted to justify the lenient terms of the plea agreement by noting that Luytjes had risked his life dealing with the Colombians.[21]

Another argument that was advanced on behalf of Rik Luytjes was that he had merely transported cocaine. He was not a street dealer. Therefore, his crime was victimless. Judge Conaboy rejected that premise and commented that there were probably more victims in a case such as Luytjes's as there were in almost any other kind of case he would see. Noteworthy was Judge Conaboy's comment about what motivated Luytjes to cooperate in the first place. "You only began to cooperate because you were caught. It's as simple as that."[22]

Conaboy sentenced Luytjes to ten years and fined him $260,000, the maximum he could receive under the plea agreement. Luytjes entered the Witness Protection Program. Luytjes would serve four and one-half years of the ten-year sentence.

In California on June 26, 1987, US District Judge James M. Ideman sentenced Max Mermelstein. He had been in custody testifying, and being debriefed for the preceding two years. The judge sentenced him to time served and put him on lifetime, special parole.

Mermelstein would later testify in Louisiana for the prosecution during the trial of Seal's murderers. He firmly established the Medellin Cartel's culpability in the killing of Seal.

Chapter 14
Time Served

Barry Seal was generally unavailable for any in-depth debriefings by Louisiana or Arkansas FBI or DEA agents after he signed his plea agreement in November 1984. He surrendered to US Marshals on June 28, 1985.

He became a federally-protected witness. He vanished for all practical purposes.

Only a few federal people knew where he was: a few Miami DEA agents and the prosecuting attorneys in the Miami Southern District of Florida and Las Vegas. They were busy prepping him for the testimony he was going to give during trials of the cases he had made for the DEA.

After spending a short time in witness protection while testifying in Florida, Seal finally surfaced somewhat publicly. He and his attorney, Thomas Sclafani, came to federal court in Ft. Lauderdale on August 14, 1985. They wanted to dispose of the second indictment to which he pleaded guilty.

In a closed session before Judge Jose Gonzalez, DEA supervisor Bob Joura, and DEA agent Ernst Jacobsen testified in glowing terms to Seal's exploits as a DEA informant.

There was evidently little or no mention of Seal's prowess as one of the largest cocaine smugglers in the US before he turned DEA informant. Judge Gonzalez disposed of Seal's indictment and prior guilty plea. He sentenced Seal to five years of unsupervised probation.

That same month Seal began testifying in the Las Vegas trial.

Seal appeared in Washington, DC, on October 7, 1985, to testify before the President's Commission on Organized Crime symposium. Among his assertions was that he had quit TWA as a pilot because smuggling was so simple and lucrative and it was easy to avoid detection.

Did Seal forget to mention his 1972 arrest in the US Customs sting?

Perhaps his most forceful pronouncement was his comment, "If you told the US Army to shoot down suspected drug smugglers it would have a decided effect. I know I wouldn't be up there."

Seal and his attorney, Tom Sclafani, appeared before Judge Norman Roettger, Jr., in a second closed session on October 24, 1985. Sclafani had filed a Rule 35 motion for a reduction of Seal's sentence. Rule 35 of the Federal Rules of Criminal Procedure permit a judge to reduce a defendant's prior sentence. Sclafani was hoping to keep Seal out of prison.

Tom Sclafani began his try for the reduction by pointing out that Seal had begun serving his ten-year sentence in June 1985 when he entered the Witness Protection Program. He noted that Seal could have been free for several more weeks except for the increased danger to his physical safety.

He lamented the fact that for fifty of the ninety-seven days in witness protection, Seal had been kept under the Miami federal courthouse. Seal was in a ten-by-twelve-foot underground room with no windows and only fluorescent light, a bed, television and a bathroom—a cubicle from which he could not see outside or hear outside noises associated with normal living.

Scalfani then told of Seal's visit to Las Vegas where he was housed for two weeks in the basement of an abandoned rifle range while testifying for the government.

From Nevada, Seal went to a permanent protection center where he could exercise outdoors for only one hour a day. He had been there for thirty days at the time of the sentence reduction hearing in Miami.

Seal cooperated fully with the government—he had become the single most important government witness in the United States, Sclafani claimed. Because of Seal's cooperation, the government had been able to convict top officials of a foreign government (Colombia) as well as nine defendants in Nevada, and to indict top people in the Medellin Cartel plus the arrest of Jorge Ochoa in Spain.

Seal had almost been killed in the crash in Colombia and a shoot-down of his plane, Sclafani said. Moreover, he had been imprisoned in Managua for a day. Worse, Seal faced an open $350,000 contract on his life from the Ochoas.

Sclafani argued that Seal's repeated risking of his life was evidence that he was not merely an adventurer—he had been rehabilitated. He was not likely to return to criminal conduct.

Sclafani's motion helpfully included a section titled "Seal's Personal Characteristics."

He argued that Seal's "incredible cooperation" far outweighed the magnitude of the offense which drew a sentence of ten years.

Sclafani was absolutely correct on that score because the case Judge Roettger heard involved several hundred thousand fake methaqualone tablets made of chalk—not about eight and a half tons of cocaine.

The timing of Seal's overture to cooperate soon after he was indicted was offered as evidence that his motive was not self-serving. Sclafani pointed out that Seal's first approach was to agents Bruce Zimet and Randy Beasley—but they had rejected him.

Next, he told of Seal's attempts to convince US Attorney Stan Bardwell to permit him to cooperate with the government—and how Bardwell had also turned him down.

Sclafani knew both side of the courtroom. He was a former assistant US attorney himself. Sclafani spoke of his client's appearance before Judge Gonzalez for sentencing. He described how Seal had tearfully told Gonzalez he was prepared to risk his life as an informer in the investigation.

In part, Seal wanted a reduced sentence, and also to "undo the wrongs that I have committed." Sclafani emphasized how Seal's "resounding candor as a witness" in the Escobar trial had so impressed the parties that all but one defendant pleaded guilty during the trial.

The lawyer cited another "incredible example" of the real Barry Seal, a true humanitarian. He and undercover DEA agents landed at the Turks and Caicos Islands not far from the Bahamas chain on their way to Colombia to pick up the cocaine for the Nevada caper.

When they landed, there was an air ambulance Lear jet on the runway that couldn't get its engines started. The air ambulance was transporting an elderly woman with a broken hip who was in critical condition. Seal spent three hours removing the batteries from the ambulance jet and replacing them with the batteries from his own Lear jet. He started the engines on the air ambulance then replaced the original batteries. The ambulance jet reached its destination in sufficient time to save the elderly woman's life.

Sclafani concluded his arguments by declaring that he believed the court should reduce Seal's sentence to time served. It was a right and just resolution of the case, he argued, and it would send a message to the community that extraordinary cooperation with the federal government would be justly rewarded.

Tom Sclafani never made any claim that his client was a long-time CIA operative — or even that he had been working for the CIA when he flew the C-123 cargo plane to Nicaragua.

If Seal had been a CIA asset or operative, this was certainly the time for his attorney to announce it. Sclafani didn't. And the reason he didn't was because the CIA had never employed Seal in any capacity.

In support of the motion to reduce Seal's sentence, Dick Gregorie, submitted an affidavit. Gregorie noted that Seal had placed his life in danger while taking part in undercover operations. He affirmed that Seal had been candid, forthright and truthful in all of his testimony in the cases in which he was a witness.

Gregorie said that it was his opinion that Seal's life was in great danger. He recommended that Seal request concealment in the Witness Protection Program. More importantly, Gregorie pointed out that if Seal chose not to participate in the protection program, the federal government had no way of guaranteeing his safety.

Neither Gregorie nor his boss, Stanley Marcus, made any recommendation to the court about a sentence.

Then it was Bob Joura's turn. He recounted Seal's exploits as an informant about smuggling loads of cocaine. He testified to having worked with a lot of informants during his sixteen-year career, and he had never met one with the potential who had produced so much as Seal.

Joura said he had never caught Seal in a lie. Joura testified that he would like to see Seal's sentence reduced to time served with a substantial period of probation. He explained that, if Seal didn't get substantial help from the government in view of all he had done, it would send a clear message to others who might be considering cooperation with DEA that informants just don't get any help.

Joura also emphasized that any mention of the CIA in his testimony absolutely did not mean to infer that Seal worked for the CIA — which Joura knew was the truth.

The next witness was Detective Chief Inspector Derek O'Connell, of the Merseyside, England police force. The inspector was on loan to the British Foreign Office as police advisor on drug matters to the Royal Turks and Caicos Police Force.

The inspector acknowledged that the islands had become a smuggling haven and a refueling stop for drug planes going to and from Colombia, and a storage spot for drugs. Seal's efforts had greatly helped to stop the illicit drug trafficking. He also testified that Seal was forthright and honest.

Donald Campbell, an assistant US attorney in Las Vegas, followed inspector O'Connell. He testified that the most significant problem in Las Vegas was cocaine trafficking by a group of criminals centered in the Cuban community. He explained that, with the assistance of Barry Seal, it had been possible to successfully prosecute one of the finest cases his office ever brought against significant organized crime traffickers in Las Vegas. Campbell added that DEA agents of the Las Vegas office had asked that he convey their strong feelings to the court that Seal would be of more use out of jail cooperating with the DEA than in jail.

The final witness was Rodney Guy Smith, deputy executive director of the President's Commission on Organized Crime. Smith explained that the President's Commission was mandated to produce a report advising the president and the attorney general about organized crime figures in America. It included the source of their income, and recommendations for legislative and administrative steps to combat them.

Smith said he selected a single witness, Barry Seal, to appear before a symposium of the committee. He wanted to give the members a look-see at an individual who was the embodiment of what their agencies were up against in terms of expertise, intelligence, and ability.

Smith acknowledged that at first there was some skepticism about Seal among the group. After listening to Seal for several hours, the members found the experience quite useful. The articulate, thoughtful, intelligent and experienced pilot described how he had managed to evade their best efforts to arrest him. Smith noted that it was a media event, open to the public, and was covered by all three TV networks and twelve to fifteen print journalists.

Attorney Sclafani rested his case on behalf of Seal.

Judge Roettger made some dramatic comments. He said that, at the time of the trial, he thought Seal was evil. After listening to the witnesses, people for whom he had a lot of respect, he changed his mind. The witnesses had exhibited a sense of personal belief that Seal had changed and that his integrity was very high.

Therefore, his appraisal of Seal, though clearly correct at one time, was no longer appropriate.

The judge said promises of cooperation didn't cut any ice with him. The only time he let anybody out of jail entirely, rather than a reduction of sentence, was when their cooperation rose to the level where they put their life in a position of peril. When they did that, they deserved to be suitably rewarded.

Judge Roettger reduced Seal's sentence to time served, suspended the remainder of the time and placed him on probation for three years.

Barry Seal was a free man for now, but he still had to face Judge Polozola in Baton Rouge, his hometown.

According to Sclafani's own statistics, out of a ten-year sentence, Barry had spent a total of ninety-seven days in custody. However, none of his custodial time was within the strict confines of a federal penitentiary. He was in the custody of US Marshals in witness protection preparing to testify — or he was testifying in trials in Miami and Las Vegas.

Seal's motion to reduce sentence was heard in a closed court session in Florida. No testimony was offered in opposition to the sentence reduction. All Judge Roettger heard was one-sided testimony concerning the major cocaine cases Seal had made against big names in the Medellin Cartel — and the personal risks he took in doing so.

The transcript of the hearing contains no testimony to indicate that Judge Roettger was told anything about the hundreds of kilos of cocaine Seal was responsible for smuggling into the United States before he became the poster-boy informant for the DEA.

This was the same judge who said at the time he first sentenced Seal: "Consider yourself lucky, Mr. Seal, because if this were a cocaine case, you would be doing at least twenty-five years."

The reduction of Seal's Florida sentence to time served stunned the Baton Rouge task force agents. US Attorney Stan Bardwell had said to reporters after Seal's guilty plea: "It is my view the sentence will not be reduced."

The next hurdle was Judge Polozola. Seal would face high school classmate Stan Bardwell in Louisiana.

Chapter 15
The Sentencing: Clash of Egos

It was high drama set in a Louisiana courtroom.

A defendant, a cocky drug-smuggler turned snitch.

A federal judge angry because his sentencing prerogatives were blunted by a plea agreement.

A defense attorney trying to portray his client as merely a drug transporter.

A federal prosecutor anxious to end the career of the smuggler who brought thousands of pounds of cocaine into his jurisdiction.

Task force agents—GS-pukes, according to the smuggler— pleased with the results, fed up with the smuggler.

TV reporters eager to film the smuggler and catch his snappy sound bites.

Members of the press, pencils poised, ready to put their spin on what was about to happen.

Here is the real story.

On January 24 1986, Seal appeared at the federal court house for sentencing by Judge Frank J. Polozola.

On one side of the courtroom stood Stan Bardwell, Brad Myers, and other prosecutors from the Middle District in Baton Rouge. They were flanked by agents from the Baton Rouge offices of the DEA, FBI, and IRS.

On the other side of the courtroom were Seal and attorney Lewis Unglesby.

The exchanges between Unglesby and Judge Polozola were contentious from the start.

The judge began by routinely asking if there were any corrections, clarifications or additions to make in the pre-sentence report.

Unglesby responded that there were no changes but there were some things he would like to say. Judge Polozola asked if the facts were true and correct.

Unglesby replied that they were.

"For example, does Mr. Seal admit to having made $25 million smuggling cocaine?" Polozola asked.

"We can't rank ourselves. I mean, where is the proof of that? We never heard of such a thing. The allegation has never been made. That's just not true." Unglesby answered that Seal had never said he made $25 million smuggling cocaine and never said he was in the top five.

Seal whispered something to Unglesby and the attorney told him to tell the judge. Seal explained that his prior court testimony had been that "we grossed" that amount—not that he had made that amount personally.

"How much was your part?" Polozola asked.

"Well, I'd rather not get into that, because that's pending before the courts in Florida right now. There is still another case pending," Seal replied.

"I don't care what's pending in Florida. This is my case." The judge's irritation was evident.

"Wait a minute, judge." Unglesby sprang to his client's defense.

"No, Mr. Unglesby. Let me tell you what. I don't care who Mr. Seal thinks he is. He is nothing special to me. He is nothing more than a person who has pled guilty to a felony. I don't treat him as different." The judge was plainly angered.

Unglesby knew he had riled the judge. He attempted to explain by pointing out that Seal was under different orders from different authorities. Seal had been told "by the United States government" not to describe his activities on behalf of the DEA to his probation officer.

"What part of the United States government?" snapped the judge.

"Justice Department." Unglesby's anger began to show.

"I don't care about the Justice Department."

"Well, he does."

Unglesby brought up the Rule 35 sentence-reduction motion outlining Seal's activities over the last few years. He pointed out that Seal was under orders of the Florida court not to talk about that matter.

"Unfortunately, I wasn't aware of the fact that a Rule 35 motion was pending. And even though my sentence is tied to that one, I wasn't given an opportunity to even confer with the judge before sentence was imposed, or reduced, I should say. I'm not blaming it on Mr. Seal or you. I'm just saying that I don't like the idea of having a sentence tied to something in Florida and not having a chance to even know what's going on." Judge Polozola was still visibly annoyed.

Unglesby tried to placate the judge and told him that his and Seal's hands were tied because of a court order in Florida that said they could not discuss what Seal's activities had been. The attorney went on to discuss Seal's role in providing the basis for the extradition warrants from Spain for Jorge Ochoa.

He emphasized that there was an "outstanding contract" to kill Seal.

Polozola pointed out that Seal had been offered witness protection and didn't want it.

Unglesby countered that Seal had taken protection during periods of time he felt it was necessary but not when he thought it was not necessary. Unglesby warned that the day Jorge Ochoa came into United States custody, Seal would have to become invisible and go back into some kind of custody.

Then Polozola called on the prosecution to respond.

Stan Bardwell pointed out that Unglesby was incorrectly attempting to explain Seal's refusal to give his Baton Rouge probation officer a statement about the cocaine offense to which he was pleading guilty. It was because of some alleged "orders" from the Florida court.

"There is nothing in the orders of Florida that deal with that offense, I think that simply is not so," argued Bardwell.

And he was absolutely correct. The fifty-three-page transcript of the Rule 35 hearing before Judge Roettger contains no orders to Seal from the judge except to "have a good day."

The cocaine count to which Seal was pleading guilty in Polozola's court involved the cocaine he bought through Robert T. LeBlanc. The cocaine was stolen from New Orleans by Fred Compton and flown to LeBlanc's place in Iberville Parish.

Seal's plea had nothing to do with any indictments in Florida. Seal was hedging. He was very reluctant to have to publicly admit that he bought a large quantity of cocaine — let alone explain why he did so.

Barry Seal and his lawyers had been carefully cultivating the image that he was only a transporter — and he wanted to keep it that way. By muddying the waters with vagaries concerning "orders" from Florida, Seal hoped to obscure the facts.

You can't do much else with 210 kilos of cocaine — except peddle it.

"Maybe we may have misunderstood," Unglesby responded.

He went on to explain that the government version of the cocaine count found in the pre-sentence report came in large part from Seal and they had agreed it was factual.

It was time for Judge Polozola to pronounce sentence. He echoed some of the complaints expressed by Judge Conaboy at the sentencing of Rik Luytjes.

Judge Polozola began by expressing his disappointment with the plea agreement. He did not think justice was being done, but he had accepted the plea and would abide by it.

"But I will state for the record, just as clear as I can that, if I had the remotest idea, the slightest idea that Mr. Seal would not receive a jail sentence in Florida, under no circumstances, absolutely no circumstances, would I have accepted this plea agreement," the judge warned.

"I will concede that Mr. Seal has helped the government on several drug cases. There is another case pending in Florida that he may or may not have to testify in. But, as far as I am concerned, drug dealers like Mr. Seal are the lowest, most despicable type of people I can think of because they have no concern for the public. They have no concern for the individual user. All they want is their money. And what effect it has on others — they could care less. They don't care if the drugs go to children. They don't care if the user has to take food money. They don't care if the user has to rob, or steal or prostitute themselves. It just doesn't matter. All that matters to you is you are making big bucks. In my own opinion, people like you, Mr. Seal, ought to be in the federal penitentiary."

Judge Polozola began laying down the conditions of the probation he had been forced to impose. He warned that if the terms he was about to set were not followed, he expected the government to move to revoke probation, at which time the judge would no longer be bound by the plea agreement.

The first condition of probation was that Polozola himself was to be the only person who could approve Seal's travel outside of the Baton Rouge Middle District.

"I don't care if it is the Drug Enforcement Administration. I don't care if is the CIA. I don't care if it is the State Department. I don't care if it is the US Attorney. I don't care who it is — you don't go any place without getting my personal written approval in advance." Polozola was adamant.

The discussion shifted to Seal's use of an armed bodyguard, an issue raised in the complaint letter Sclafani sent to Bardwell. This concerned the incident at the Holiday Inn when Crittenden of the LSP photographed Seal's secretary.

The judge made it very clear that he was not ruling on the issue, then he issued a warning. Polozola pointed out that Seal was a convicted felon. Having armed people around him might be held to be constructive possession of firearms under the law. It could lead to a revocation of Seal's probation.

Unglesby interrupted. He didn't mean to be disrespectful, but the case had engendered a great deal of animosity between his client and some law enforcement agencies. He noted that there was nothing in the pre-sentence report about armed guards. Since the judge had brought it up, Unglesby wanted to know who the bodyguards were.

"They are his guards, his bodyguards. This is what I understand. He has bodyguards. And the police officers didn't advise me of this," answered the judge.

Unglesby responded that it was "news to us."

Polozola questioned Seal directly. "Mr. Seal, do you have bodyguards that carry guns?"

"Not in the car with me, not around me."

"Do you have bodyguards that carry guns?"

"They don't live with me."

"Do you have bodyguards that carry guns?"

"Not at this time I don't, no, sir."

"Did you have bodyguards in that past that carried guns?"

"Yes, sir."

"But I want to tell you on the record that you can't have a gun." The judge was unbending.

Barry Seal wasn't going to let a federal judge tell him what he could do. He could be cocky and downright uncooperative with authority figures—judges, cops, GS pukes.

"I don't possess a gun, and I don't intend to. But I do intend to have bodyguards."

"Well, your bodyguards are going to have to be without guns." The judge's anger was rising again.

Seal pressed the issue. "Well, why is that, if they have legal permits to carry them?"

"You take your chance, Mr. Seal. Take your chance. Have bodyguards with guns and take your chance." The judge was through arguing with Seal.

Judge Polozola began to pronounce sentence.

On Count One, he fined Seal $25,000 and suspended a sentence as to imprisonment.

On Count II, the judge fined him $10,000 then placed him on active probation for five years.

Then the judge began to explain the conditions of the probation he had been obligated to impose under the terms of the plea agreement. —Seal was to comply with local, state, and federal laws as well as with the rules and regulations of the probation office.

—He must notify the US Attorney of any change of address.

—He was not to travel outside of the Baton Rouge Middle District without prior written approval of the court.

—Continuing with the terms of the probation, Seal was required to carry a pager at all times and to be able to respond to a signal from the probation office within one hour of receiving it.

—Seal was required to produce a complete financial accounting of his business and personal finances on a quarterly basis, beginning January 1, 1986 and continuing throughout the five years of his probation.

—And he was forbidden all contact with other co-defendants.

—Then came the bombshell.

—Seal was ordered to reside at the Salvation Army Community Treatment Center on Airline Highway in Baton Rouge at night for six months. He was to be in the facility by 6 pm and remain there until 6 am

A stunned Unglesby spun around. He began to protest to Bardwell and Brad Myers.

The judge scolded Unglesby for talking to the government lawyers while he was explaining the conditions of probation. Polozola told him to pay attention because he wanted him, as well as Seal, to clearly understand the travel restrictions and that Seal had to live for six months at the Salvation Army facility.

"Well, we want to talk about that," said Unglesby. He was now furious and struggling to maintain composure.

"Well, there is nothing to talk about."

"That's a double-cross by the government." Unglesby was livid.

Polozola countered that it was not a double-cross. Read the plea agreement, he said.

"I've read it," snapped the lawyer. "I'm very familiar with it. I hammered it out. Okay? It says no incarceration."

Unglesby was insistent. He continued to argue that spending the night in the halfway house was incarceration—and not in accordance with the plea agreement.

Polozola denied that it was incarceration. He invited Unglesby to file a motion and appeal the sentence. He would love for the plea agreement to be "broken right now."

The sentencing session ended with Unglesby vowing to appeal.

Some of the GS pukes who were in the courtroom wore smiles.

Unglesby, Seal, and their entourage left the courtroom visibly angered.

Local television reporters were outside on the courthouse steps waiting for Barry Seal. When he stopped to talk to them, he complained bitterly about the latest turn of events and the fact that he would be staying at the Salvation Army at night.

And, in keeping with his character, Seal attempted to deprecate Judge Polozola. "I'm trying desperately to understand the logic behind Judge Polozola's ruling. At the sentencing he said he wanted to make sure I didn't bring any more drugs into the Middle District. I brought 20,000 pounds of cocaine into the Middle District of Louisiana, nowhere else, and I never left my home. I did it all by phone."

Seal's pronouncement would later backfire when the IRS used his own statistics to calculate his income.

The IRS slapped a $29 million federal tax lien against Seal and his property.

Here's what the law says: the judge may require a person, as a condition of probation, to reside in a residential community treatment center for all or part of the period of probation. (Provisions of Title 18, Section 3651 of the US Code.)

Apparently, someone had failed to deal with that provision in the plea agreement.

Judge Polozola followed the terms of the plea agreement and gave Seal the sentence of five years' probation that it called for. However, he put conditions on the probation that Section 3651 gave him the statutory authority to do.

Any claims that Judge Polozola violated the terms of the plea agreement and jailed Seal are false.

Seal got the sentence of probation he had been promised. He was not put into a federal penitentiary where many big-time convicted drug smugglers end up.

Seal brought too much cocaine into the United States to allow him to walk away a free man.

By Seal's own admission, he had brought all of the cocaine into Louisiana. US Attorney Stan Bardwell and rest of the federal and state law enforcement community in Baton Rouge thought he deserved some jail time, no matter how successful he had been as a DEA informant.

In the end, Barry Seal would not spend any time in a federal penitentiary—although his ability to travel, especially to Florida and South America, was greatly curtailed.

Critics sometimes ignored the fact that Seal wasn't the only target in Louisiana or Arkansas. They overlooked the most significant result of the plea agreement.

Seal's entire organization of accomplices and co-conspirators were targets. Agents were targeting three pilots, four or five ground personnel, a mechanic, the drivers of the cars who took the cocaine to Florida, a secretary, a communications expert and others such as Fred Hampton and Joe Evans.

After Seal signed the plea agreement, the remnants of his drug smuggling organization were vulnerable to prosecution. No one had immunity.

The plea agreement called for total cooperation from Barry Seal. He was required to submit to debriefing whenever requested by government agents and prosecutors. He had to be truthful and candid and had to appear before grand juries and at any trials.

It was further agreed that any statements or testimony Seal gave could be used as leads against other persons.

Many agreements have escape clauses. This one certainly did. This one allowed the government to go after Seal again. Seal had no escape.

The escape clause reserved to the government the right to bring a new indictment if Seal did not fully comply with the terms of the agreement.

Barry Seal was between the proverbial rock and a hard place. He would have been required to provide information about the involvement of his underlings in his cocaine smuggling operation. And he would have been required to testify against them at trial had they been prosecuted.

Regrettably, there were no further prosecutions of Seal's accomplices.

Chapter 16
"Murder Most Foul"

At approximately 6:00 pm on Wednesday, February 19, 1986, Barry Seal pulled his white Cadillac into the parking lot of the Salvation Army Treatment Center on Airline Highway in Baton Rouge. He backed his car into a parking spot and turned off the engine. He was still sitting in the car.

That's when two Colombians walked up to the vehicle and opened fire with MAC-10 and Uzi machine guns.

This was the smuggler's end.

According to the autopsy report, death was instantaneous, resulting from multiple gunshot wounds, seven in all, to the head and body.

The Medellin drug lords who considered themselves betrayed by Seal finally had their revenge.

Robert Lane, an employee of the Salvation Army Treatment Center, happened to be sitting on a sofa overlooking the parking lot. He saw the shooters.

They were subsequently identified as Bernardo Antonio Vasquez and Miguel Velez.

The two backed their gray four-door Buick into a parking slot and remained seated in the car. At first he thought nothing of it. Moments later Lane was stupefied when he saw them walk to the Cadillac and blast away at Seal.

Colleen McGehee was stopped in her van at a red light on Airline Highway in front of the Salvation Army center. She saw a man with a machine gun jump from behind a used clothing drop box. She thought it was a joke — until she saw him shoot the driver who was sitting in his Cadillac.

After the shooting, the two gunmen walked back to their vehicle and drove away. Within minutes, the Buick containing the two machine guns was found abandoned in the parking lot of the Hi

Nabor supermarket about three blocks from the Salvation Army center. Detectives quickly located an eyewitness who saw the killers get out of the Buick and switch to a red Cadillac.

Miguel Velez was arrested at approximately 11:00 pm that same day.

A deer and a taxi cab collision helped.

The cab he hired at New Orleans International Airport to take him to Montgomery, Alabama, struck a deer near Meridian, Mississippi. Mississippi State Highway Patrol officers responding to the accident recognized Velez based on information contained in the all-points bulletin put out by the Louisiana State Police.

Meanwhile, Vasquez abandoned the red Cadillac at the New Orleans International Airport. Agents learned Vasquez caught a flight to Miami. Federal agents apprehended him when he arrived there.

Within 48 hours of the killing, the six Colombians who had conspired with the Medellin drug lords to murder Barry Seal were in custody.

This was a result of the combined efforts of the Baton Rouge Police Department, Louisiana State Police, Mississippi Highway Patrol, Immigration and Naturalization Service (INS), US Border Patrol, US Customs Service, FBI, IRS, and DEA agents in Baton Rouge, New Orleans and Miami.

An editorial was published in the *Miami Herald* on February 23, 1986, the Sunday following Seal's murder. Headlined "Murder Most Foul," the editorial asked why Seal was permitted to go unprotected when the DEA knew Colombian drug lords had put out a contract on his life. The US Justice Department said their most important snitch had shunned witness protection, the newspaper noted. Since when did the personal prerogative of a convicted drug smuggler supersede the government's interest in keeping a witness alive? These tough questions came from the largest newspaper in Florida. The paper reported on the front lines of the wars among the cocaine cowboys on Brickell Avenue, Dadeland Mall, and Cuban communities.

Seal's attorney provided his answer when he said that federal agents in Louisiana weren't interested in protecting his client. They regarded Seal as little better than the big-league smugglers he helped put away. The newspaper editorial called for federal agents in Louisiana to be drummed out of law enforcement forever if investigation substantiated allegations that Seal was hung out to dry. The editorial went on to say that US District Judge Frank Polozola ought to explain why he ignored warnings that Seal was marked for assassination and ordered him to report to a halfway house every night.

Admittedly, Polozola's requirement that he spend his nights in the Salvation Army Halfway facility made Barry Seal more vulnerable. Hitmen could learn his whereabouts for a twelve-hour period.

Realistically, the judge's order magnified very little the danger Seal was already facing.

Pablo Escobar and Carlos Lehder were ruthless cutthroats. The men they sent to kill Barry Seal were cold-blooded killers. They were motivated by a half-million dollar bounty.

Escobar was the man who was said to have planned the bombing of an Avianca 727 flying from Bogota to Cali. The plane blew up, killing a hundred passengers and the crew. Two passengers Escobar suspected of being informants died in the explosion.[1]

Seal's fans, family and Unglesby used the term "double-cross" to describe the Baton Rouge Middle District's handling of the smuggler's case.

The most bizarre accusations would come from the conspiracy disciples who touted the entire scenario as a CIA plot. It was all a plot to silence Barry Seal. The agency wanted him gone lest he spill the beans about his involvement at Mena in their drugs-up-guns-down program on behalf of the Contras. Judge Polozola was following in lock-step.

Of course, there was no believable evidence that Barry Seal worked for the CIA. And there were facts that proved that such allegations were nothing more than the malicious bilge of a few screwballs.

The first orders to kill Seal were given to Max Mermelstein by Rafael "Rafa" Cardona Salazar, after he viewed the tape *Uncle Sam Wants You*. Salazar played John Camp's videotape for Max Mermelstein. The tape confirmed that the man they all thought was Ellis McKenzie was actually Barry Seal.

By this time, Mermelstein had so ingratiated himself with the Ochoa smuggling organization that they assigned him the "contract" to kill Barry Seal.

Pablo Escobar and Fabio Ochoa concurred with Salazar. Jorge Ochoa sent a representative to Miami. He was equipped with a MAC-

10 compact submachine gun, a rapid fire gun developed by the US Army and others then soon adopted by drug assassins. They included $100,000 in cash for Mermelstein to help him get the job done. [2]

Obeying the order he was given, Mermelstein traveled to Baton Rouge on January 15, 1985, to hunt for Seal.

He couldn't find Seal. Between January 15 and March 10, 1985, he made three more unsuccessful trips to Baton Rouge hunting for Seal without finding him. He finally told the Ochoas he couldn't find him, although he once eye-balled Seal's wife, Debbie.

After reporting back from one of his unsuccessful trips, Cardona told Max, "F--- that, go to the house some night and take everybody there.[3]

Cardona didn't mean take them out to dinner.

In June 1985, the government caught up with Max Mermelstein when an eleven-count indictment was brought against him in the Central District of California. He was charged with multiple counts of cocaine importation, possession, and conspiracy, as well as the big one, operating a continuing criminal enterprise. Federal agents arrested him at Ft. Lauderdale, Florida on June 5, 1985.

He was faced with the possibility of a life sentence plus ninety years. Mermelstein started to talk. One of the things he talked about was his contract to kill Barry Seal.

Over the next six years, Max Mermelstein served as one of the government's top witnesses against Cartel members. He testified in Lake Charles, Louisiana, for state prosecutors during the trial of the three Colombians responsible for the murder of Seal.

Mermelstein's personal knowledge of the conspiracy to murder Seal was extensive. He was able to tell government agents that the MAC-10 used to kill Seal had been test-fired into a basement wall of a Miami residence. Federal agents were able to recover spent slugs then match them to the weapon.

Al Winters regarded Mermelstein as being as good a witness as he had ever encountered during his career as a prosecutor.

Max Mermelstein had failed to get the hit job done. In January 1986, Jorge Ochoa ordered a Colombian named Carlos Uribe-Munera to kill Seal. Ochoa set the price for the hit at ten million pesos. Uribe refused to carry out the order when he learned that he himself was going to be killed after he murdered Seal.

On January 22, 1986, on orders from Jorge Ochoa, gunmen shot Uribe-Munera five times in the head and upper body. They left him for dead.

Miraculously, he survived the shooting. He went into hiding until May 1986 when he showed up at the US Embassy in Bogota asking for asylum. Uribe-Munera told US officials about the plot to murder Seal and he tied it to Jorge Ochoa.

Uribe-Munera was brought to the United States where, on October 28, 1986, in Baton Rouge, he pleaded guilty before the late federal Judge John V. Parker. The guilty plea was entered to an indictment charging one count of conspiracy to import cocaine and one count of conspiracy to distribute 11,000 pounds of cocaine. Judge Parker handed down a sentence of fifteen years on each count, to be served consecutively.

Uribe-Munera was promised protection while he was in federal custody. He was sent off to Springfield Medical Center for treatment of the residual effects of his gunshot wounds. Uribe-Munera testified for the state of Louisiana against the Colombians who had carried out the murder.

The national PBS series, *Frontline*, reported an interview with Fernando Arenas, who was the personal pilot for Carlos Lehder for many years.

Arenas said the Ochoas ordered Seal killed. What Seal did was such an act of betrayal that Fabio Ochoa wanted to kill Seal himself.

The murder of Barry Seal was carried out by the collective efforts of three Colombians: Miguel Velez, who obviously received the permission he sought, Bernardo Antonio Vasquez, and Luis Carlos Quintero-Cruz.

The three went to trial in Lake Charles, Louisiana, where the state's case was prosecuted by Prem Burns, lead attorney and Joe Lotwick. Both prosecutors were assistant district attorneys from East Baton Rouge, the Nineteenth Judicial District. They were skilled and experienced in the courtroom.

Attorneys for the murder suspects put on a tenacious courtroom defense. All three defendants were convicted of murder and received life sentences.

No evidence was introduced during the trial to prove that any of these killers were involved in a conspiracy with the CIA to silence Barry Seal.

There is a Supreme Court case that deals with the government's responsibility to protect informants. The case involved a man named Jessie Swanner, who had been acting as a "special employee" of the US Treasury, Bureau of Alcohol Tax and Firearms (ATF). Swanner was assisting the agency in the undercover investigation of illegal whiskey making in Tennessee. One night a bomb exploded under Swanner's house, injuring him and members of his family and causing much damage to the house and contents.

Swanner sued ATF for damages under the Tort Claim Act. He alleged that the ATF was negligent for not protecting him against retaliation from those on whom he was informing: a man named Ed McGlocklin. Somehow, McGlocklin discovered Swanner was an ATF informant and threatened him.

Swanner learned of the threats and notified ATF agents who advised him that, in their judgment, he was safe from McGlocklin as long as he remained in Alabama. The ATF took no more action. Swanner remained in Alabama.

Swanner won the lawsuit and collected monetary damages.

In the Swanner case, the Supreme Court concluded that the ATF owed a special duty to use reasonable care to protect Swanner. The court cited evidence that he had collaborated and assisted the government in the arrest and prosecution of criminals and there was reasonable cause to believe he was endangered because of his assistance to the ATF. It was the act of assisting the ATF to catch criminals that gave rise to the duty to protect the individual from any form of retaliation.[4]

The same logic ought to apply to the DEA with regard to their relationship with Barry Seal. His life was endangered because he assisted the DEA in their efforts to jail members of the Medellin Cartel — and the agency certainly knew about the threat.

What distinguishes Jessie Swanner from Barry Seal is that Swanner sought help from the ATF and was told everything would be okay if he stayed in Alabama. Seal didn't ask the DEA to protect him from the Colombians.

Even if Seal had asked, the only thing DEA could have done was to try to convince him to enter the Witness Protection Program, or else organize their own off-the-books protection program and assign bodyguards to him or relocate him — or do both.

The FBI, the DEA, or whichever federal agency it may be, has a duty to conceal an informant's identity as well as to provide protection from retaliation. The duty is unequivocal and fundamental to the concept of using informants in law enforcement.

The problem for an agency, such as the DEA or the FBI, is how to fulfill this obligation when there is no lawful means of forcibly imposing protective measures on someone who doesn't want them.

As the Barry Seal case demonstrated, there is no way.

Managed by the US Marshals Service, the federal Witness Protection Program is strictly a voluntary program — and there is the dilemma. Participation in the program is by request only. Federal judges do not have the authority to order an individual to enter witness protection. Without a request to enter the Witness Protection Program, there is little, if anything, the government can do to protect an informant.

Some say that DEA or FBI agents should have guarded Barry Seal. Being a bodyguard is not in the job description of FBI or DEA agents and they do not receive the necessary training.

There is much more involved in providing personal physical protection than carrying a gun and standing around in sunglasses wearing a hearing aid. Secret Service agents do it for the president, the vice president, and others. Providing personal protection is a complex task involving complicated logistics, threat assessments, round-the-clock vigilance, and a lot of personnel. Secret Service agents are trained and equipped to do it. FBI, DEA, IRS, Customs and ATF agents are rarely, if ever, trained to act as bodyguards.

Seal employed a bodyguard for a time. Retired deputy US Marshal Clint Hebert, now deceased, told of one incident involving his bodyguard and two postal inspectors. The two postal inspectors, who were from New Orleans, were working a pornography case believed to be operating out of a building across the street from Seal's downtown office building. They were conducting a surveillance and made several drive-by checks of the building. They had no idea they were anywhere near Barry Seal — and didn't even know who he was.

Seal and his bodyguard confronted the two inspectors and demanded their identification. Fortunately, there was no violence. The inspectors complained and Judge Polozola was made aware of the incident.

We can explore some of the alternatives to the Witness Protection Program for someone in Seal's position.

Self-help would be one alternative but it would involve either employing armed guards or carrying a gun. Neither is a desirable solution. A convicted felon can't legally possess a firearm and, as Judge Polozola noted, having armed bodyguards might be ruled to be constructive possession of a firearm. Furthermore, it is absurd to think that a US citizen, even a convicted felon, has to hire and pay bodyguards to protect themselves from criminals like Pablo Escobar and Jorge Ochoa. The presence of armed bodyguards brings the risk of a shootout in the streets and, with it, the danger of flying bullets to innocent bystanders. Shootouts like this were front page news in South Florida in the 1980s.

What about fleeing? Going on the lam for a cooperating defendant on probation would defeat the purpose of any plea agreement calling for cooperation with the Department of Justice. Also, fleeing the jurisdiction would likely be a violation of the conditions of the defendant's parole — not a good idea.

How about incarceration in a prison cell? That would be a reasonably safe environment, though not totally safe. However, the government can't put someone in prison who has no prison sentence or who is on probation or who has been released from prison after time-served.

The truth of the matter is that Seal would have been safest had he been locked up and serving the ten-year sentence he was originally given by Judge Roettger in Florida.

Attorneys Unglesby and Sclafani were aware of the danger their client faced.

It was Unglesby who told Judge Polozola at the sentencing that Seal had taken witness protection during periods of time he felt it was necessary. Other times Seal refused. His course of action was both arrogant and impractical in the face of an authentic death threat.

Seal was in danger every place he went. He could have been gunned down at a pay phone, or in his driveway along with his wife and kids, or perhaps at one of his favorite restaurants along with innocent patrons. That was the reality of his situation. It was obvious that his attorneys, family members, Dick Gregorie, and the DEA could not get him to enter the Witness Protection Program.

Some misinformed people insist that Seal was never offered witness protection by Judge Polozola. That is simply not true. Judge Polozola suggested to Seal that he enter the Witness Protection Program but he lacked the authority to order him to do so.

Jim B. Brown, the former chief deputy marshal for the Baton Rouge Middle District, was present in Judge Polozola's conference room, along with Unglesby, Brad Myers, and Stan Bardwell. Brown heard the judge make the suggestion. Clint Hebert was also present when Judge Polozola suggested that Seal enter witness protection and heard him refuse to do it. Seal was adamant that he was not going into witness protection because it was too "restrictive."

Florida attorney Tom Sclafani came to Baton Rouge to attend Seal's funeral.

While in town, he was interviewed by Keith Lawrence, a reporter for the Baton Rouge *Advocate*. Lawrence wrote an article that quoted Sclafani as saying that Seal rejected being placed in the Witness Protection Program after having been placed in it once previously. "It was the most harrowing experience he ever had," said the attorney.

The attorney said Seal was not able to see his family for four months, and he did not like the fact that his family would be forced to relocate wherever the US Marshal's office decided he should go. Seal was concerned for his children's schooling and his family's comfort.

Sclafani said Seal cooperated with the federal government for two reasons: "to reduce his jail sentence" and to "disabuse his children of the notion he was a drug dealer." He didn't want to go to jail. More importantly, he didn't want his children to go to school and have kids tell them their daddy was a drug dealer.

Donald Campbell, the former Chief of the Organized Crime Task Force in Las Vegas, also attended Seal's funeral. He told the *Advocate* reporter that the government should have moved Seal from Baton Rouge and should have allowed him to have armed bodyguards. Campbell said that Seal was prepared to hire three ex-FBI agents who had retired or left the FBI under honorable circumstances.

Could Seal have gone somewhere other than Baton Rouge? The answer is yes.

Sclafani said Judge Polozola agreed to let him find an alternate location—and that one had been found.

With the help of the US Attorney's office in Miami, he found a place for Seal and his family in Pensacola. When Polozola and Bardwell found out, they rejected it on the grounds they couldn't let him go to Florida because it was considered a drug state.

Bob Sibille, chief probation officer for the Baton Rouge Middle District, said he had talked to the chief probation officer in the Northern District of Florida about transferring Seal. Sibille said he was preparing to send his file to Tallahassee. When Seal found out he would have the same restrictions he had in Baton Rouge, he told his probation officer, Lionel Jardell, that he was no longer interested in going.

Seal also turned down an offer to move to the Eastern District of New York for similar reasons, according to Sibille. The headquarters of the court is in Brooklyn.

Sibille said it was Bardwell's office, after consulting with the US attorney's office in Miami, who recommended that Seal be placed in a halfway house. Sibille agreed with Judge Polozola's order.

In hindsight, "we made a bad judgment" by putting Seal at the halfway house, said Sibille.

It took Seal too long to realize and accept how deadly his situation was.

He knew he had a contract on his head.

He knew there was danger.

But he had the mentality that it wouldn't happen to him. As he neared entry into the halfway house, Seal had become a desperate man.

William Bottoms watched his personality change and said, "It was not a pretty sight."

Bottoms finally convinced Seal of his great peril.

Once Seal accepted the fact, he got desperate and decided to leave the country. Seal contacted William Roger Reaves and told him to move some money to the Cayman Islands, a well-known financial center, like the Turks and Caicos Islands.

Seal sent a New Orleans CPA and Ellis McKenzie to the Caymans where they were to meet with Reaves and receive money from him that was to be deposited into another bank account.

Contrary to popular belief, Seal had no huge bank accounts in the Caymans. "There was some money in Panama, but Reaves had control of it," said Bottoms.

Each evening that Seal went to the Salvation Army halfway house, either William Bottoms or Ellis McKenzie was with him.

One of them met him every morning when he left the center. Bottoms didn't ride with Seal but he did follow him in his pickup truck. He kept a weapon on the seat.

Bottoms still feels some responsibility for Seal's death and believes things might have gone differently had he been there the evening of the murder.

On the evening Seal was killed, Bottoms was supposed to meet with him to pick up two bank account numbers. Because of heavy traffic, he was running late. When he realized he would be late, he stopped and called Seal from a pay phone to tell him he couldn't make it by six o'clock.

Seal told him to meet him the next morning.

Shortly after their phone conversation, Bottoms learned that Seal had been killed.

Had they met that evening, the plan was for Bottoms to fly to the Caymans that night and transfer the money from one account to another account that only he and Seal knew about.

Bottoms was to fly back to the States, bringing McKenzie and some cash. Seal would meet the plane the following day and they would refuel and depart the country prior to Seal's six o'clock curfew.

The plan was to fly to Cancun, refuel, fly to Honduras, refuel, and fly on to Costa Rica, where Seal had a hideout on the southwestern coast.

Barry Seal was already making plans to use Coco Island, Costa Rica, as a staging area to develop a larger smuggling operation.

"Barry was not a good person," said Bottoms. "He had talents but he also had major flaws that exceeded his talent. His ego is what did him in and his fear of jail. Had he simply gone to jail, he would have survived his mistakes, but only to go on and make larger ones."

Seal was not "hung out to dry" as the *Miami Herald* suggested.

The fact remains that the only method the government could utilize to fulfill the duty to protect Seal was to get him into the Witness Protection Program. Judge Polozola offered him witness protection. It was recommended by Richard Gregorie. Yet Seal refused to request it. According to his attorney, Seal accepted witness protection only when he thought he needed it.

It is absurd to believe that Seal had the ability to foresee where and when he would need witness protection—and when it was not necessary. Such thinking was egotistical and characteristic of the man that he was.

Barry Seal was not the only one who was in danger. His wife and children, and anyone else who might have been near him when the killers decided to strike, were also at risk.

Recall that Jorge Ochoa told Max Mermelstein to go by Seal's house and "take everybody" — and he meant kill them.

Barry Seal was fully cognizant of the danger he was facing yet confident that he was smarter than the Medellin drug lords who were hell-bent on having him executed.

He made the doubly fatal error of underestimating the capacity and determination of the Colombians to kill him and overestimating his own ability to outwit them.

In the final analysis, Barry Seal's death was the consequence of a combination of factors—all working against him. Among the factors must be included animosity, a clash of egos, and obstinacy on both sides of the table.

No one associated with the task force investigation and the prosecution of Barry Seal took any delight in his death. Everyone knew the Ochoas wanted Seal dead and were willing to pay to get it done. Few thought they would succeed. When the murder went down, the reaction was shock and then sadness.

Several hundred family members, friends, and associates—and the media—attended Seal's funeral. He was buried in a sky blue casket. On top of the casket was a wreath containing a tiny TWA model plane.

No one from the Baton Rouge task force attended the funeral.

Several DEA agents from Florida were planning to attend Seal's funeral and had planned to do so at the expense of the government. They were ordered by the Department of Justice to stay away.

PART TWO: THE MYTHS

ഇ൦രൂഇ൦രൂ

Chapter 17

The Crimes of Mena

To the "vast government conspiracy" crowd, Mena, Arkansas, became as infamous as Roswell, New Mexico. The reputation came after public knowledge that Barry Seal used the town's airport as a base for his smuggling planes. He parked the famous C-123 cargo plane there.

Although there were no alien sightings, it was generally presumed that he laundered millions and millions of dollars through Mena banks and smuggled hundreds of kilos of cocaine and tons of arms and munitions through the Mena Intermountain Airport on behalf of the CIA.

Barry Seal may have brought some unwelcome notoriety to Mena. The airport was popular with aircraft owners long before Seal could fly.

A rough flying field was started on the McBride property south of town in the early forties. In 1942, Hartzell Geyer built the first hangar and opened a small flying school. In 1946, serious construction began when the Civil Aeronautics Board (now the FAA) chose the site as an emergency landing strip for commercial aircraft.

In the early years, the grass field was maintained by an agreement with a farmer who mowed and baled the runway in exchange for the hay.

After development of the airstrip, several businesses opened. Pilots began to bring their planes in for overhaul and repair. It was remote but centrally located. The aircraft industry at the Mena airport grew and now employs several hundred people in the areas of upholstery, painting, engineering, engine overhauling, and general maintenance. These businesses bring millions of dollars into the local economy, and the popularity of the airport has continued to grow.

In 2015, the regional airport has a lighted and paved six thousand-foot runway and five thousand-foot paved runways, with support and mechanical services for most aircraft including small- and mid-sized commercial airliners.[1]

The Mena airport was in the jurisdiction of Polk County Sheriff A. L. Hadaway. It didn't take him long to get word of Barry Seal's arrival and to learn what kind of business he was in.

Sheriff Hadaway and the author had a long phone conversation on May 18, 1983. The sheriff said he had what he considered to be reliable information that someone named "Barry" from Baton Rouge was running a drug smuggling operation out of Rich Mountain Aviation, an aircraft service facility at the Mena airport. Rich Mountain was owned by a man named Fred Hampton. The sheriff had a first name of "Barry" and a pager number and little else. His source was reliable.

Hadaway described one specific event that took place. A Piper Seneca, plane number N8049Z, was observed to take off. The informant said the plane was flown by "Red" Hall. It carried one duffel bag of cocaine.

The Piper Seneca involved in the incident had been purchased from Louisiana Aircraft Rental on March 12, 1982, by Seal. He had personally handed one of the owners a fruit carton containing $160,000 cash.

The plane had been registered in the name of Interstate Aviation to a bogus address in Jackson, Mississippi. FAA records revealed that the individual who was listed as president of Interstate Aviation was a helicopter pilot who resided in Baton Rouge and was known to be associated with Seal.

The author's phone conversation with Sheriff Hadaway was cordial and informative. He was provided with the registration information and history of the Seneca, and some background information on Seal. The pager number the sheriff had was confirmed to be Seal's pager number at a Baton Rouge answering service.

It was good news to learn that another law enforcement agency was pursuing Seal.

Baton Rouge agents eventually learned that Sheriff Hadaway was getting his information from a woman named Lucia Gonzalez, also known as Lucia Williams. She worked for Fred Hampton.

One of Hadaway's auxiliary deputies named Terry Capehart operated a business in a hangar near Hampton's hangar. Lucia was providing the information to Capehart.

Seal knew who Terry Capehart was. He suspected that the

deputy might be snooping around the hangar. Although he may have worried about Capehart, Seal was smart enough to know that the fruits of any illegal searches could never be used against him in court. Still, Capehart's presence concerned him and he was always wary of him. Seal scrupulously avoided keeping anything in the hangar or in his planes that might incriminate him.

The May 1983 incident involving Red Hall and the Piper Seneca was the only explicit allegation the Baton Rouge task force heard that cocaine was anywhere near the Rich Mountain Aviation center.

It is extremely doubtful that federal or state investigators could have convinced a magistrate or judge that a search warrant for Rich Mountain Aviation's hangars should be signed. What Lucia was alleged to have said was not enough. Whoever swore to the affidavit for a search warrant could not state truthfully that there was reasonable belief that more cocaine was on the premises. In fact the "informant" reportedly said the cocaine was flown away in the Piper Seneca.

Red Hall, now deceased, was subsequently subpoenaed to appear before the Baton Rouge Middle District of Louisiana grand jury. Hall had lived in Baton Rouge in the mid-1950s, knew Barry Seal and was considered a key witness with firsthand information about Barry Seal's planes and the sophisticated avionics aboard. Hall was to have been questioned under oath in front of the grand jury. Instead, he was allowed him to come to the US Attorney's office, where he was thoroughly interviewed on February 8, 1984, by task force agents and assistant US attorney Brad Myers.

Hall described Seal as a customer who purchased aircraft avionics from his employer and said Seal was a friend he had known for years. Hall denied that he had ever flown any cocaine for Barry Seal from the Mena airport — or from anywhere else.

Several years before the Mena airport and Barry Seal came to the attention of Congress[2] and the media, the DEA, FBI, and US Customs agents, and Louisiana State Police narcs were investigating the smuggler. They had a good idea where he was delivering cocaine.

Seal's first major cocaine flight was in December 1978 when he delivered a load to his private airstrip in Ascension Parish, Louisiana along the Mississippi River.

When William Bottoms started flying for brother-in-law Seal in 1980, he airdropped cocaine at the Opelousas airport, near the small Cajun community north of Lafayette.

After Seal moved his planes to Mena, he continued to have Bottoms deliver the cocaine into Louisiana. He made airdrops at predetermined locations usually in the Atchafalaya Basin.

William Bottoms is certain that the Mena airport was used strictly as a storage and maintenance center for the planes, and not as a cocaine delivery site. He flew twenty-five cocaine flights that were arranged by Barry Seal and he always airdropped to pre-selected locations in Louisiana, mostly in the Atchafalaya Basin, a swampy expanse between Baton Rouge and Lafayette. It's perfect for secluded fishing — and smuggling. Bottoms said he never delivered a load of cocaine to the Mena airport. He also knows that Seal regularly arranged for decoy flights to confuse the investigators.

Seal was too cautious to risk having any of his people busted while delivering a load of cocaine to the Mena airport. Seal could airdrop over thousands of acres of desolate and unpopulated swamps. He had access to three or four private airstrips near Baton Rouge.

Without a doubt, Seal was involved in money laundering at Mena. The source of that cash was positively from his smuggling activities. He had little, if any, other income.

However, the estimated amount of money Seal actually laundered has ballooned over the years in the retelling, from a few hundred thousand dollars to millions upon millions of dollars. This is simply not true.

IRS special agent William Duncan was assigned to a money laundering investigation. It began in April 1983, when he first learned of the allegations at a meeting in the US Attorney's office at Fort Smith, Arkansas.

Duncan was an "experienced and highly regarded" agent for the IRS's Criminal Investigation Division (CID). He was assigned to a grand jury investigation that was opened in the Western District of Arkansas by then-US Attorney Asa Hutchinson. Duncan's investigation began shortly after the drug task force in the Baton Rouge Middle District of Louisiana started its investigation of Barry Seal.

At the onset, the grand jury investigation was not aimed at Barry Seal. The targets were "individuals believed to be associated with and/or doing aircraft modification and repair work for Barry Seal."[3]

The targets were a banker, Rich Mountain Aviation, Fred Lee Hampton, and Joseph Nevil Evans.

Arkansas State Police Investigator Russell Welch was already investigating allegations of drug trafficking and FAA violations at the Mena airport. He was eventually made an agent of Hutchinson's federal grand jury and worked with Duncan much of the time.[4]

Duncan issued subpoenas to various banks in Mena and Waldron. He began interviewing bank employees.

The investigation and the paper trail led him to the Union Bank of Mena, where he eventually uncovered evidence proving that money laundering was taking place.

Here's how it worked: The money laundering activity consisted of obtaining cashier's checks in amounts of less than $10,000 at various financial institutions in and around Mena. If cash in amounts of less than $10,000 was exchanged for cashier's checks, the institution was not required to prepare and file a Currency Transaction Report (CTR), which would have identified the individual who was the source of the funds. This type of activity was known as "structuring." It was designed to defeat the federal bank reporting requirements.

Bill Duncan found out that Fred Hampton once took a suitcase full of cash, about $70,000, to the bank. There an officer went down the line of tellers handing out packets of currency and obtaining cashier's checks. Duncan told Jerry Bize, his IRS counterpart in Baton Rouge, about it shortly after it happened. Bize began checking local banks for similar activity — and he found it.

Several investigators interviewed a woman who worked for Fred Hampton. Russell Welch, Bill Duncan, and US Attorney J. Michael Fitzhugh interviewed Lucia Gonzalez-Williams on October 10, 1985, in Fitzhugh's office. Fitzhugh had replaced Asa Hutchinson. The woman was Sheriff Hadaway's informant.

Lucia said she worked for Fred Hampton from sometime in 1981 to July 1983. Lucia said that Joe Evans stored two Piper Navajo Panthers belonging to Seal in one of the two hangars owned by Fred Hampton. She said the planes were identical in appearance and had plane N numbers that were very similar. Both planes had cargo doors that she believed were installed at Rich Mountain Aviation. She once noticed that Barry Seal's Piper Seneca had the N number altered with black tape when the airplane was in Hampton's main hangar. She couldn't remember the number but that it had been something like a one changed to a four.

Lucia said she never saw any cocaine at Rich Mountain Aviation and had no knowledge of Red Hall ever taking off with a duffel bag of cocaine. She said deputy Terry Capehart was lying if he ever said differently.

Lucia said there was never any paperwork or files maintained on Barry Seal's airplanes. She said that Hampton was very angry one time and asked her what she was telling Terry Capehart and Sheriff Hadaway about the operation of Rich Mountain Aviation. She said he told her he wasn't doing anything illegal.[5]

Lucia later acknowledged to investigators that on several occasions she received cash of approximately $30,000 from her boss and was instructed to deposit the money in amounts of less than $10,000.

On December 5, 1985, Duncan took a sworn statement from Jim Neugent, vice president of the Union Bank. Neugent said he analyzed bank records concerning transactions involving Fred Hampton that exceeded $10,000. The first such transaction was in November 1982 in the amount of $65,937 involving seven checks all less than $10,000.

Neugent's conclusion was that an employee of Rich Mountain Aviation had acted to avoid the filing of federal banking rules. Neugent found that Kathy Corrigan, an employee of Rich Mountain Aviation, had purchased some checks. The remitter on two checks was Adler B. Seal and the payee was Union Bank of Mena. Neugent told Duncan he had found that a total of $106,870 in deposits in cashier's checks had been made between September 1982 and January 1985. And cash deposits between May 1981 and March 1985 were in excess of $235,000, bringing the total cash and cash-equivalent transactions with this bank to a little more than $341,000.[6]

The amount involved in proven structuring—$340,000—was a small percentage of the millions of dollars Seal was handling. Still, it was a significant amount at this community bank. It was all the money-laundering activity Duncan could uncover during his very thorough investigation.

Duncan has never said he found millions of dollars in CTR violations. He testified that he proved between $250,000 and $300,000 had been laundered in more than twenty-five instances. Duncan said he could prove the first instance of money laundering concerned a deposit of cash that was used to build Seal's hangar at the Mena airport.

Duncan's investigative reports detailing the evidence of the structuring of cash transactions by Seal, Hampton and the banker were given to US Attorney Michael Fitzhugh. A special assistant US attorney from Miami, who was a money laundering specialist, reviewed the evidence in January 1986. He helped Duncan and Fitzhugh to draft a series of indictments numbering 29 counts.

No one was ever indicted by the grand jury. This disappointed Bill Duncan.

Later, false rumors alleging government malfeasance, a cover-up, and the bribery of an FBI agent or the US attorney general would begin to circulate.

No one got bribed. There were no money laundering violations because of a court decision.

Duane Larson was convicted in US District Court, District of Minnesota. He was money laundering by making numerous monetary transactions of less than $10,000 to avoid the Currency Transaction Reporting (CTR) statute. He bought cashier's checks from separate branches of two banks.

Larson was structuring his cash transactions to keep the bank from filing CTRs. Bill Duncan proved Barry Seal, Fred Hampton, and the banker were doing the same thing at the Union Bank of Mena.

Larson was convicted of two violations: concealing material facts from the government because his structured transactions caused the banks to fail to file CTRs [violating Title 18, Section 1001], and aiding and abetting in violation of Title 18, Section 2.

Larson appealed and he won. Both convictions were reversed by the 8th Circuit Court of Appeals, whose jurisdiction includes the state of Arkansas.[7]

The appeals court ruled that the CTR Act did not require the customer to disclose to the bank that the transactions were structured for the purpose of avoiding the CTR reporting requirements. Therefore, the customer was not guilty of concealing information from the government. The court also held that Larson's due process rights were violated because he had no fair warning that his conduct was illegal.

Duane Larson's appeal had been pending for months. The court finally decided the case July 26, 1986. From then on, no US Attorney within the boundaries of the 8th Circuit would have brought an indictment for the type of money laundering Duncan uncovered. If they did, it would have been dismissed by the district courts based on the decision in the *Larson* case.

There were reversals of structuring convictions in other circuits as well as the 8th.

The Department of Justice may even have told US attorneys not to bring structuring indictments, preferring to wait for Congress to act. That is precisely what happened.

Congress added Section 5324 to the Bank Secrecy Act which became effective January 1987. The new law made it clear that it was a crime for any person to "structure or assist in structuring, or attempt to structure or assist in structuring, any transaction with one or more domestic financial institutions."

The decision in the *Larson* case was the reason there was no prosecution of Fred Hampton or anyone else for money laundering in Mena, Arkansas.

However, it has always been far more appealing to self-styled investigators, pundits and conspiracy buffs to attribute the absence of a prosecution to the payment of a $350,000 bribe.

Bill Duncan's quarrel was with two US attorneys who would not prosecute anyone he proved involved in the structuring of cash transactions. Fitzhugh had a grand jury in session, but Duncan and his boss in Little Rock, CID Chief N. Paul Whitmore, felt that he was not taking the necessary action. He wasn't issuing subpoenas to key witnesses including Barry Seal, who would probably take the Fifth.

Former US Attorney Fitzhugh, an Arkansas circuit judge in 2015, said he was aware of the decision in the *Larson* case and the impact it would have on structuring indictments within the 8th Circuit. He would not comment on what evidence was presented to the grand jury in the case of Hampton and Seal because of grand jury secrecy requirements. However, he made a presentment and a no true bill was returned. He also recalled that he discussed the ruling in the *Larson* case with Bill Duncan.

The House Judiciary Committee had become aware of Duncan's complaints. They gave him a subpoena to appear before the Subcommittee on Crime. In December 1987, IRS disclosure attorney Mary Anne Curtain was assigned to advise Duncan. She prepared him for testimony on tax return information (Title 26 of the IRS Code), and to review grand jury secrecy. Tax returns were not the issue because Duncan's investigation was about money laundering (under Title 21) and not a Title 26 tax case. Duncan was functioning as an agent of the grand jury, so the evidence and testimony he had gathered was secret. He gave his testimony on February 26, 1988.

The origin of the allegation of a bribe being paid to a high Justice Department official started with a telephone conversation between Russell Welch and Bill Duncan. The call took place in January 1988. Duncan confirmed this on June 21, 1991, during his deposition that was taken in an investigation named "Joint Investigation by the Arkansas State Attorney General's Office and the United States Congress." The joint investigation was conducted by Rep. William Alexander and Arkansas Attorney General Winston Bryant and two attorneys from his office.

Duncan said he had received an allegation from Russell Welch that Attorney General Edwin Meese received a several hundred thousand dollar bribe from Barry Seal directly.

Duncan was preparing for his appearance before the House Subcommittee on Crime. He reported the information about the alleged bribe to his handler, Mary Anne Curtin, but only as being information provided to him by Russell Welch and something about which the committee might question him.

Russell Welch said it was Terry Capehart, the Polk County auxiliary deputy, who made the phone call to tell him about the alleged bribe.

Duncan got nothing more than hearsay twice removed.

The story of the alleged bribe got out and was hawked, twisted, and bootstrapped upward by the media and by repetition. Finally, it became a factoid that a bribe had been paid to a high Republican administration appointee—and the IRS was attempting to muzzle Duncan to keep him from disclosing the facts. This was a completely distorted account of what actually happened. It was nothing but hearsay or rumor in the first place.

Bill Duncan's lengthy investigation did not turn up one shred of evidence that Barry Seal bribed anyone to block the money laundering investigation, a drug investigation or an indictment in the State of Arkansas or anywhere else.

Furthermore, the former IRS agent gave testimony before two House subcommittees. Never once did he say that he had discovered evidence of a bribe being paid to any federal official by Seal or anyone else.

In a subsequent appearance before the House Subcommittee on Commerce, Consumer, and Monetary Affairs Duncan had the following to say about the alleged bribe: [8]

Barnard: Mr. Duncan, do you believe that the information on the $350,000 bribe to a high-level Justice official was valid?
Duncan: That is not a determination for me to make. I can only communicate that the law enforcement officer who received that information told me on numerous occasions that the informant that provided the information had provided in the past nothing but good information.

As an IRS agent with subpoena powers, Bill Duncan had access to bank records from all over Arkansas and access to Rich Mountain Aviation's records. Duncan could get all other records belonging to Barry Seal that had been seized by IRS and were available in Mena and in Baton Rouge.

Admittedly, financial records and cancelled checks are rarely, if ever, notated as being for a "bribe" or a "payoff." However, $350,000 is a significant amount of money, and odds are great that Bill Duncan would have uncovered the evidence to prove it somewhere among the 7,000 documents he said he examined — but he didn't. The only thing he had was hearsay from Russell Welch.

What is obvious is that Bill Duncan believed that a vast government conspiracy was carried out at the Mena airport and the evidence is his statement to the same House subcommittee.

Duncan: Evidence gathered during the last year and a half indicates that during the period 1984 through 1986, the Mena, Arkansas, airport was an important hub/waypoint for transshipment of drugs, weapons and Central American "Contra" and Panamanian Defense Force personnel who were receiving covert training in a variety of specialties in the Nella community, located ten miles north of the Mena, Arkansas, airport. The evidence details a bizarre mixture of drug smuggling, gun running, money laundering, and covert operations by Barry Seal, his associates, and both employees and contract operatives of the United States Intelligence Services. The testimony reveals a scheme whereby massive amounts of cocaine were smuggled into the state of Arkansas, and profits were partially used to fund covert operations. Two witnesses testified that one of the Western District of Arkansas assistant US attorneys told them that the US Attorney's Office received a call to shut down the investigations involving Seal and his associates.

What was Duncan's "evidence" about the Mena airport? He suggested it was an important hub/waypoint for transshipment of drugs, weapons and Contra and Panamanian Defense Force personnel receiving training. Who provided the "testimony" revealing a scheme whereby massive amounts of cocaine were smuggled into the state of Arkansas? He never told us —and we still don't know.

During his June 21, 1991, deposition to the "Joint Investigation by the Arkansas State Attorney General's Office," Duncan was asked:

Question: Regarding the allegations of drug running and weapons running and any other things that you might have heard, what information do you have to, number one, substantiate that there might have been drugs brought to the Mena airport?

Duncan: We were receiving information from a variety of sources that Barry was doing work for the United States government, but that he was smuggling on the return trips for himself. We knew from his modus operandi in Louisiana that he many times dropped the drugs in remote areas and retrieved them with helicopters. He had helicopters in the hangers (sic) at Mena and a variety of aircraft, smuggling type aircraft on the ground in Mena. And we heard, you know, all the time that he was making on return trips– Terry Capehart, a deputy at Polk County Sheriff's Department, had received information from an informant on the inside at Rich Mountain Aviation that drugs were actually brought into Rich Mountain Aviation, and on one occasion guarded with armed guards around the aircraft. He also received information from this informant that Freddie Hampton had personally transported a shipment of drugs to Louisiana from Rich Mountain Aviation.

A significant part of that answer was totally at odds with what Lucia Gonzalez-Williams, Capehart's "informant on the inside at Rich Mountain Aviation," told Duncan, Welch and US Attorney Fitzhugh on October 10, 1985. She said she had never seen any cocaine at Rich Mountain Aviation. She called Capehart a liar if he said otherwise.

Duncan was quizzed further:

Question: What specific physical evidence did you observe at the Mena airport that would indicate to you, in your professional opinion, drugs were brought to Mena, or that Mena was used as a base for drug smuggling?

Duncan: Primarily I was reviewing evidence gathered by the law enforcement agencies, surveillance logs, their representations to me. I was focusing on the money laundering and financial analysis end of it, and did not conduct a lot of physical surveillance myself. But we had a lot of intelligence reports of various airplanes in there being refueled, leaving in the middle of the night, N numbers being changed, typical modus operandi of a smuggling.

Duncan didn't name one piece of "specific physical evidence" he had observed.

He didn't describe any of the "evidence gathered by law enforcement agencies."

And he didn't disclose any law enforcement agency "representations to me," which would likely have been hearsay.

The period between mid-1982 and February 1984 was Barry Seal's most active cocaine smuggling years. The Mena airport and Rich Mountain Aviation's hangar and Seal's hangar were all under periodic surveillance and continuous and intensive investigation. This included the county sheriff, an Arkansas State Police investigator, and federal investigators from Customs, DEA, and the FBI.

Despite their best efforts, no cocaine belonging to Seal was ever seized at the Mena airport. And none of the investigators were able to obtain search warrants for any of Seal's planes, for his hangar or for Fred Hampton's hangar.

The reason was that none of the investigators could ever develop enough credible evidence (probable cause) to convince a judge or a magistrate that there was cocaine stored or flowing through any of the airport's facilities. Hearsay is not enough—and essentially that was all they had.

No weapons, munitions, or other war-fighting material were found and seized at the airport—and no Contras or Panamanian Defense Forces were apprehended at Mena or Nella.

In March 1989, publicity surrounding the activities of Seal and Hampton at the Mena airport had surfaced. US Rep. Bill Alexander (D-Ark) contacted the FBI and asked for a briefing on the case. By then, the case was closed.

On April 20, 1989, FBI representatives met with the congressman and gave him a briefing. The FBI memorandum reporting this briefing states that the evidence concerning Fred Hampton was presented to the US attorney who advised that he had obtained a no true bill.

Jeffrey Stinson writing in the *Arkansas Gazette* on December 22, 1990, quoted Rep. Alexander saying, "Basically what you have here is a massive cover-up."

It is obvious Bill Alexander believed there was a cover-up in the Barry Seal case — but he never offered any credible evidence to support his belief.

Bill Duncan's highly publicized quarrel with the IRS was about what he considered to be the bad legal advice he was getting from Mary Anne Curtin. He testified that Curtin told him not to express his opinion, which was critical, about how Fitzhugh handled the Seal case. Duncan was also told to say that he had no information of an alleged bribe being paid to a Justice official.

Duncan viewed the instruction on how to answer questions concerning the alleged bribe as asking him to commit perjury. This he would not do — and he was absolutely right to refuse to do it.

His supervisor, Paul Whitmore, corroborated Duncan's testimony.

Whitmore and Duncan were of the opinion that Curtin's real function was to preserve the image of the IRS. Concern was the agency might be linked to bad publicity about an alleged bribe and mishandling of a major drug trafficking case.

Duncan thought the extensive briefings provided by Curtin and her supervisor, prior to his testimony before the committee, were designed to control his testimony and to limit the committee's ability to oversee and scrutinize the integrity of the IRS investigation of Seal. Whitmore and Duncan took polygraph tests as to the truth of what they said Curtain instructed Duncan to do. They both passed. Curtain as well as her supervisor declined to be tested.

The outcome of the investigation of Barry Seal and Fred Hampton conducted at Mena by Bill Duncan has been distorted. It's been misrepresented by a few writers and "investigators" to support their own notions of what they believe occurred at Mena — or rather, what they wish had occurred there.

The fact is that Bill Duncan developed evidence proving that Seal and Hampton, with the help of a local banker, laundered a bit more than $340,000 cash through the Union Bank of Mena.

Clearly, Duncan was satisfied that he had completed a

comprehensive and in-depth investigation that was ready for prosecution. He took his findings to the US attorney and then assisted him and a money laundering expert from Miami in drafting a 29-count indictment.

Regrettably, the decision in the *Larson* case stymied prosecutions for structured banking transactions in Arkansas for a period of time.

Because no cocaine or other drugs had been seized at Rich Mountain Aviation, a prosecution for conspiracy to smuggle, possess, or distribute cocaine was the likely alternative for the US Attorney.

The government would have had to prove that Hampton and Evans knowingly performed illegal alterations to aircraft fuel systems and cargo hatches of planes they knew were intended to be used to transport cocaine.

This may have been a somewhat difficult conspiracy to prove to the satisfaction of a jury for a number of reasons.

It would have been pointless for the government to put Lucia Gonzalez-Williams on the stand to try and prove that cocaine was flowing through Rich Mountain Aviation with the knowledge and help of Hampton and Evans.

During her October 1985 interview with the US Attorney Fitzhugh, Duncan, and Welch, she said she worked for Hampton for close to three years. She never saw any cocaine at Rich Mountain Aviation. That statement by Lucia was *Brady* material, which would have delighted a defense attorney.

Lucia also called Terry Capehart a "liar," which was a further bonus for the defense. If the government put Capehart on the stand, Lucia's characterization of him as being a liar was *Giglio* material that had to be disclosed. It would quite likely have caused a trial jury to question Capehart's believability.

Barry Seal was also a problem. Seal would have been the key government witness—had he lived long enough. He had told the world while standing on the federal courthouse steps in Baton Rouge that he brought 20,000 pounds of cocaine into the Middle District of Louisiana—and nowhere else.

Moreover, in August 1985 while on the stand as a government witness during the *Reyes* trial, Seal testified, "I always brought the cocaine back into Louisiana." Those statements were *Brady* material for the defense of Hampton and Evans.

William Bottoms had been granted limited use immunity

in Florida in return for being the pilot in the *Reyes* undercover investigation. At that time he told US Attorney Stanley Marcus, Assistant US Attorney Dick Gregorie, Bob Jura and Ernst Jacobsen that he didn't bring cocaine into Mena. He always airdropped the loads into Louisiana.

What he told the Miami contingent of federal officers was more *Brady* material for the defense of Hampton and Evans. Seal had also told Baton Rouge task force agents that all the cocaine he transported came into Louisiana—and none went into the Mena airport.

What if there been an indictment and trial of Evans and Hampton? Their attorneys could have created quite a spectacle by putting an assemblage of agents from the FBI, the DEA, and the IRS, plus a US Attorney and a few assistant US Attorneys on the witness stand. They might testify that to their knowledge Seal dumped all of his cocaine loads into Louisiana and not Mena.

Federal prosecutors in Arkansas faced that dilemma if they tried to prove that hundreds of kilos of cocaine were flowing through Rich Mountain Aviation with the help of Hampton and Evans.

Jury confusion was also a real possibility. Remember that one Piper Navajo and the Lockheed? They had altered cargo hatches and were equipped to utilize illegal fuel systems for smuggling runs. Both planes had been used by Barry Seal on two undercover operations while he was acting as an informant for the DEA. When was Seal smuggling for himself? When was he flying an undercover operation for the DEA?

Furthermore, Joe Evans was an FAA-certified aircraft mechanic— and the logical suspect. But there was a paucity of evidence to prove exactly who made the illegal plane alterations, what they consisted of and when they were made. Lucia said no records were kept of work done on Barry Seal's planes.

It is likely that only Barry Seal, Fred Hampton, and Joe Evans had that knowledge. Hampton and Evans had Fifth Amendment privileges. Barry was no longer alive to testify.

Russell Welch has said publicly that he developed evidence of Joe Evans and Fred Hampton's complicity in Seal's drug smuggling operation at Mena.

Welch described the case against the two as "strong." The strongest case was against Evans because of his more hands-on involvement with the planes. Welch gathered evidence that included forged signatures on fuel truck receipts that were used to establish a fictitious business that would account for the hundreds and hundreds of gallons of aviation fuel used on the drug flights.

Evidence of what was going on at Rich Mountain Aviation was developed during the Coinroll investigation from intercepted conversations and the admissions of drug pilot William Earle, Jr., after his arrest.

Earle was interviewed in New Orleans where he admitted flying a Piper Navajo to Rich Mountain Aviation to have an illegal fuel bladder installed. He did not see who installed the bladder in the plane because Barry Seal had put him in an office while the work was being done. Seal told him it was for his own good — he didn't want him to know who did the plumbing job.

Seal acquired the plane, with Venezuelan registration number YV 189 CP, and made some of the arrangements for the flight with Earle over a pay telephone. The plane was observed by FBI and Customs agents at Hammond, Louisiana while enroute to Rich Mountain Aviation.

DEA and FBI agents observed the plane at Rich Mountain Aviation until it departed Mena at approximately 1:18 am on Dec. 14. They could not see what work was being done. FBI and Customs agents had it under observation when it landed in Baton Rouge at 3:07 am and again at Hammond at 6:45 pm when it was refueled. Seal was seen paying for the gas.

The installation of the illegal fuel bladder on the Piper Navajo at Rich Mountain Aviation took place on December 13 and 14, 1983. That was almost four months before Seal began working for the DEA. Therefore, neither he nor anyone else involved could make a credible claim that the work was done to further some secret DEA undercover operation. However, the government didn't have the Navajo and agents had scant evidence to prove exactly what was done and by whom.

Joe Evans was the licensed FAA mechanic. Logically he could be presumed to have done the plumbing job but presumptions aren't evidence.

Seal was dead.

A prosecution would have boiled down to Billy Earle's word against the words of Fred Hampton and Joe Evans.

Earle was a convicted felon who would not have had an easy time on the stand during cross examination.

Three "use of a telephone" violations had occurred when

arrangements were made to do the plumbing job on the Navajo. The calls were intercepted in the Baton Rouge Middle District of Louisiana. The violators were Barry Seal who was dead, and Billy Earle, Jr., who had cooperated with the government and had already been prosecuted in the New Orleans Eastern District of Louisiana. Earle was on his way to federal prison.

It was Barry Seal's work as a DEA informant that provided the greatest roadblock to prosecutions for criminal activity at Mena. Hampton and Evans may have succeeded in convincing a jury that they were merely assisting Seal to help the DEA and the CIA — or at least they thought they were.

Without Barry Seal's testimony, there was little evidence to refute what Hampton and Evans may have told a jury.

Barry Seal, had he lived, and Billy Earle, Jr. would have been the government's key, and possibly its only witnesses against Fred Hampton and Joe Evans in a prosecution in Arkansas for a conspiracy to smuggle cocaine.

The feds had no big load of seized cocaine or piles of cash and guns to display to a jury to jazz up the government's case. The conspiracy would have hinged on proving to the satisfaction of a jury that Joe Evans knowingly prepared specific planes for use in smuggling ventures with the knowledge and cooperation of Fred Hampton.

Kathy Corrigan seemed willing enough to testify. Her knowledge was generally limited to structured cash transactions at the bank — money laundering.

An article written by Joe Stumpe was published in the December 23, 1990, edition of the *Arkansas Democrat*. Captioned "Grand jury in drug case mishandled, juror says," the article reported on Stumpe's taped interview with an unidentified member of Fitzhugh's grand jury, who said the jury was "mishandled." The juror felt there could have been an indictment of "two Polk County businessmen" on charges of money laundering and conspiracy to traffic in drugs. US Attorney Fitzhugh was contacted for comment. Reporter Stumpe quoted his response: "Any criminal case that is developed by this office has to meet certain rigid standards of prosecution that are set forth in our guidelines and appropriate under federal law, and this office does not bring any case until those standards are met."

Department of Justice guidelines for prosecution set forth in the 1980 edition of *Principles of Federal Prosecution*, state that the attorney for the government should commence or recommend prosecution if he believes that the person's conduct constitutes a federal offense and that the admissible evidence will probably be sufficient to obtain and sustain a conviction.

US Attorney Fitzhugh did not think the available evidence met the guidelines. Therefore he didn't prosecute Hampton or Evans for conspiracy to smuggle cocaine. The decision in the *Larson* case brought money laundering prosecutions to a standstill in Arkansas until the law was changed by Congress.

Chapter 18

Spooks at Mena

The airport at Mena, the CIA and Barry Seal created headlines only after it became public knowledge that he based his C-123 at the airport. After that same cargo plane was shot down in 1986 while on a Contra supply mission for the CIA, the focus on Mena intensified. This stoked outlandish theories and wild speculation about what Barry Seal and the CIA were involved in at Mena.

The CIA admitted in their Inspector General's Report of November 8, 1996, that it contracted with some businesses at the Mena airport. The purpose? To perform routine aviation-related services on equipment the agency-owned. The companies were selected based on their ability to perform, competitive pricing, and their reputation within aviation circles.

The service companies and their employees were not informed that CIA owned the equipment that was to be serviced. Therefore, some military-type planes belonging to the CIA probably flew in and out of Mena from time to time.

So what?

Barry Seal wasn't involved. There is nothing insidious or criminal about the CIA bringing its planes to Mena for repairs and maintenance. They probably did not want the whole world to know about it. What better place than a relatively out-of-the-way airport with a variety of aircraft-related repair and maintenance services available?

As distasteful as it may be for some to accept, the CIA Inspector General's report gave a reasonable and believable explanation for one reason the CIA had a presence at the Mena airport.

The same CIA report admitted that the agency participated in a joint training operation at the airport with "another federal agency." The CIA's role in the two-week exercise was not disclosed. The report stated that coordination and contact with local Mena officials was handled by the other federal agency.

Russell Welch spent several years investigating Seal and the Mena airport. His investigation turned up information of activity at the airport involving C-130 cargo aircraft that may have been — or at least appeared to be — CIA-related.

A company named Southern Cross Aviation began operating at the Mena airport in late 1986. Southern Cross owned an affiliate company named Multitrade that claimed it could deliver any kind of aircraft anywhere in the world within 24 hours.

In 1991, Welch seized a twin-engine Otter for the DEA at the hangar of Multitrade. The de Havilland DHC-6 Twin Otter is a Canadian 19-passenger STOL (short takeoff and landing) utility aircraft developed by de Havilland of Canada.

Later, Welch saw newspaper clippings from an Australian newspaper in which it was reported that the Otter pilot had attempted to buy two C-130s in Australia. The sale was halted by the US State Department when it was established that the planes were to be used to haul cocaine for the Cali Cartel. One of the C-130 planes was at Multitrade when Welch seized the Otter. He subsequently found out that US Customs agents were also aware of the C-130. They were monitoring the activity at Southern Cross Aviation involving the plane.

Earl Covel, a former partner in Southern Cross Aviation, came to Mena in July 1987 to set up and manage the company's operations at the airport. The company had a base in Camarillo, California. The move to Mena represented an expansion of the company's business of ferrying aircraft. His customers were companies and individuals who sent their planes for work at the various aviation-related businesses operating at the Mena airport. He recalled that his company did ferry a C-130 to the Mena airport. One of Covel's partners in Southern Cross Aviation was part owner of Multitrade, but that company was not a subsidiary of Southern Cross Aviation.

Covel knew who Russell Welch was and eventually learned that Welch had become convinced Southern Cross Aviation was a CIA front and Covel was a CIA agent.

Covel said Southern Cross Aviation had nothing to do with the CIA. Southern Cross is no longer operating at the Mena airport but still has operations in Camarillo, California. Covel dropped out of the Southern Cross partnership and stayed in Mena to form his own aircraft ferrying service, Ultimate Aircraft Services, Inc.

There is a reasonable history behind the appearance of a few

C-130s at Mena. The United States Forest Service (USFS) contracts with private companies to provide tanker aircraft for fighting forest fires. In the 1980s, the bulk of the aerial tanker fleet consisted of C-119 Flying Boxcars, which were grounded in 1987 because of safety concerns.

In December 1987, the deputy director of fire and aviation for USFS requested the Department of Defense to cooperate in a plan to replace the firefighting fleet. It would involve surplus military transport aircraft stored at Davis-Monthan Air Force Base in Tucson, Arizona.

In December 1987, the US Air Force agreed to declare C-130s to be excess property and transfer them to General Services Administration (GSA) which could then legally make the planes available to other government agencies.

Ultimately some C-130As were distributed to six contractors. Twelve of the C-130s came from Davis-Monthan Air Force Base in Tucson, and sixteen were retired from Air Force Reserve units. The program was quietly terminated in January 1990 because the general counsel of the US Department of Agriculture (USDA), the parent agency of the USFS, did not have authority to conduct the program.

The intent of the exchange program was to keep the C-130s under US control to be used for firefighting within the US. However, some of the aircraft were used for more than firefighting. In October 1997, one of the C-130s was seized by Mexican federal officials for hauling drugs.

In 1991, an aircraft broker named Gary Eitel heard about the program and tried to obtain C-130s for his clients. The Forestry Service told him there were no more aircraft available, and that only three planes had been involved. He didn't believe what he was told and launched his own investigation. One of the things he learned was that some of the planes were resold for profit. Eventually he came to believe he had uncovered a covert CIA operation that funneled C-130s into the hands of private companies which then provided clandestine air services to the CIA.

In 1994, Gary Eitel filed a *qui tam* civil suit on behalf of the federal government against six tanker operators, and a number of other defendants, which alleged fraud and unjust enrichment. In a *qui tam* action the plaintiff must pay legal expenses out of his own pocket. If he prevails, he is entitled to receive fifteen percent to thirty percent of the money that the government recovers. Among the issues raised by the suit was whether the US Justice Department and Forest Service covered up a CIA and drug cartel link to some of the planes.

Assistant Inspector General James R. Ebbitt of the Office of Inspector General, USDA testified that he found no evidence of CIA involvement in the program. The CIA and the Forest Service denied CIA involvement. The Justice Department never found any evidence of CIA involvement.

Insight magazine published a piece by James Dettmer which sheds more light on what went on at Mena airport involving C-130s. The story offers an explanation for some of the sightings and the activity that Welch and others encountered.

Two C-130s, Air Force numbers 570517 and 570518, came into possession of T & G Aviation of Chandler, Arizona. William "Woody" Grantham, who had once been a pilot for the CIA-owned Air America, founded T & G Aviation. In 1992 and 1993, T & G Aviation filed applications with the Department of State and received approval to sell the C-130s to a company named Aero Postal.

The planes were to be used for legal cargo-shipping purposes or for aerial pesticide spraying. The sale to Aero Postal was approved. Either by design or because of a bureaucratic foul-up, the planes eventually ended up in possession of the Arellano-Felix Cartel. They were major traffickers running the Tijuana Cartel. The planes were eventually impounded but for a time one of the C-130s, the one seen by Russell Welch and watched by US Customs agents, was parked at Mena Intermountain Regional Airport.

Dettmer's piece said the DEA revealed in 1994 court documents involving a major Chicago-based drug case that Luis Carlos Herrera-Lizcano, a top Cali and Medellin Cartel operative, had in the mid-1980s attempted to purchase mothballed C-130s from the Australian government.

Australian newspaper accounts—probably some of the same articles seen by Russell Welch—identified the middleman in the deal as John Ford, III, an attorney and corporate secretary from T & G Aviation. Dettmer wrote that Ford had sent an "associate" named Frank Battison-Posada to check out the Australian C-130s. Battison-Posada, who was not charged, was the pilot of the twin Otter. The plane was seized in 1991 at the Mena airport by Russell Welch at the request of the DEA on suspicion of drug smuggling.

Darrell Baker, the former manager of Mena Intermountain

Airport, was chairman of the Airport Commission from 1990 to 1994. He remembered that a company named Eagle Aviation operated at the Mena airport for a short time. The company rented a small office in the hangar owned by Mena Air Center. A company representative made a presentation to the Airport Commission during the time Baker was chairman. In essence, this company wanted financial help to go into the C-130 refurbishing business on a large scale. "They had an idea but no plan," said Baker. Their proposal was rejected.

Baker said the company brought two C-130s to the airport and had work performed on them outside on the ramp near their office because there was insufficient hangar space. One plane eventually left. The second plane, by then little more than a cannibalized hulk, sat at the airport for more than a year. Curious visitors, probably law enforcement personnel, kept coming by to photograph it. Baker said Southern Cross Aviation, had no connections to Eagle Aviation that he was aware of.

There was other activity at the Mena airport that would likely have generated rumors of CIA paramilitary operations in this small west Arkansas town. The US Air Force and the Army conducted joint exercises involving Patriot missile batteries at the airport for several years. The administrative headquarters and troop facilities were set up at the Mena airport. Fighter planes participated along with C-130s. The big cargo planes flew many low-level flights over the airport. The Patriot batteries were set up, usually on private property with the owner's permission, within a five-mile radius of the Mena airport. The exercises brought many personnel and their equipment.

Michael Haddigan, in a June 28, 1988, article in the *Arkansas Gazette*, wrote that in October 1987, Army anti-aircraft units taking part in Air Force exercises made their headquarters at the Mena airport. Haddigan quoted Army Major Frank Theissing, public affairs officer at Fort Chaffee, as saying there would likely be more exercises at the Mena airport in the future.

After the 1991 Gulf War ended, one of the Patriot batteries that had once trained at Mena came back. It was put on a static display at the airport. Darrell Baker thought it was the battery that shot down the first SCUD missile because he remembered that pieces of a SCUD were on display. He knows the town of Mena was quite proud to have been associated with the Patriot missile training exercises and the Army wanted to show its appreciation.

Other activity centered at Fort Chaffee also involved the Mena airport. In the early 1980s, the Department of Energy, the FBI, and an Army Ranger unit participated in a joint three-day exercise involving the simulated theft of a nuclear weapon device. During the exercise, FBI counter-terrorism specialists hunted down Army Rangers who were playing the role of terrorists. Local residents occasionally saw participants in these paramilitary exercises in the Mena area. Such encounters with armed civilian and military personnel were likely to have stimulated stories of mysterious goings-on. These exercises are known as Nuclear Weapon Accident Incident Exercise. They take place regularly across the country throughout the year.

For example, in April, 2012, it was publicly announced in newspapers that members from the North Dakota National Guard's 81st Civil Support Team from Bismarck, North Dakota, were participating in a three-day NUWAIX on the Minot Air Force Base. The exercise involved nearly four hundred people and several agencies, including the Department of Energy, the Federal Bureau of Investigation, the US Air Force 5th Bomb Wing, US Army North Command, and several others. Foreign dignitaries from the United Kingdom, France, Netherlands and Turkey came to observe the exercise. NUWAIX 2015 took place May 5-8, 2015 on Naval Base Kitsap-Bangor located on the Kitsap Peninsula in the state of Washington.

By its own admission, the CIA was engaged in activities at the Mena airport. They participated in field exercises with another federal agency and they sent some of their planes there for repairs and maintenance. The agency was very likely to have been involved in some testing related to an experimental surveillance aircraft.

There is no evidence that Barry Seal was involved with the CIA in any "black operations" at the Mena airport — except for the cameras the CIA placed on the C-123 at the time Seal flew it to Nicaragua,

Russell Welch believes rumors of Seal's involvement with the CIA at Mena began to circulate in 1984 when Fred Hampton started a whispering campaign that he and Seal had been working for the CIA. The evidence of this is found in the petition filed in Hampton's federal suit. Hampton alleges that Barry Seal told him he was working for the CIA. As Welch sees it, the CIA story was circulated by Hampton to save face locally and to downplay his culpability in the money laundering and drug smuggling operations of Barry Seal. It is also likely that Seal himself greatly exaggerated the extent of his association with the CIA. Such hype would be typical of Barry Seal.

Rumors of CIA "black operations" and strange paramilitary activity taking place at the Mena airport stem largely from legitimate military and federal law enforcement activity that was observed by the local residents. The stories were amped up by the appearance of a pair of C-130s that had nothing to do with Barry Seal. The rumors were further fueled by exaggeration and speculation regarding Seal and the C-123 that he based at the airport for a period of time.

Admittedly the CIA did have a presence at the Mena airport, but there is little credible evidence that any of the agency's activities involved Barry Seal.

Chapter 19
The Cadillac Papers and Barry's Bank

The search of Barry Seal's Cadillac is more remarkable for what it did not show investigators.

No links or paystubs from the CIA.

No links to the White House, George H. W. Bush, Bill Clinton, or Oliver North.

No paper trail linking cocaine smuggling to Seal himself or to his Air Seal airplane fleet.

After Barry Seal's's murder, rumors persisted about hundreds upon hundreds of documents that supposedly proved he worked for the CIA and smuggled drugs into Mena on behalf of the CIA and Oliver North. They were found in his Cadillac. Conspiracy advocates claimed that government agents destroyed these documents soon after Seal's death as part of a cover-up.

Such assertions are pure nonsense and more of the Barry Seal mystique.

The morning after Seal's murder near the Salvation Army center in Baton Rouge, IRS agent Jerry Bize went to the State Police Crime Lab. That's where Seal's Cadillac had been taken for processing. Bize removed all of the Permafile boxes from the vehicle. Some documents in the boxes in the back seat were splattered with blood and brain matter.

Bize loaded the boxes, five or six as he recalled, into his government vehicle and took the boxes to Stan Bardwell's office. There they were thoroughly examined by task force agents, Brad Myers and a few other government attorneys.

The great bulk of the documents consisted of old bank statements and canceled checks from Seal's accounts at Capital Bank and Trust, a bank that had failed several years earlier. There was documentation of a loan made by Capital Bank that was secured by a few small, loose diamonds.

Other documents revealed that the same diamonds valued at less than $3,500 had become collateral for another loan made to Seal's long-time buddy, Joe Mazzuka. Recall that it was Mazzuka who got Seal involved in the 1972 Customs sting that resulted in Seal's first arrest.

There were some tape cassettes in the boxes. Agents listened to all of the tapes. None contained conversations with Terry Reed, George H. W. Bush, Oliver North, or any CIA representatives.

One tape in particular was typical of Barry Seal. It was a recording of a phone call between himself and DEA agent Bob Joura. The DEA operator answered. Seal asked for "Group Seven."

There is a brief conversation between Joura and Seal.

At one point Joura asked Seal if he was taping the call.

"I wouldn't tape you," Seal answered.

Among the documents were repair bills and receipts for work performed by Fred Hampton's company, Rich Mountain Aviation in Mena, on various aircraft belonging to Seal. None of the invoices, however, were for the installation of illegal fuel systems or alterations to cargo hatches. Seal had covered his tracks.

There were other documents indicating that Seal was paying some of Hampton's legal bills.

Millionaire smuggler Barry Seal wrestled with taxes and mortgages just like most Americans. Only larger. There was a diary with a notation written on February 5, 1986, the day after IRS filed the jeopardy assessment and a tax lien totaling $29,487,718. "29 million—should have had mortgages on everything."

Again, there were no entries in his diary that made any reference to Oliver North, George Bush, Bill Clinton, Michael Tolliver, or Terry Reed.

Among the material in the boxes was a copy of a charter, issued by Turks and Caicos Islands, for a bank that was organized by Seal. He had named it Lawyers Deposit and Trust.

There were receipts from a Miami department store for the cash purchase of a diamond bracelet for $17,000, and two ermine ladies' jackets for $8,500 apiece.

There were no videotapes of President Bill Clinton or President George H. W. Bush or Bush sons receiving a delivery of cocaine.

And there were no documents, contracts, letters, payroll stubs, or other evidence that Barry Seal had ever worked for the CIA.

Russell Welch and Bill Duncan came to Baton Rouge in April 1986 to spend several days studying the Cadillac documents at the

US Attorney's office. Welch made the only uncontaminated copies of the documents. There were absolutely no documents of any kind that would support any of the claims made by authors Terry Reed and John Cummings in their book, *Compromised, Clinton, Bush and the CIA,* Welch said.

Jerry Bize thought the Seal Cadillac papers were brought to Lake Charles during the trial of three Colombians who murdered Seal. The two prosecutors, Prem Burns and Joe Lotwick, had no recollection of boxes of documents.

The "Cadillac papers" were examined by government lawyers, federal and state criminal investigators from three federal and two state agencies. They were all experienced in white collar, political corruption and financial fraud and drug investigations.

The investigators and government attorneys were all looking for evidence of any crimes and for assets, such as foreign bank accounts, or assets in possession of other persons, hidden or in plain sight. No such documentary evidence was found.

There were no smoking guns. Nothing among the documents remotely tied Barry Seal to the White House, Bill Clinton, Terry Kent Reed, Oliver North, or the CIA and their Contra supply program.

Almost a year after Seal's murder, task force agents began to hear rumors that there were records concerning Barry Seal's money that government agents couldn't find.

The rumor source was Baton Rouge city policeman, Bobby Seale, the husband of Barry's secretary, Dandra. He was not related to Barry.

Bobby Seale was reported to be telling people that the "stupid feds" were running around looking for Seal's money, when all the information was in the police officer's possession.

Well, wouldn't you know it, the stupid feds got a federal search warrant. In February 1987, FBI agent FBI Jerry Phipps, along with IRS agent Jerry Bize and DEA agent Bob Briard, served it on Bobby Seale. They searched his residence.

The affidavit for the search warrant revealed that the search was based on statements from Marjorie Groht, another Baton Rouge police officer, who told FBI agent Jerry Phipps that Bobby Seale told her, "The feds think they have all of Barry Seal's records, but Dandra and I have them in boxes in a closet at our house."

At the time of the search, Bobby Seale denied to reporters that he told Groht anything like that. He said he told Groht that he and Dandra were gathering quite a bit of information for the book they were writing. The book was complete but hadn't been published. Bobby Seale said he thinks the search warrant was retaliation for a complaint he filed against another city police officer for alleged harassment of the local police union.

The agents seized a box containing miscellaneous records and correspondence belonging to smuggler Barry Seal. The only items of value they found were the original island bank charter for Lawyers Deposit and Trust bank and two stock certificates. One certificate was issued to North Haven Holding, Inc., for 100 shares and the other was issued to South Haven Holding Inc. for 100 shares. There were no documents revealing the existence of other assets.

And conspiracy buffs can take note that North Haven Holding Inc. has nothing to do with Lt. Col. Oliver North.

So much for the Cadillac papers — just another myth.

Chapter 20
Congress Investigates

He wanted to embarrass the Republicans and glean some publicity. Early in 1986, Democratic Senator John F. Kerry of Massachusetts launched an investigation into illegal gun running and narcotics trafficking alleged to be associated with the Contra forces involved in the war against the Nicaraguan government.

Beginning in April 1986, hearings were held by the Senate Sub-committee on Terrorism, Narcotics, and International Operations of the US Senate Committee on Foreign Relations.

Senator Kerry's investigation came largely in response to newspaper accounts alleging links between the Contras and drug traffickers that first appeared in December 1985 in an Associated Press story. This investigation took place long before the publication of the controversial *Compromised: Clinton, Bush and the CIA.*

Four Companies Named by Kerry Committee to Help Contras

The Kerry Committee, as it came to be known, identified four companies that had been contracted by the Department of State to supply humanitarian assistance to the Contra forces The companies were also involved in drug trafficking.

The companies were:

SETCO Air, a company set up by Honduran drug trafficker Ramon Matta Ballesteros, a class I DEA violator.

DIACSA, a Miami based air freight company operated as a drug trafficker enterprise for convicted drug traffickers Floyd Carlton and Alfredo Caballero.

Firgorificos de Punteranas, a firm owned and operated by Cuban-American drug traffickers.

Vortex, an air service company partially owned by admitted drug trafficker Michael Palmer.

Payments made to these four companies totaled $806,000 between January and August 1986.

Prior to the time that the State Department entered into contracts with these four companies, there was information in possession of federal law enforcement agencies that individuals associated with the companies were involved in narcotics trafficking.

Interestingly enough, none of the four companies had operations at Mena, the place conspiracy buffs claim was the hub of a secret CIA drugs-up, guns-down operation in support of the Contras.

The Kerry Committee also identified a handful of pilots who were working for the CIA and who were known to be associated with drug trafficking and smuggling.

Barry Seal wasn't one of those pilots.

Officials of the Nicaraguan Humanitarian Assistance Operation (NHAO), the entity that was set up to handle the assistance program, told Government Accounting Office (GAO) investigators that the four supply contractors being used were to have been screened by US law enforcement and intelligence agencies to insure they were not involved in criminal activity. No one knew for certain whether they were ever actually vetted.

Whether by design or negligence, it was certainly a slipshod arrangement that gave the four companies a cover for their drug trafficking.

The security foul-up also provided "vast government conspiracy" theorists as well as some Kerry Committee Democrats with more ammo to use to further criminalize the CIA's Contra operations.

Although none of the four companies identified by the Kerry Committee were found to have ties to Barry Seal, could he have been working behind the scenes to help the CIA?

Beginning in March 1983, Barry Seal became the target of the drug task force of the Baton Rouge Middle District of Louisiana. From April of that year and continuing until mid-January 1984, he was usually in Baton Rouge under the surveillance of FBI agents. They, along with DEA agents, were also monitoring his phone conversations from as many as ten pay phones. Seal carried a pager and rolls of coins in a camera bag.

Spring 1984 was a busy time for Seal.

During February 1984, Seal was in Florida preparing for the trial that started February 14 and ended March 17.

On March 25, he flew to Washington, DC, and met with representatives of the Vice-President's Task Force on Drugs.

On March 28, Barry Seal inked his deal with the DEA in Miami. Seal debuted as an informant.

When the congressionally appropriated Contra funding ran out in the summer 1984, Barry Seal was already totally engrossed in setting up his Nicaraguan undercover operation. He was usually in the company of DEA agents Joura and Jacobsen.

Seal made two unsuccessful attempts to transport the large load of cocaine — on May 28 and June 4. His efforts finally paid off on June 26, 1984. On that day he flew his C-123 cargo plane, the *Fat Lady*, into Los Brasiles airport in Managua. He picked up 1,465 pounds of cocaine.

Seal's identity was leaked as a DEA informant in July 1984.

Seal spent the remainder of the year battling the Baton Rouge Middle District task force in his hometown and consulting with his attorneys trying to arrive at a plea agreement with US Attorney Stan Bardwell. The two had known each other since Baton Rouge High.

Seal finally succeeded in November 1984.

Seal didn't have the time to be involved with the CIA in a covert plan to resupply the Contras. Most of all, it was a program that was not yet in place.

Lt. Colonel Oliver North, the point man on the Contra project, did not begin to recruit until May 1984 when he brought in Robert Owen to be his personal liaison with the Contras. In mid-1984, retired Air Force Major General Richard Secord was brought aboard to handle arms-procurement and covert resupply activities.[1]

By April 1984, Seal was a DEA informant busily at work trying to keep himself out of federal prison. He had very little time and few opportunities to be of any help to North.

The first Contra resupply mission wasn't flown until April 11, 1986 when North, Owen and Secord arranged for the use of an L-100/C-130 plane. It was leased from Southern Air Transport to be used in the humanitarian assistance program.[2]

Nine more weapons drops were made between March and June 1986. By that time, Seal was dead.[3]

Nevertheless, attempts were made to link him to the CIA and their Contra resupply effort. The linkage was provided by the C-123 that was shot down over Nicaragua on October 5, 1986, while on a Contra resupply flight.

The C-123 was the same plane Seal used when he took delivery of the large load of cocaine and obtained the famous hidden camera photographs.

So, the CIA just had to be in the drug business and Seal had to be a CIA operative, right? That was the flawed logic applied by those who arrived at this conclusion. Many did so because they were more interested in embarrassing the Reagan administration and hanging Oliver North than they were in getting the facts straight.

The fact is that when Barry Seal flew the C-123 two years earlier, he was a DEA informant — and not a CIA spook. The only connection the CIA had with the flight was to get permission from the DEA to install two cameras on the aircraft. The Kerry Committee developed no credible evidence to refute this.

The notoriety generated by the Kerry Committee hearings became a boon to some dopers. It did not help when the government failed follow up with prosecution.

Smugglers were able to claim, with little fear of contradiction, that were assisting the CIA and helping the Contras. When Miami US Attorney Leon Kellner and Richard Gregorie met with committee staffers in November 1986, they told them that many Miami cocaine traffickers used the "I was working for the CIA" story as a defense. Some drug traffickers made such a claim to avoid prosecution or get lighter sentences. Others did it to indulge investigators and the media. Or maybe to write a book.

When reporter Edmond Jacoby's story of Seal's flight to Nicaragua appeared on the front page of the *Washington Times* on July 17, 1984, it was apparent that someone in the know had leaked word of the operation.

The Kerry Committee tried to find out who it was. In July 1988, three top level DEA managers provided statements to the committee. They were Assistant Administrator for Operations Frank Monastero, Deputy Assistant Administrator for Operations Dave Westrate, and Ron Caffrey, Chief of the Cocaine Desk.

The testimony given by the DEA officials revealed that a meeting took place in the Executive Office Building on June 27, 1984, the day after Seal's first flight in the C-123. Those in attendance were:

Dave Westrate, Ron Caffrey,

Lt. Colonel North,

Dewey Clarridge of the CIA,

Kennedy Grafinrid, assistant to the president,

Greg Johnstone, Office of Indian Affairs, Department of State.

Caffrey testified that he had been instructed by Dave Westrate to give a briefing. He gave the group a briefing and displayed the photos taken by Seal the previous day. Dewey Clarridge identified Frederico Vaughn as an associate of Nicaraguan government officials.

Congressman William J. Hughes (D-NJ) asked Caffrey if Oliver North "wanted to go public" with the information.

Caffrey did not recall that North had suggested going public but said he had mentioned one time during the briefing that Congress was getting ready to vote on funding for the Contras. It would be helpful to be able to report publicly that the Sandinistas were involved with the Medellin drug cartel.

Congressman Bill McCollum (R-Fla.) asked Caffrey if he had any knowledge that Oliver North or anyone at the National Security Council had leaked the information to the press. Caffrey answered that he did not have that knowledge.

Dave Westrate testified that the June 27 meeting opened with a presentation of the photographs by Dewey Clarridge. This was followed by a general discussion of whether or not a release of the facts in the case would in any way influence the pending congressional vote on funding for the Contras.

Westrate told the committee that the group had concluded that the knowledge would probably not have any influence on the pending vote in Congress. It was clear to Westrate that the White House felt that having derogatory information on members of the Sandinista government handling cocaine would be helpful with regard to the vote on funding.

A second meeting was held June 29, 1984, attended by Dave Westrate, Ron Caffrey, Oliver North, Dewey Clarridge and Greg Johnstone. North conducted the meeting. According to Westrate's testimony, it was a general discussion of the case and of the DEA's future plans to use Barry Seal.

A few weeks later Jacoby's story was front-page news in the *Washington Times*. The conservative newspaper's circulation was only a fifth the size of the *Washington Post*, yet the Seal story had impact.[4]

Frank Monastero told the Kerry Committee that he briefed Carlton Turner, the White House drug policy advisor, on July 17, the same day the Jacoby article appeared in the paper.

Monastero said that the inference he drew from their conversation was that Turner was accusing the DEA of leaking the story. Monastero became quite irritated and let Turner know in no uncertain terms that he thought the White House was responsible for the leak.

Many fingers pointed to Oliver North as the source of the leak. On October 9, 2000, millions of television viewers saw and heard him during a PBS *Frontline* television special titled *Drug Wars, Part One*. He said that he had been ordered to brief Florida Republican Senator Paula Hawkins about Seal's undercover flight to Nicaragua and he had done so.[5]

On August 7, 1984, Senator Hawkins held a press conference about the Sandinista involvement in drug smuggling. Four photos taken during Seal's June 25 flight were shown. Colonel North's disclosure on the *Frontline* special does not answer the question of how Edmond Jacoby got the information to write his story some three weeks before Senator Hawkins held her news conference.

The Kerry Committee report correctly treated the mission flown by Barry Seal as an example of a bona fide DEA investigation that was prematurely disclosed in an effort to block passage of the Boland amendment.

The Kerry Committee never determined precisely who leaked the story of Seal's mission to Nicaragua. The circumstances lead to the inescapable conclusion that the motive was largely political.

It is doubtful that the DEA was responsible for the leak because the agency had no motive. They were after the leadership of the Medellin Cartel. They had every reason to believe that Seal would come through for them.

On the other hand, it was the CIA that had the frontline responsibility to keep the Contras in the fight. The agency has admitted that it "maintains relationships with reporters from every major wire service, newspapers, newsweekly and TV network."

Therefore, the CIA has an admitted penchant for using the media to its advantage. It can't be let off the hook.

Logic has always pointed to someone in the White House or the CIA. The collective thought was that discrediting the Sandinista government in the eyes of Congress would protect funding for the Contras.

Senator Kerry attempted to bring William Bottoms to Washington during the hearings but the DEA would not let him go. At that time Bottoms was working undercover with the DEA and they did not want to risk exposing him.

OCA 95-2274
16 August 1995

MEMORANDUM FOR THE RECORD

SUBJECT: Briefing for Representative James Leach (R-IA)
Regarding [   ] in Arkansas in the
(b)(1)   Late 1980s with NSA - 21 July 1995
(b)(3)
(b)(6)

1. On 21 July 1995, at 1000 hours, in room 2186
Rayburn House Office Building, Chairman James Leach (R-IA),
Committee on Banking and Financial Services, and staffer
Jamie McCormick, received a briefing, at Leach's written
request to the DCI, on allegations of [   ]
in Arkansas in the late 1980s. Agency participants were:
[   ] Investigative Staff, Office of Inspector General;
[   ] Chief, Legislation Group, Office of
Congressional Affairs; and the undersigned. NSA participants
were: Frank Newton, Inspector General, and [   ]
Congressional Affairs. [ ]

2. Representative Leach began the briefing by saying
that he was not interested in opening a new probe of U.S.
Contra-policy or suggesting wrongdoing by either Agency,
especially since he served on the October Surprise Task
Force, where he was convinced that the Marcos' walked away
with billion of dollars. Leach, however, did say he based
his request for the briefing on reports that have appeared
in the press that refer to secret foreign bank accounts held
by prominent people in Mena, Arkansas, [   ]
[   ] and an Arkansas-centered network of
banks formed to [   ] (see attached incoming letter).
Leach also said that over a period of time he had talked to
a lot of people regarding this issue. He said that most of
the allegations contained within the articles were probably
false, but he felt an obligation to look into Whitewater
related allegations on behalf of the Banking Committee.
That said, some allegations may be credible, some totally
unbelievable, but as information goes out to the American
public in non-traditional ways, it becomes more believable.
[ ]

3. [   ] along with Frank Newton,
responded to Leach's questions regarding each Agency's
current knowledge on involvement with any of the alleged
allegations contained in his letter. Newton responded
[   ] to all of the questions posed in the incoming
letter, but did, however, provide a brief broadbrush

I-102J
+1 Leach

APPROVED FOR RELEASE
DATE: JUL 2002

*US Rep. Jim Leach received a broad briefing about allegations involving the CIA,
Barry Seal, drug smuggling and other activities at Mena, Arkansas.*

SUBJECT: Briefing for Representative James Leach
          (R-IA) Regarding [   ] in
          Arkansas in the Late 1980s - 21 July 1995

background briefing on how NSA conducts it normal daily
activities [   ] said that the
capability of the IG to conduct its function depends in part
on cooperation by others with CIA and thus far the IG had
not look into any of these allegations. However, [
said as he understood the current issue, a thorough search
had been conducted by CIA regarding PROMIS/Inslaw issues
relating to Systematics, Inc., Mena, and Hadron, during a
much earlier timeframe. Also, he understood that thus far
very little information had been found to be responsive to
the exact allegations contained in the current letter. [
[   ] however, did say that the Agency had perhaps made
some connections within the larger picture of things. The
Agency was aware of Barry Seal, but had no relationship with
him nor any records regarding his activities in Mena. Seal's
association with the Drug Enforcement Agency (DEA) was widely
publicized, [

                          As for PROMIS, that issue had been
looked at in-depth by the Senate Select Committee on
Intelligence (SSCI) and the House Judiciary Committee in 1991
and 1993. The conclusion then and still is that the Agency
never purchased any INSLAW/PROMIS software. [

                  ] Chairman Leach was also informed that we
had not found any records related to Systematics of Arkansas,
a banking software firm, [

     4. [

SUBJECT: Briefing for Representative James Leach
(R-IA) Regarding [   ] in
Arkansas in the Late 1980s - 21 July 1995

5.

6. Leach, after listening to the responses to his
earlier questions, proceeded to ask approximately 45 other
questions regarding the issue, basically repeating many
of the issues already addressed. For those questions and
responses, please see attached pages from a draft memorandum
provided by staffer Jamie McCormick and checked against the
personal notes of the undersigned. The responses in the
draft memorandum correspond correctly to the personal notes
of the undersigned. [   ]

7. Leach concluded by once again saying he has an
obligation to look into the matter on behalf of the
Committee, and asked us to inform the DCI and DIRNSA that
he may hold hearings on these allegations in the fall. (U)

8. The briefing lasted approximately 90 minutes.
Leach was informed that the Agency would continue to
check its records, especially on questions relating to:
1) Park-o-Meter; 2) CIA's relationship, if any, with Terry
Reed; and 3) whether the CIA had any connection to Seal's
cargo plane (serial number 54-0679). [   ]

CIA Liaison Group
Office of Congressional Affairs

Attachments

Responses to Chairman Leach's Prepared Questions of 7/21

Q: Have any of you or anyone else at either the CIA or NSA
discussed this inquiry from us with anyone at the White House, the
Department of Justice, or any other governmental organization?

A: No, not in response to Chairman Leach's letters
requesting a briefing.

Q: Does the CIA or NSA have knowledge of or any involvement
in clandestine activity by the U.S. Government or any private
parties in or near Mena, Arkansas, in the 1980s?

A: CIA's knowledge [   ]
[   ]   NSA [   ]

Q: Have any reports on activities in and around Mena been
prepared for the DCI, specifically, for former Director Woolsey?

A: No.   The only reports the CIA has were prepared in
conjunction with the Chairman's requested briefing.

A.   Gun Smuggling

Q: Did the CIA or NSA have any involvement in, or knowledge
of, any operation by the U.S. government or the so-called "private
benefactors" (led by retired Gen. Richard Secord) to train pilots
and/or ship arms from the Rich inter-mountain regional airport at
Mena to the Nicaraguan Contras?

A: NSA, [   ] CIA representatives replied that they "did
not think so." CIA noted that the IG had checked back records
on this issue in 1994 and had discovered no responsive
information. CIA noted parenthetically that the operational
activities of the private benefactors were mainly conducted
from southern Florida.

Q: (Skipped) If so, did any such activities take place with
the knowledge or approval of other Federal officials?

Q: (Skipped) Did any such activities take place with the
knowledge or approval of Arkansas state government officials?

Q: (Skipped) Did the CIA contract with any Arkansas
manufacturers to build automatic weapons for the Nicaraguan
Contras?

Q: Does the CIA or NSA have any contractual or other
relationship with, or knowledge of, an Arkansas company called
Park-o-Meter, also known as POM? Do you have any reason to believe
that POM produced disposable fuel tanks for use by Barry Seal and
possibly others in connection with supplying arms to the Contras?

A: NSA ⬚   CIA had no knowledge, but would check and get back to the Chairman.

B.   Barry Seal and Associates

Q: (Skipped) Did the CIA or NSA have any contractual or other relationship with the late Adler Barriman "Barry" Seal (Seal was murdered, allegedly at the direction of Columbian drug lords, in Feb. 1986)?

Q: To your knowledge, did any other government agency (such as the DEA or DIA) have any contractual or other relationship with Barry Seal?

A: NSA, ⬚ CIA had no confirmation from any other USG agency, including DEA, that Seal had any government contracts.

Q: Is the CIA or NSA aware of any IRS determination that money earned by Seal between 1984 and 1986 was not illegal because of his alleged CIA-DEA employment?

A: NSA, ⬚ CIA, no.

Q: Did the CIA have any involvement in, or knowledge of, the installation of cameras on Seal's C-123K transport plane for use in a 1984 "sting" operation against the Sandinista official Federico Vaughan?

A: CIA, no.

Q: Was Seal's C-123K cargo plane, christened Fat Lady (serial number 54-0679), sold by Seal to the CIA or any other U.S.-government related entity? Was this the plane later shot down over Nicaragua with a load of arms destined for the Contras?

A: CIA, no records suggested it was.

Q: Did the CIA have any contractual or other relationship with Terry Reed, a former Air Force intelligence officer (who claims he had a relationship with the CIA in the 1980s) and author of Compromised: Clinton, Bush and the CIA?

A: CIA had no knowledge, but would check further.

Q: Did the CIA ever have dealings with former Arkansas State Trooper L.D. Brown?

A: CIA no, not beyond as stated earlier in their presentation.

Q: Is the CIA or NSA aware of any attempts by federal or state officials to interfere with or terminate any investigation [by] the IRS, Justice Department, Arkansas State Police or any other law-enforcement authorities into Mena-related criminal conduct?

A: CIA, no. NSA, [ ]

C. Narcotics Smuggling

Q: Did the CIA or NSA have any knowledge of or involvement in illicit narcotics trafficking, possibly by rogue operatives, in or near Mena, Arkansas? As you know, there have been allegations that on their return flights from Central America, pilots smuggled more than 20 tons of cocaine into Mena.

A: NSA, [ ] CIA no. [ ] noted that CIA had also checked with its counter-narcotics center, which reported no responsive information available.

D. Money Laundering

Q: Did the CIA or NSA have any indication that [ ] local businesses and Arkansas [ ]

A: NSA, [ ] CIA, no.

Q: Does the CIA or NSA have any indication that Barry Seal or his associates attempted to [ ]

A: NSA, [ ] CIA, no.

Q: Does the CIA or NSA have any indication that the proceeds from illicit narcotics trafficking might have been laundered through the Arkansas Development Finance Authority (ADFA)?

A: NSA, [ ] CIA, no.

E. [ ]

Q: Does the CIA or NSA know of any secret [ ] or more ever held by U.S. citizens domiciled in Arkansas at anytime between 1988 and now?

A: NSA [ ]

[ ] CIA representatives stated

A: CIA, no. NSA, [ ]

Q: Is it possible, and does CIA have any information that might suggest, that alleged Mena-related activities stemmed from private Nicaraguan assistance groups, perhaps under the supervision, or at least knowledge of, Colonel North?

A: NSA, [ ] CIA was not aware of any such activity in or around Mena

Q: Did either NSA or CIA ever request that any government organization cooperate or not interfere with aircraft operating out [of] Mena?

A: CIA, no. NSA, [ ]

Q: Is either the NSA or the CIA aware of any foreign governments who might have provided arms, money or any assistance to any group operating out of Mena?

A: NSA, [ ] CIA, no.

ER 95-3123

U.S. HOUSE OF REPRESENTATIVES

COMMITTEE ON BANKING AND FINANCIAL SERVICES

ONE HUNDRED FOURTH CONGRESS

2129 RAYBURN HOUSE OFFICE BUILDING
WASHINGTON, DC 20515-6050

July 11, 1995

Hon. John M. Deutsch
Director
Central Intelligence Agency
Washington, D.C. 20505

Dear Director Deutsch:

I am writing to seek your agency's help in verifying or laying to
rest various allegations of money laundering in Arkansas in the
late 1980s. For that purpose, I would request a briefing from
the CIA's Inspector General on Friday, July 14 before 1:00 p.m.;
if that is not possible, Monday, July 17, would also be a conve-
nient day.

The reports I have in mind have appeared in the general press
and, sometimes in sensational form, in more narrow-gauged out-
lets, including the Internet. They speak of secret foreign bank
accounts held by prominent people in Arkansas, special software
to monitor bank transfers, an Arkansas-centered network of banks
formed to launder money, and similar tales. I would like to
determine whether there is any substance at all to these stories.

Specifically, I would like your Inspector General to tell me
whether the Agency:

(1) knows of any secret bank accounts held by U.S. citizens
domiciled in Arkansas at any time between 1988 and now;

(2) is aware, directly or indirectly, of any efforts by computer
hackers, U.S.-government related or otherwise, to penetrate banks
for the purpose of monitoring accounts and transactions;

(3) knows of or has participated, directly or indirectly, in
efforts to sell software--notably versions of a program in use at
the Justice Department called PROMIS--or clandestinely produced
devices to foreign banks for the purpose of collecting economic
intelligence and information of illicit money transfers;

US Rep. Jim Leach asked the CIA Director about money laundering, Mena and Barry Seal.

In December 1988, Senator Kerry sent an investigator to Miami to take his deposition. That's when Bottoms admitted his role in Seal's cocaine smuggling organization. He fully explained what activities he and Seal had engaged in at Mena. Bottoms denied that they had any connections with the CIA. His testimony was classified and remains so today in 2015.

In 1996, Representative Jim Leach (R-Iowa) began another investigation to find out what had gone on in Mena. Thirteen years after the fact, Leach's House Banking Committee started looking into money laundering, among other things.

Representative Leach knew about the deposition William Bottoms had given to the Kerry Committee. Shortly before the 1996 election, Leach sent an attorney named Steve Ganis to Baton Rouge to interview Bottoms.

The meeting between Ganis and Bottoms took place in attorney Lewis Unglesby's office on September 6, 1996. From the onset, it was obvious the purpose of the interview and Leach's investigation was political.

Ganis began by saying "We know what is in the court records. We want to know what happened under the table, you know, guns, drugs, CIA, money laundering, Clinton's involvement—anything you can give us along those lines." William Bottoms told Ganis the truth about Seal's activities at Mena.

Congressman Leach was obviously aware of Terry Reed and the story he told in *Compromised: Clinton, Bush and the CIA*, because in July 1995 he asked the CIA for a briefing from their inspector general. That same month the CIA gave Leach the briefing and answered some of his questions. A CIA summary of the briefing noted that Leach said that he was aware that "most of the allegations were false" and some were "totally unbelievable."

Leach's letter to Director John Deutch and the agency's "memorandum for the record" and their answers to his questions are found in this chapter. The documents reveal that CIA was aware of Barry Seal but had no relationship with him and no records of his activities at Mena.

The doubters and conspiracy advocates will disbelieve the disclosures but they are on the public record and are essential to telling the complete story of Barry Seal.

The questions provide evidence that Leach's investigation included a look into Seal's activities at Mena and the claims made by Terry Reed in *Compromised*.

CIA Questions and Answers about Mena, Smuggling

(1) Did CIA have any contractual relationship with Terry Reed, a former Air Force intelligence officer (who claims he had a relationship with the CIA in the 1980s) and author of *Compromised: Clinton, Bush and the CIA?*

The answer was "CIA had no knowledge, but would check further."

(2) Is the CIA aware of any attempts by federal or state officials to interfere with or terminate any investigation by the IRS, Justice Department, Arkansas State Police or any other law-enforcement authorities into Mena-related criminal conduct?

The CIA answer was no.

(3) Did CIA have any knowledge of or involvement in illicit narcotics trafficking, possibly by rogue operatives, in or near Mena, Arkansas? As you know there have been allegations that on their return flights from Central America, pilots smuggled more than 20 tons of cocaine into Mena.

The CIA answered no.

(4) Did CIA have any involvement in, or knowledge of, any operations by the US government or the so-called "private benefactors" (led by retired Gen. Richard Secord) to train pilots and/or ship arms from the Rich inter-mountain [Sic] regional airport at Mena to Nicaraguan Contras?

CIA representatives replied that they "did not think so." CIA noted that the IG had checked back records on this issue in 1994 and had discovered no responsive information. CIA noted parenthetically that the operational activities of the private benefactors were mainly conducted from southern Florida.

(5) Did CIA have any involvement in, or knowledge of, the installation of cameras on Seal's C-123K transport plane for use in a 1984, "sting" operation against Sandinista official Federico Vaughn?

To this question the CIA answer was "no."

Source: www.foia.cia.gov/

This writer can offer no logical explanation for the CIA's false answer to question 5. Leach must have had knowledge of the C-123 story to have been able to raise the question. The media had the story in 1984, shortly after Seal flew the mission although he was not then publicly identified as the pilot. After the C-123 was shot down over Nicaragua, Seal's prior association with the plane was all over the media.

Regardless of the false answer, paragraph eight in the August 16, 1995, memorandum states that the agency would continue to check its records, especially on questions relating to CIA's relationship, if any, with Terry Reed and whether the CIA had any connection to Seal's cargo plane.

Eventually CIA Inspector General Frederick Hitz disclosed the agency's relationship with Seal. His report dated November 8, 1996, divulged that in 1984, CIA personnel did have limited contact with Seal when they provided technical support to a DEA sting operation by installing of two 35mm cameras into the C-123 airplane flown by Seal.

Leach's Committee took the testimony of Ron Kelly, the former Little Rock FBI supervisor, who had direct supervision over the investigation of Barry Seal, Fred Hampton, and activities at the Mena airport. When Kelly testified, he had access to all of the investigative reports and other documents connected with investigations because the FBI had previously turned over to the committee all of its investigative files.

Kelly's testimony, originally scheduled to take four hours, went on for nine hours. And when it was over, the committee members knew everything there was to know about Barry Seal, Fred Hampton, Joe Evans, Rich Mountain Aviation, and activities at the Mena airport. Kelly said that Congressman Leach was not present the day he testified.

Barry Seal's work as an informant produced meaningful and spectacular results in a relatively short period of time.

It is very likely that he could have done much more, had it not been for the leaked release of the photographs and Edmond Jacoby's newspaper piece. The administration wanted Congress to continue military aid to the Contras. They hoped that releasing Seal's photographs would do the job. The plan failed. The war on drugs took the hit.

Dick Gregorie said later, "The narcotics war was never the priority of the US government. They were more concerned about fighting the godless communist conspiracy and the spread of communism in Latin America than they were about the extent of the narcotics trade."[5]

Had the administration paid attention to the DEA, the people who were actually fighting the drug war, the results might have been even better than they were.

Barry Seal could very likely have continued in his undercover role and eventually delivered the entire Medellin Cartel on the celebrated silver platter to the government. That goal, as a national interest affecting the welfare of this country, should have taken precedence over the funding of another revolution in a banana republic.

As a result of two largely politically-motivated congressional inquiries, the truth about Seal, his activities at Mena and his limited connection to the CIA is known.

Republican Congressman Leach focused his investigation on what went on at Mena in the hope it would implicate Bill Clinton. His investigation was widespread. Many people were asked to testify — and did.

When it was over, no credible evidence was unearthed to incriminate Bill Clinton or to tie him or the CIA into Barry Seal's smuggling operation. If there had been a smoking gun, Leach would have released a scathing report and announced it in numerous press conferences.

Leach never released a report. Instead, in December 1996, a C-SPAN TV news audience heard Leach say that not as much happened at Mena as was originally thought.

Senator Kerry focused on allegations that some drug traffickers who worked for the CIA to help the Reagan administration keep the Contras supplied had used their affiliation with the agency as a cover to further their drug business. The administration suffered some embarrassment. Senator Kerry racked up some headlines and soundbites but developed little evidence about traffickers involved with the CIA.

Kerry released a report of the results of his investigation and it did not disclose any credible evidence that Barry Seal had any connection with CIA and their Contra resupply efforts.

Most of the writers and self-styled investigators who want to pin the blame for the leak on Oliver North cite the Kerry report where at page 121 the following statement appears:

"However, the operation was disclosed prematurely by an administration official who leaked to the press evidence supposedly collected by Seal in an effort to influence a pending congressional vote on Contra aid. Law enforcement officials were furious that their undercover operation was revealed and agents' lives jeopardized because one individual in the US government— Lt. Col. Oliver North—decided to play politics with the issue." In a footnote, that information is attributed to the testimony of DEA administrator John C. Lawn taken July 12, 1988.

This writer had no success trying to locate the footnoted testimony, so John Lawn was contacted to find out what he had to say, and it was this: "I did not testify about North because I had no such knowledge. A staffer came to me after learning that North's schedule on his White House computer indicated North had visited me. His visit had nothing to do with Barry Seal or the Seal investigation. DEA had guessed that North might have leaked the photo, but I gave no such testimony."

In an attempt to resolve the footnote issue, the author sought the services of Mary Curry, PhD. She is Public Services Coordinator and Research Associate at the National Security Archives, George Washington University. Dr. Curry was not able to find the footnoted testimony of John Lawn. She did, however, find other relevant testimony provided by Lawn, but it was not to a Senate subcommittee. On October 5, 1988, he gave testimony to the Subcommittee on Crime of the Committee on the Judiciary of the House of Representatives.

Lawn's testimony clearly refuted the Kerry report's attempt to portray him as the man who pinned the leak on Oliver North.

Representative William J. Hughes, was the person asking the questions and, not surprisingly, he was a Democrat from New Jersey. The relevant documented testimony can be found in this chapter.

Who Leaked the Story about Barry Seal?

Hughes: Okay. Well certainly the Barry Seal case falls into that category. You wouldn't quarrel with that would you?
Lawn: At this point certainly, the Barry Seal case was compromised. The problem we have is we don't know who leaked the information.
Hughes: Well, I think it's pretty clear. It was either the CIA or North, Colonel North or both. I mean the CIA, from the very beginning, wanted to expose the case because of the contraband coming in from Nicaragua and Colonel North went to great lengths to persuade the DEA. In fact he tried to persuade you, didn't he?
Lawn: No, sir.

H521-85

ENFORCEMENT OF NARCOTICS, FIREARMS, AND MONEY LAUNDERING LAWS

OVERSIGHT HEARINGS

BEFORE THE

SUBCOMMITTEE ON CRIME

OF THE

COMMITTEE ON THE JUDICIARY
HOUSE OF REPRESENTATIVES

ONE HUNDREDTH CONGRESS

SECOND SESSION

JULY 28, SEPTEMBER 23, 29, AND OCTOBER 5, 1988

Serial No. 138

Printed for the use of the Committee on the Judiciary

U.S. GOVERNMENT PRINTING OFFICE

93-627

WASHINGTON : 1989

For sale by the Superintendent of Documents, Congressional Sales Office
U.S. Government Printing Office, Washington, DC 20402

H521-85

US Rep. William J. Hughes questioned John Lawn on the leak about Barry Seal.

Mr. LAWN. Perhaps not, sir, but on the other hand, they could have told us that their law required that they seize all of it and would have kept all 752 pounds.

Mr. HUGHES. That's right. They could tell us anything.

Mr. LAWN. In this case, we made arrests in the United States, seized $1.3 million in cash, arrested the defendants, and that was the level of cooperation that we received.

Mr. WESTRATE. Mr. Chairman, there's a little confusion here, I think, over what is a representative sample. Part of the reason for the 52 pounds was that we weren't certain at the time whether or not there would be a prosecution of some of these people in Panama. Remember, this was an aircraft transiting, so this happened within a matter of hours.

As the follow-up investigation occurred, it was determined there would not be a prosecution in Panama and the defendants were expelled to the United States for prosecution as opposed to Panamanian prosecution. But I don't think the decision to retain 52 pounds in Panama for prosecution there is at all unusual. They would want to have a substantial amount for their prosecution, as we would up here, as opposed to maybe a half a gram or a gram.

Mr. HUGHES. Mr. Westrate, I've never heard of keeping 52 pounds for a representative sample. I mean, I've heard of taking photographs of the contraband, and I've heard of taking a sample in case you have to establish that it's marijuana or cocaine. It's like holding on to $15 million in the bank vault because you want to show a jury that we have $15 million. That's stupid. I don't know of any countries in this hemisphere that requires that, do you, Mr. Lawn?

Mr. LAWN. No, sir, but I can tell you that it was done in the United States, that despite the initial release of the Attorney General's guidelines on destruction, U.S. attorneys——

Mr. HUGHES. Oh, I know.

Mr. LAWN [continuing]. Said that they were going to retain every bit of the cocaine that was seized, to the effect that just the guard service to protect the cocaine we seized in Florida was costing us on the average of $10,000 a day.

Mr. HUGHES. Sure, and it was dumb.

Mr. LAWN. Yes, sir.

Mr. HUGHES. I don't know why any U.S. attorney, first of all, would maintain that as a policy. It's stupid. And frankly, if you can identify for us U.S. attorneys that are doing that, we'd be very happy to conduct future oversight hearings—not in this session of Congress, but maybe in future sessions of Congress, because that doesn't make sense. Let me just move on, if I could, because we're running out of time and I promised to free you up by 4:00 and I'm sure my colleagues have some other questions.

I want to pick up on something that Lamar Smith just dealt with—the problem of law enforcement and the intelligence community, and that that line, trying to maintain that balance between good law enforcement and, at the same time, being a good partner when it comes to national security goals.

Barry Seal comes to mind. Now, that's an example of a case that was jerked around by the intelligence community, in my judgment, to serve purely political ends, and blew probably one of the most important cases that perhaps DEA has worked on, at least in my eight years in the Congress, and it may be one of the most important cases that you remember.

My question is, how much of a problem is that for you at DEA? Do you find that the intelligence community, whether it be the CIA or whether it be the National Security Council, basically interferes with the criminal justice system, to carry out other political objectives?

Mr. LAWN. No, sir, I don't perceive it to be a major problem. We have CIA personnel who work at DEA Headquarters. The cooperation, I would say, is generally excellent. I chair the intelligence committee for the National Drug Policy Board. There is an exchange of information. While the Barry Seal case certainly was a major case, you are certainly aware of another major case that was compromised, not by the National Security Council, but by another component of the Government.

Mr. HUGHES. But my question deals with national security.

How many instances are you aware of where the intelligence community has, for one reason or another, decided to expose a case for other objectives—nonlaw enforcement?

Mr. LAWN. I'm not aware of any, sir.

Mr. HUGHES. Okay. Well, certainly, Barry Seal falls into that category. You wouldn't quarrel with that?

Mr. LAWN. At this point, certainly, the Barry Seal case was compromised. The problem we have is that we don't know who leaked the information——

Mr. HUGHES. Well, I think it's pretty clear. It was either the CIA or North, Colonel North, or both. I mean, the CIA, from the very beginning, wanted to expose the case because of the contraband coming in from Nicaragua and Colonel North went to great lengths to persuade the DEA. In fact, he tried to persuade you, didn't he?

Mr. LAWN. No, sir.

Mr. HUGHES. He tried to persuade those within DEA that he talked with, including Mr. Westrate, including yourself, that, in fact, the matter should be public or that we shouldn't be sending Barry Seal back into Nicaragua, or both.

And I have no doubt that that's an instance where, in fact, there was a political objective, and that is to attempt to provide some embarrassment to the Sandinista government before a vote in the Congress. It's rather clear from the hearing record that that was the case.

Your testimony is that that's the only instance you know about?

Mr. LAWN. Yes, sir. In my eight years, that's the only incident that I can recall.

Mr. HUGHES. What is the policy of DEA when we send a confidential informant into another country to operate?

Mr. LAWN. That's something, sir, that we would have to discuss in executive session.

Mr. HUGHES. All right. That's something that we'd have to take up in executive session?

Mr. LAWN. Yes, sir.

Mr. HUGHES. I have a number of concerns, getting back to the Michael Palmer case. Let me just say at the outset that I believe the Drug Enforcement Administration does an outstanding job and we're very proud of the work they do. I regret that there is some suggestion that we're attempting to reduce, in fact, what they do and undercut their operations because that's not the purpose of an oversight hearing.

But there are things about the Michael Palmer, confidential informant, operation that gives me some great concern. We both know that if you don't watch operatives, they have their own little business on the side. We know that we often use these operatives because they have all kinds of contacts in the underworld, that they have all kinds of nefarious relationships, that we attempt to use.

And nobody's ever suggested—at least I've never heard any member of this subcommittee suggest that we should not be using confidential informants. So, if anybody suggests that anybody is proposing we don't use confidential informants, he has missed the target because that's not the point.

In the Michael Palmer instance, it would appear that when he set the operation up, he had a great deal of freedom. Now, we heard the testimony and there was some effort to try to suggest that there was supervision all along the way, but the facts show that that was not the case.

There's some suggestion, although it's now in doubt so I'm not totally persuaded, but there's some suggestion that he picked out his targets and gave them to DEA. Over a period of weeks, there seemed to be a transition on the part of Michael Palmer and certainly the testimony that suggests that what he did was he picked out a number of different targets and then DEA decided what the operation would be.

But what concerns me most of all is the operation itself. We ended up going from Miami into Colombia and back into Mexico. Most of the evidence suggests that that's always what at least Michael Palmer and Haas intended—to bring it back into an airfield in Mexico. The facts are beyond dispute that we lost most of that load.

We contend that we may have gotten as much of it as a half, but half of that that we say we finally got in this country, we can't really trace to that load that was dumped in Mexico. We certainly concede that we lost probably 10,000 to 11,000 pounds of marijuana, at the very least.

And the evidence was, in my judgment, pretty clear that at least the operatives, the confidential informant Michael Palmer, always intended to take it into Mexico because the big fish was going to be that bargeload, perhaps up to 500,000 pounds of marijuana. That was to be the next trip and we had to persuade those traffickers that we're on the level, number one, and we could deliver. So, that was one thing that troubled me greatly.

The second thing that troubled me was that Michael Palmer is a con man, A-number one. I've come across a lot of cons in my life and he might be the granddaddy of the cons. But in any event, he was able to assimilate anywhere between $1.3 million and maybe $2.5 million. As much as $1 million at one time that he had in a tool chest and up to $1.3 million that the traffickers paid him and we have very little control over that. It's very hard to pin him down.

To finally resolve the question of who leaked the Barry Seal story, the author contacted reporter Edmond Jacoby and asked him if Oliver North was the source for his article.

Now living in Placerville, California, Jacoby replied, "I can state absolutely that Oliver North had nothing to do with my story as far as I knew, or as far as I know today. My direct source was a fellow named Ted Lunger [he's now deceased]; he was a former Special Forces and CIA guy who worked on the hill for Dan Daniel (D-Va.) in those days."

Chapter 21
"I Have No Knowledge..."

Rumors that Barry Seal might be associated with the CIA began in 1972 after his arrest and trial in New Orleans. This rumor was investigated in 1983, before the Baton Rouge Middle District task force made him their target.

Neither the FBI nor the DEA were willing to invest a lot of agent-hours, equipment, and budgetary dollars on surveillance and the expenses associated with the operation of a Title III wiretap, only to have the CIA step in and put the kibosh on a prosecution in the name of national security.

If Seal had been a top-level spy for the CIA, an agency representative would have gone to the FBI director or the US attorney general, or both, and whispered in their ears.

CIA would have claimed it was a "matter of national security." The word from Washington would have come down to Baton Rouge to knock it off. There wouldn't have been any approval for a Title III wiretap from Department of Justice. There wouldn't have been any investigation of Seal in Mena or New Orleans.

The obvious thing to do was to ask the CIA if Seal was an asset or had any relationship with the agency. That is exactly what was done.

A written request prepared by this author was sent to FBI head-quarters early in March 1983 asking that the CIA be contacted and queried about Seal's status. The request was sent through the Department of Justice to the CIA. The question prepared by this writer and submitted was: "Is Adler Berriman 'Barry' Seal an asset, informant, employee, contractor, or a proprietary of either the CIA or of a CIA proprietary?"

The CIA replied that Barry Seal was not then and never had been connected with the agency in any capacity. The CIA response was prompt and unambiguous. The answer was relayed through the

Department of Justice to FBI headquarters to New Orleans and to Baton Rouge.

The CIA issue was resolved. The Baton Rouge Middle District's task force investigation of Barry Seal went forward.

There were times when Barry Seal was asked under oath about his rumored association with CIA. In August 1985, he was testifying for the government in federal court in Nevada in the case of *US v. Reyes*. On cross-examination he was asked about the 1972 New Orleans arrest when he was scheduled to pilot a plane loaded with explosives:

What Seal Said about Working for the CIA

Question: Was it connected with the CIA?
Seal: It was alleged to be. I had no direct knowledge of that.[1]

During the same trial Seal was questioned about his Nicaragua cocaine flight:
Question: And, the first time, I believe that you testified that you recall working for the CIA in what has been referred to as the Nicaraguan affair.
Seal: State that question again. You say I worked for the CIA?
Question: Yes.
Seal: I have no knowledge of ever working for the CIA.[2]

During the sentence reduction hearing on October 24, 1985, DEA supervisor Robert Joura told the court that the CIA approached Seal about putting cameras on his plane at the time they learned that he was shot down in Nicaragua. Joura said that his testimony about the CIA placing a hidden camera on Seal's aircraft was "absolutely not" intended to infer in any way that Seal was working for the CIA.

If Seal had ever been a CIA employee, this was certainly the time for someone to mention it.

The CIA addressed the allegations that Barry Seal was on their payroll. On September 3, 1996, CIA Director John Deutch, ordered an inquiry into allegations stemming from the three-part newspaper investigation, *Dark Alliance*. It was published in the San Jose *Mercury News* in August 1996. Gary Webb, the author of the series, suggested that the CIA might have been involved in drug trafficking, specifically bringing cocaine into American cities such as Los Angeles.

CIA Inspector General Frederick Hitz conducted the investigation and released his findings in a report dated November 8, 1996. One of the questions addressed was what, if any, contact or relationship did the agency have with Barry Seal. This was the CIA's answer:

What the CIA Says About Barry Seal

"Adler Berriman "Barry" Seal was never employed by CIA in any capacity. The only limited contact any CIA personnel had with Seal was during a two-day period in 1984 when Seal was involved in a Drug Enforcement Administration (DEA) sting operation that subsequently implicated a Nicaraguan government official and members of the Medellin drug cartel in a conspiracy to smuggle cocaine into the United States. CIA provided technical support to this operation, which involved the installation of two 35mm cameras into the C-123-K airplane that Seal used during the operation. CIA personnel discussed with Seal options for installing the cameras in the aircraft, and instructed him on the methods of operating the cameras. Other CIA personnel who were present had passing or otherwise brief discussions with Seal. During the course of these discussions, Seal was escorted by DEA personnel. No evidence has been found to indicate that the CIA knew Seal's true identity prior to the operation, or that CIA personnel had any other contact with Seal either before or after this 1984 operation."[3]

Except for the explanation about the use of the cameras which had not taken place as yet, the CIA told the Department of Justice and the FBI the same thing in 1983.

It has usually been Barry Seal's connection with the C-123 cargo plane that has been accepted and cited as proof that the CIA employed him.

This ignores the evidence. Here is what the paper trail shows:

According to the FAA aircraft bill of sale, Colonel Richard L. Uppstrom, USAF, Director of the Air Force Museum, sold the C-123 on June 17, 1983, to Roy Stafford of Jacksonville, Florida.

Stafford sold the plane in August 1983 to Harry Doan, a Daytona Beach aircraft broker and the owner of Doan Helicopter, Inc.

Doan advertised the plane for sale in the magazine, *Trade-A-Plane*.

And Barry Seal, on his own initiative, acquired the plane in June 1984 to use on the Nicaragua mission after his two previous smuggling attempts had failed.

In April 1984, Seal traded his Hughes 500 helicopter and the vessel, *Lauren Lee*, to Jorge Ochoa and Pablo Escobar for a Merlin III B, tail number N1012T.

According to Harry Doan's records, Seal traded that Merlin for the C-123 on June 18, 1984.

Seal testified in the Las Vegas trial that he traded the Merlin to Doan. There was corroboration from Seal's DEA handler, Ernst Jacobsen, who testified in July 1988 before the House Subcommittee on Crime. Jacobsen said that Seal traded the Merlin aircraft for the C-123. The DEA made arrangements with the Pentagon to fly the plane to an air force base near Columbus, Ohio (Rickenbacker), where some structural and engine repairs were done, which cost DEA approximately $40,000.

Seal's avionics expert and long-time friend, Red Hall, corroborated the C-123 plane saga. Hall first met Seal in 1956 when he was living in Baton Rouge.

The only connection Hall ever knew Barry Seal to have with the CIA involved the hidden cameras that were installed on Seal's C-123. After the second unsuccessful attempt to fly cocaine out of Colombia, Seal told Hall he wanted to buy a larger military-type aircraft.

Seal called Hall when he found the C-123 advertised for sale in *Trade-A-Plane*. Hall went with him to Daytona Beach when he met with Harry Doan. Seal flew the C-123 to Rickenbacker Air Force Base near Columbus, Ohio where the engines were overhauled. Hall installed new radar and a selcall UHF radio communication system. The selective calling radio allows a radio to call another radio with a sequence of tones that each recognize.

Red Hall said that while Seal's cargo plane was at Rickenbacker, a DEA agent from Cleveland started investigating Seal and the plane.

Seal found out. He called the DEA in Miami. He raised hell about the investigation. The Cleveland agent was soon ordered to drop the matter. After the work at Rickenbacker was completed, Seal flew the plane to Mena where additional work was done in preparation for the Nicaragua cocaine smuggling flight.

After the Nicaraguan mission ended, the plane was flown back to Mena and parked at Seal's hangar.

Polk County Sheriff A. L. Hadaway said that when he once threatened to seize the plane, he received a call—not from the CIA—but from Bob Joura of the DEA. Joura told the sheriff if he seized Seal's plane, the government would take it back.

Seal's plane made several more flights while based at Mena but none to South America. One flight was a maintenance and engine test flight. The other flight was during the filming of *Uncle Sam Wants You* and the third flight was a trip to England to pick up a

Rolls Royce for Peter Everson.

The big plane sat on the ground at the Mena airport until June 15, 1985. That's when Seal sold it back to Harry Doan. William Bottoms flew the plane to Doan's hangar at the airport in New Smyrna Beach, Florida.

Former Arkansas State Trooper L. D. Brown was Bill Clinton's bodyguard while he was governor.

Brown claimed to have flown to Central America in the C-123 with Seal.

Brown's story does not seem to square with the facts.

On October 23, 1984, the day Brown said he made the flight, the plane was being used in Mena by Barry Seal and John Camp to film the TV special *Uncle Sam Wants You.*

There are those who continue to insist that Barry Seal worked for the CIA.

They offer little in the way of proof.

Most pundits and "vast government conspiracy" advocates have relied on the fact that his C-123 was equipped with hidden cameras by the CIA as proof that Seal worked for the agency.

This ignores Seal's own testimony, the testimony of DEA agents Jacobsen and Jura, Red Hall, information from the CIA, FAA records, and bank records.

Then there is former DEA administrator Francis M. "Bud" Mullen. He said that the CIA approached the DEA about utilizing Seal's services. Mullen gave the approval.

When Seal's C-123 was shot down in Nicaragua on October 5, 1986, the only survivor was the "air freight specialist," a former Marine paratrooper, Eugene Hausenfus, who parachuted to safety.

Hausenfus admitted in a nationally broadcast news conference from Managua, that he worked with the CIA and had made ten similar flights. He never mentioned that Barry Seal was his boss.

While the wiretap was operating in Baton Rouge, FBI and DEA agents and an assistant US attorney listened to a large number of phone conversations between Barry Seal and people in cities all over the United States, including Mena, Arkansas.

The conversations took place over a period of almost three months from ten Baton Rouge area pay phones that Seal obviously thought were secure. The individuals and companies he placed calls to and received calls from were identified through the issuance of subpoenas to the telephone company.

There were no calls by Seal to the CIA.

None of Seal's conversations carried any hint he was working for the CIA — or that a CIA representative was on the other end of the conversation.

Seal never discussed the delivery of supplies to the Contras or the training of their pilots in Arkansas.

Seal never had a conversation with Bill Clinton, or Oliver North on these monitored calls.

During the lengthy investigation, no member of the Baton Rouge task force was ever contacted by a representative of CIA requesting that they lay off of Seal, Fred Hampton or Rich Mountain Aviation.

Likewise, there were never any CIA contacts with government attorneys in Louisiana, Arkansas, or Florida on behalf of Seal during his plea negotiations or at any other time while the investigations were underway.

More importantly, at no time did either of Seal's lawyers, Tom Sclafani or Lewis Unglesby, claim, in mitigation of Seal's crimes, that their client had been working as a CIA operative. Undoubtedly, the attorneys would have done so had it been true because it would have nicely enhanced Seal's resume.

Federal agents debriefed Seal on several occasions after he signed his plea agreement. This was before the exaggerated stories about his involvement with the CIA and his activities at Mena became topics of public interest and much speculation.

Seal never mentioned that he had ever had any type of affiliation with the CIA other than when the hidden cameras were put on his plane.

Seal never claimed to have flown supplies to the Contras or to have known or met Oliver North.

Seal and Red Hall took video films of several flights made by the C-123 during the time it was at Mena.

Seal also took a video of the Lockheed after the modified cargo doors were installed at Hampton's hangar. Seal wanted a record of the work done on his planes. The videos could also have been used to help convince a jury that his planes were altered only to help the DEA.

After Seal was killed, Hall said an investigator from Washington called him and demanded that he turn over the "film" of an airplane.

The investigator was insistent that the film had something to do with Seal loaning an airplane to Bill Clinton.

"That never happened," said Hall. "Barry never met Clinton — and he never lent him a plane."

Red Hall set up the radio station and monitored the radio when Seal, Emile Camp and Peter Everson flew in the C-123 to Nicaragua to get the cocaine. Hall also prepared the numerical codes that were used to communicate by radio with Seal during the flight. Before the flight began, Hall was with Seal in Miami when he went to the CIA office to discuss the installation of the cameras on the plane.

Hall didn't sit in on the CIA meeting. Seal had previously assured Hall that the deal with the C-123 was legal and approved by the DEA—and they would be fully protected from prosecution.

After the second Nicaragua flight, Seal brought the C-123 back to Mena where it remained until he sold it back to Harry Doan. Hall said he never heard a word from Seal about the training of Contra pilots and he never saw Terry Reed or any "Latino pilots" at Mena.

William Bottoms was with Barry Seal on virtually a daily basis beginning in June 1980 and continuing to the day before he was murdered.

He believes it would have been extremely difficult—if not impossible—for Seal to work for the CIA without it coming to his attention.

Bottoms is certain that Seal never worked for the CIA.

The first CIA rumor can be traced back to Barry's 1972 arrest and the subsequent trial in New Orleans. The rumor was revived in 1984 when it became public knowledge that the CIA had hidden cameras on the C-123 in connection with the Nicaragua flight.

The rumor spread further when Fred Hampton filed his civil suit in November 1984 in which he alleged that Barry Seal was involved with the CIA. Not surprisingly, Hampton named Seal as the source of the story.

Claims that Seal had a long-time association with the CIA and was involved in the Contra resupply operations are speculation. Some are wishful thinking and are based on rumors that have been foisted off on a gullible public by ill-informed writers, publicity hounds, self-proclaimed investigators—and, at times when it suited him, by Barry Seal, himself.

The truth rests Barry Seal's sworn, public testimony during the *Reyes* trial in Nevada when he said, "I have no knowledge of ever working for the CIA."

Chapter 22
The Christic Institute

The first public airing of an allegation that Barry Seal was involved with the CIA's efforts to resupply the Contras can be traced to a complex civil law suit filed in Florida. It was filed in 1986 by the Christic Institute, a public-interest litigation organization, shortly after Seal was murdered in Baton Rouge.

This controversial law firm had a history of backing the underdog and so-called lost causes. Its founder was Daniel Sheehan, his wife, and a partner.

Sheehan's suit was filed on behalf of two American journalists, Anthony Avirgan and his wife, Martha Honey. Anthony Avirgan had been present at a press conference held by Nicaraguan Contra leader Eden Pastora, at a jungle camp in La Penca, Nicaragua.

On May 30, 1984, a bomb exploded, killing eight people and wounding approximately thirty others.

Avirgan was slightly cut and bruised, and his camera equipment was destroyed. At the time of the La Penca bombing, Avirgan was employed as a television cameraman for ABC News.

Martha Honey was not present at the bombing. She was a journalist who reported for the Canadian Broadcasting Corporation, the British Broadcasting Company (BBC), *London Sunday Times*, and the *Times of London*.

The two journalists accused a Libyan terrorist named Amac Galil as being the person responsible for the bombing. They wrote and said he was tied to a drug-financed "Secret Team" of Contras and CIA agents. Beginning in August 1985 and continuing into April 1987, in newspaper articles and personal appearances all over the world, Avirgan and Honey told their version of the La Penca bombing. They proclaimed the existence of a CIA-Contra Secret Team that was linked to drug trafficking.

Christic Institute and Romero Institute at a Glance

unmask the shadow government

CHRISTIC INSTITUTE

Christic Institute Founders: Daniel Sheehan, his wife Sara Nelson and their partner William J. Davis, a Jesuit priest, in 1980.

Key Cases: The firm filed suit on behalf of the children of Karen Silkwood, who died in a mysterious crash during a nuclear plant investigation. The firm represented victims of the nuclear disaster at Three Mile Island. The firm prosecuted members of the KKK for killing demonstrators in Greensboro.

Headquarters: Washington with offices in other cities.

Christic dissolved 1991: Succeeded by the Romero Institute, with Daniel Sheehan as chief counsel and Sara Nelson as executive director.

Funding: Grassroots donors and organizations like the New World Foundation.

Activities in 2014-2015: The Romero Institute announced that two South Dakota Native American tribes had received foster care grants as a result of its work since 2005. The institute supported climate change positions by Pope Francis. It worked for protection against unlawful detention in Santa Cruz, California.

Daniel Sheehan, the attorney who headed the Christic Institute, took up the cause of the two journalists. He filed the lawsuit under provisions of the Racketeer Influenced and Corrupt Organization Act (RICO).

The RICO suit was filed in the Miami Southern District of Florida on May 26, 1986, a little more than three months after Barry Seal was murdered.

Twenty-nine individual defendants were named, including retired Army General John Singlaub, CIA agents Thomas Clines and Theodore Shackley, and Medellin Cartel drug lords Pablo Escobar and Jorge Ochoa.

Most of the defendants had also been implicated in the Iran-Contra arms investigation. Some had hands in Seal's murder.

Sheehan asked for $22,465,000 in actual and punitive damages. He declared that the Christic Institute was acting in the dubious role of a "private attorney general" to remedy a pattern of criminal violations of a wide range of federal and state criminal racketeering laws. They included gun running, drug trafficking, and political assassinations that had been committed by "the enterprise" over a thirty-year period.

A lengthy and detailed *Declaration of Plaintiffs' Counsel* written by Sheehan contained summaries of the testimony provided by numerous witnesses. They included Michael "Mickey" Tolliver, an American pilot and drug smuggler. Tolliver was deposed on March 10, 1987, at Miami's Metropolitan Correctional Center, where he was serving a 40-month sentence for conspiracy to import marijuana.

Mickey Tolliver was the first person to create a nexus between Barry Seal and the CIA's Contra resupply effort. Tolliver did it in 1987, a year after Seal's murder.

At the time Tolliver came up with his story, the details of Seal's flight to Nicaragua in the C-123 and the shoot-down of the same plane on a CIA mission to resupply the Contras had been widely reported in the media. More importantly for Tolliver, Barry Seal was not around to refute his tale.

Tolliver claimed that he had been contacted in "late July or early August" of 1985 by Barry Seal. Then, Seal "was known for his ties to the CIA." At the time of this alleged contact with Seal, Tolliver was serving time in a federal halfway house in Atlanta. Tolliver had been sent there after being released from the Federal Correctional Institute at Butner, North Carolina. He said Seal asked him to meet with some people about working on a "covert" operation. He told of being passed off to a string of people until he finally met with Rafael Quintero, a Cuban living in Florida.

Tolliver said he flew a DC-6 cargo plane loaded with military supplies in March 1986 from Miami International Airport to Aguacate, Honduras. There he unloaded and reloaded with 25,360 pounds of marijuana that he flew to Homestead Air Force Base.

Tolliver tried to paint Seal as a CIA operative in another legal case. This one involved a bank that owned a plane that crashed during a smuggling run with Tolliver as pilot.

Tolliver gave a second deposition in November 1987, in a civil suit in federal court in Kansas in a case titled *Midland National Bank versus Conlogue and American Aircraft*. The plaintiff bank alleged that in late 1982, an undercover US Customs agent leased a Beech King Air plane, claiming that it would be used in an undercover operation.

On January 3, 1983, Michael Tolliver, the pilot of the leased plane, was returning from Colombia with a load of marijuana. Tolliver ran out of fuel and ditched the plane off the coast of Grand Cayman Island.

Midland Bank, the lien holder, sued to recover the value of the plane. The bank called Tolliver for a deposition. Tolliver took the Fifth Amendment protection to key questions.

A procedure was instituted which granted Tolliver limited immunity at which time he claimed to be involved in "drugs-for-guns" activity. Tolliver then said Quintero told him Barry Seal was one of the recruiters for crews to fly military aid to Honduras.

DEA agent Ernst Jacobsen and William Bottoms both worked with Mickey Tolliver in an undercover operation called "Sky King." At that time Tolliver was a DEA informant being handled by Jacobsen.

Bottoms and Tolliver worked together on several undercover stings, one of which involved a trip to Haiti to meet some people who were in need of pilots.

Tolliver and Bottoms flew a DC-3 cargo plane from Haiti to Colombia to pick up some marijuana. The plane had mechanical problems and they had to return empty.

Tolliver learned a lot about Seal and the Nicaraguan operation from talking to Bottoms and Jacobsen—and from reading newspaper accounts.

Tolliver's story of the flight to Homestead Air Force Base with Seal is a fabrication. His story is based on his experiences with Bottoms. Tolliver simply related some of the things he had experienced while he was a DEA informant, then added Barry Seal to the mix. Then he told Sheehan what he wanted to hear.

Tolliver's deposition became public knowledge in 1987. DEA agent Jack Hook, a spokesman for the Miami DEA office, acknowledged that Tolliver had been a DEA informant. Hook called him a "fanatical liar" totally lacking integrity and honesty. "He was never recruited by Barry Seal. He didn't know Barry Seal and he never met Barry Seal. I know that for a fact."

Hook said the DEA investigated Tolliver's claims. The agency found no evidence that Barry Seal was involved in clandestine drug or weapons smuggling during his stint as an undercover DEA informant.

Hook pointed out that Tolliver made no mention of his involvement in the Contra arms shipments to DEA officials when he was recruited as an informant.

Tolliver was terminated as an informant because he was "dealing drugs behind our backs," said Hook.[1]

DEA agent Ernst Jacobsen subsequently arrested Tolliver in another cocaine case. Not long afterwards, Tolliver fled. He was out on bond awaiting trial, left the country, and went to Spain.

He was eventually killed there by the people he was dealing with.

One of Sheehan's investigators was Bill McCoy, a former warrant officer 4 investigator with Army Criminal Investigation Division (CID).

McCoy contacted this writer in 1987. McCoy, seemingly a competent and experienced investigator, was committed to the investigation. He explained Mickey Tolliver's allegations and said he was looking for evidence to support them. He said he had no evidence other than Tolliver's story. He wanted to know whether the Baton Rouge Middle District task force investigation had developed any evidence that Seal was working for the CIA or had been flying supplies to the Contras from Mena.

McCoy was told there was no evidence that Seal was involved with the CIA or was linked to Tolliver.

About Judge James Lawrence King

James Lawrence King (born 1927) is one of the longest-serving federal judges in the US. Judge King received his BA from the University of Florida in 1949 and his LLB from the University of Florida School of Law in 1953.

From 1953 to May, 1955 he was lieutenant on active duty in the office of the Judge Advocate General, US Air Force.

He was in private practice until 1964. From 1964 to 1970 he was circuit judge in the 11th Judicial Court, Florida.

In 1970 he was appointed to the federal bench in the Southern District of Florida by President Richard Nixon. From September 1984 to September 1991, he was chief judge of the Southern District. He assumed senior status in 1992.

Source: Author research 2015.

On June 23, 1988, after several years of discovery and motions, Sheehan's RICO case came to an end.

US District Judge James Lawrence King signed an order granting summary judgments to the defendants.

In February 1989, Judge King awarded the defendants a total of $1,034,381.36 in attorney fees and costs.

Allegations that Barry Seal was connected to the CIA's Contra resupply program can be traced to Michael Tolliver and the RICO suit. They boil down to Tolliver's claim that Seal tried to recruit him to participate in a "covert" operation not further described.

Oddly enough, Sheehan didn't complain that the CIA was running their "guns-down, drugs-up" operation from the Mena airport with the knowledge and blessing of Bill Clinton, as many conspiracy advocates claim was the case.

Sheehan's silence in this regard was probably because Hillary Rodham Clinton's actions. When she was chairman of the Legal Services Corporation, she ordered that a $20,000 grant go to the Christic Institute.[2]

After March 28, 1984, the date of his letter of understanding with the DEA, Seal was involved in very little activity that didn't also include Ernst Jacobsen, Bob Joura, and other DEA agents.

US Marshals in Miami took Seal into custody on June 28, 1985, to begin serving his ten-year sentence — but it was not in a federal penitentiary.

Seal was kept in custody in a cell in the basement of the federal courthouse as a protected witness. While there, he was in regular contact with federal attorneys who were preparing to try the Norman Saunders case and other criminal cases in which Seal been involved.

Norman Saunders was chief minister of Turks and Caicos Islands. He was indicted in Miami on federal charges of conspiring to further drug-smuggling. He was taking payoffs to allow cocaine smugglers headed north to Florida to use the islands southeast of the Bahamas as a trans-shipment point and for refueling. He was convicted and sentenced to 8½ years.

On July 9, 1985, Seal began testifying in federal courts. On July 30, 1985, he was in a federal court in Miami testifying in the trial of Carlos A. "Lito" Bustamonte.

Bustamonte oversaw cocaine distribution in the Miami area for the Ochoas. He was convicted and given a 40-year sentence.

Beginning on August 19, 1985, Seal was in federal court in Las Vegas testifying in the trial of the *Reyes* drug case he had put together with the help of William Bottoms.

It would have been nearly physically impossible for Seal to have a meeting with Tolliver in "June or July of 1985" at a halfway house in Georgia without the knowledge and presence of his DEA handlers. No such meeting has ever been acknowledged or proven to have occurred.

One thing Sheehan's RICO suit did accomplish was to document the history of the C-123 cargo plane after Seal sold it back to Harry Doan.

Documents obtained by Sheehan through discovery provided evidence that Harry Doan owned the C-123 after Seal used it.

Doan subsequently sold the plane to the CIA on March 28, 1986, for $425,000. Payment was by a cashier's check from Udall Research Corporation made payable to Harry Doan. The cashier's check was paid for with a check drawn on account number 47363801 at the Sun Bank in Daytona Beach, Florida.[3] This was an account maintained by Southern Air Transport, a known CIA proprietary. The Udall Corporation was the company established by Richard Secord that ultimately purchased land and built an airstrip in Santa Elena, Costa Rica. It was to help the Contra supply effort.

Sheehan, like Terry Reed, wrote a book. He called it *The People's Advocate: The Life and History of America's Most Fearless Public Interest Lawyer.*

He has uncovered another conspiracy.

He lost his RICO suit because Judge King was "actively litigating against us since the very inception of our case, as an active and conscious operative of the CIA."[4]

What's his evidence?

Mitchell Rogovin, a deceased lawyer, told another lawyer, in confidence, that he attended a "training" for "CIA legal counsels" with Judge King.

When asked if he would respond, Judge King said he does not comment on cases he's heard or the lawyers involved.

Sheehan's RICO suit shined one of the earlier spotlights on Barry Seal.

Next: learn how one of Sheehan's investigators, Milton Gene Wheaton, unraveled the mysteries of Mena.

Chapter 23
Mister Wheaton

Another voice heard during the course of the Christic Institute litigation was that of Milton Gene Wheaton. He was a retired Army chief warrant officer who had been a CID investigator. He did some investigation for Daniel Sheehan.

Warrant Officers are the technical experts of the military. They have single specialty technical skills. They are made officers by a warrant. In the military pecking order, they stand between the senior enlisted ranks of non-commissioned officers, and commissioned officers. Many warrant officers in the Army fly helicopters. Some, like Wheaton, are investigators.

Wheaton was deposed by Sheehan between March 1 and March 8, 1988.

Wheaton did not seem to let the facts get in the way of his alleged investigation of Seal, Mena and the CIA.

Michael Haddigan, a reporter for the *Arkansas Gazette*, analyzed Wheaton's allegations in an article published on June 26, 1988.

Wheaton said Seal moved to Mena in 1982. And, after he became a government informant in 1984, Seal began flying missions out of Florida into Central America. He hauled weapons down and drugs back "under the control of the DEA and CIA."

According to Wheaton, Seal made Fred Hampton his associate and financially supported his company, Rich Mountain Aviation.

Fred Hampton told a different story. According to the Haddigan newspaper story, Hampton said Seal was strictly a customer. Hampton's company performed maintenance on six or eight of Seal's planes between 1981 and 1986. He said Seal paid cash for the work but was slow to pay. Seal owed him $13,000 at the time of his murder.

Wheaton said Seal bought an isolated piece of land near Nella. Seal and Fred Hampton built a two-thousand foot dirt landing strip and began training pilots for night takeoffs and landings. At the same time covert paramilitary training operations began there and continued into late 1987.

Haddigan wrote that Fred Hampton totally contradicted Wheaton. Hampton bought the land as an investment and for recreation. He planned to build a house there but never did. Hampton called Wheaton's speculation that the land was used for a private smuggling operation and had something to do with the Iran-Contra affair "totally ludicrous."

In his *Gazette* article, Haddigan reported that residents and law enforcement officers in Scott County where Nella is located said they noticed no unusual activity in the area. Colonel Tommy Goodwin, director of the Arkansas State Police was also quoted as saying he had "no knowledge" of military training or smuggling in the area.

William Bottoms had a lengthy telephone conversation with Gene Wheaton in March 1997. Wheaton said he had become aware of some of the things Bottoms said about him publicly which were critical. He wanted Bottoms to know he had been misrepresented on many occasions.

John Cummings is co-author with Terry Kent Reed of the book *Compromised: Clinton, Bush and the CIA.*

From time to time, Wheaton has claimed that he introduced Reed to Cummings at a party in Washington, DC. Bottoms had heard the same story and he asked Wheaton about it. Wheaton said it was true that he introduced the two. He assured Bottoms that he did not collaborate with Reed or Cummings on their book. Wheaton acknowledged that he had talked to Terry Reed and thought he had picked up a lot for his book from their conversations.

Wheaton made it clear that he thought much of Reed's story was fabricated.

Wheaton told Bottoms that Daniel Sheehan asked him to come to work for the Christic Institute, but he had turned down the offer. He said he wanted to remain independent and he did not agree with the Christic Institute's social and religious beliefs. He admitted that he had been reimbursed by the Christic Institute for expenses incurred while doing some investigative work that was directly related to RICO lawsuit.

Bottoms began to question Wheaton about his deposition in the Christic Institute case. Wheaton became evasive and said that, unless one had all of the hundreds of pages of his testimony, brief abstracts were misleading.

Bottoms asked Wheaton point-blank if he thought Seal flew guns for the CIA, laundered huge sums of money at Mena, or brought large quantities of drugs into Mena.

Wheaton answered, "No, Seal was a scapegoat."

Bottoms pointed out that Wheaton said otherwise in his depositions.

Wheaton responded that "context was not presented correctly."

In the final analysis, Gene Wheaton made it quite clear to Bottoms that he wanted to get on with his life and forget about depositions and Mena.

John Cummings repudiated Wheaton's story. He said he was aware of Wheaton's claim that he introduced him to Terry Reed but could never figure out why he would make the statement. Cummings said it was CID investigator Bill McCoy — not Gene Wheaton — who introduced him to Terry Reed.

A reading of Wheaton's deposition is fascinating. Here was a guy who just happened to be driving through Arkansas in December 1987 when he heard a radio newscast about an investigation going on concerning Barry Seal. The smuggler was murdered in 1986.

Wheaton went to the local radio station, talked to the newscaster and was put in touch with the Arkansas State Police. He then continued his trip to California but returned to Arkansas in January 1988. He met with Russell Welch of the Arkansas State Police and county attorney Chuck Black.

Wheaton said both men had been working on the investigation of Seal since 1982, but they did not quite understand the national and international implications concerning Seal's background.

Wheaton said the Arkansas State Police asked for his help. He worked with them for ten days then left on other business, only to return and work ten more days. At the time of his deposition, Wheaton said he was still working with Welch and Black.

Russell Welch contradicted Wheaton on every point. Welch said he had little contact with Wheaton and never asked him to do any investigating on behalf of the Arkansas State Police.

Retired Army Maj. Gen. John K. Singlaub, was one of the defendants in the Christic Institute suit. He described Wheaton as a former warrant officer whom Sheehan falsely claimed had been an intelligence officer.

Wheaton was paid $20,000 cash for expenses but failed to provide any substantiation for the major claims about Singlaub that Sheehan had attributed to him.[1]

Wheaton's testimony has also been characterized as "paid, rambling hearsay."[2]

The details of Wheaton's investigation are contained in Sheehan's affidavit where his identity is concealed and he is referred to as Source 24 and Source 48. "Basically, I found an operation there of guns-down, drugs-up out of Mena, modification of drug smuggler's aircraft, and paramilitary training operations going on there on a large scale."

This is the crux of Wheaton's tale but it is difficult, if not impossible, to determine exactly what he found independently.

It is extremely doubtful that Wheaton could have conducted much of an investigation during the twenty days he claimed to have worked for the Arkansas State Police.

Russell Welch has refuted that Wheaton worked there for the state police.

Wheaton surfaced again in 1995 when he approached the Assassination Records Review Board (ARRB) with information about the John F. Kennedy assassination.

Former FBI agent Anne Buttimer, the chief investigator for the ARRB, interviewed Wheaton. She reported: "Wheaton told me that from 1984 to 1987 he spent a lot of time in the Washington, DC area and that starting in 1985 he was 'recruited into Ollie North's network' by the CIA officer he has information about. He got to know this man and his wife, a 'super grade high-level CIA officer' and kept a bedroom in their Virginia home. His friend was a Marine Corps liaison in New Orleans and was the CIA contact with Carlos Marcello. Wheaton said he also got to know many of the Cubans who had been his friend's soldiers/operatives when the Cubans visited in Virginia from their homes in Miami. His friend and the Cubans confirmed to Wheaton they assassinated JFK."

Wheaton's friend was Carl Elmer Jenkins, a former Marine and CIA officer. He described Wheaton as, "a piece of work, a paranoid character of grandiosity and conspiracy. He's got to be in the middle of everything. Always seems to be one of these little guys on the fringe. . . everything is a conspiracy."[3]

Sheehan described Wheaton as a "former chief of security for the United States Marine Corps at Khe Sanh, and a former master sergeant in the United States Marine Corps CID."[4]

Retired FBI agent Earle G. Breeding was a US Marine captain

and the commanding officer of Echo Company, 2nd Battalion, 26th Marines in 1968 during the siege at Khe Sanh. He and his Marines withstood numerous attacks and held Hill 861A from January 1 to July 8, 1968. He was awarded the Silver Star.

Breeding said he never heard of Gene Wheaton. The only security at Khe Sanh he was aware of was provided by "our 45s, M-16s, hand grenades, mortars, machine guns, artillery and airstrikes."

At various times between 1999 and 2004, Gene Wheaton provided written documents to Matt Ehling of Public Record Media, a government transparency nonprofit organization.

The documents Wheaton gave to Ehling indicate that he was a chief warrant officer and an investigator in the US Army CID. From May 1971 to July 1973, he was narcotics and smuggling advisor of the US Military Mission in Iran, which was providing assistance to the Imperial Iranian Police. He received the Legion of Merit for this work. He subsequently conducted and supervised criminal investigations and physical security matters for the US Army Logistics Center at Cam Ranh Bay, Vietnam.

Documents obtained by the author from the National Personnel Records Center reveal Milton Gene Wheaton, Serial Number 1410325, enlisted in the Marine Corps July 16, 1953 at Oklahoma City. He was released from active duty July 15, 1956.

He served in Korea from approximately January 6, 1954, to February 1956 as a wireman in Headquarters & Service Company, 1st 90 mm. Anti-Aircraft Gun Battalion, 1st Marine Air Wing. He held the ranks private, private first class, corporal, and sergeant. He received the Korean Service Medal, United Nations Service Medal, and the Good Conduct Medal. He didn't have any trigger time because the Korean cease fire was signed July 27, 1953.

Notwithstanding, the vagaries in his assertions and the questionable authenticity of his Mena investigation, Gene Wheaton has sometimes been referred to as an authoritative "reliable source" on Barry Seal and what went on at Mena.

Wheaton is not an authoritative or a "reliable source" on Barry Seal and what went on at Mena.

Wheaton's conflicting record of military service and questions about his Mena investigations show otherwise.

Chapter 24
Terry Reed versus *Time* Magazine

Barry Seal was murdered in 1986. In 1994, *Compromised: Clinton, Bush and the CIA* was published. The book was the collaborative effort of Terry Kent Reed and John Cummings but the heart and soul of the book was the story told by Terry Reed.

The book was proclaimed to be an exposé that leveled serious charges of wrongdoing against the FBI and the CIA and implicated Bill Clinton. Congressman Jim Leach's investigation which began in 1996 was prompted, in part, by the publicity generated by the arrival of *Compromised*.

Was it nonfiction or fiction? A court battle between a co-author and a *Time* magazine reporter would show some details.

As Terry Reed's story unfolds we learn that the FBI introduced him to Oliver North who in turn put him in contact with Barry Seal, who then hired him to train Contra pilots in Arkansas.

When the pilot training program ended, Reed went to work for the CIA. He soon discovered that the agency was involved in a drugs-for-guns-conspiracy at Mena, Arkansas. It was said to be a covert effort that was being carried out with the knowledge and consent of then-Governor Bill Clinton. Most shocking of Reed's many claims was that Barry Seal told him he had evidence that President George H. W. Bush's sons were involved in drug trafficking.

Compromised was published six years after Senator John Kerry's committee reported that a few pilots who worked for the CIA to provide support to the Contras were also involved in drug smuggling.

This public information provided a factual basis upon which a story with some believability could be built.

Also available to make the story more palatable was the public information contained in Daniel Sheehan's RICO suit.

As Reed tells it, on March 12, 1983, he and his wife Janis were flying to Florida when their plane, a Piper Arrow, developed engine trouble.

Reed landed at the Joplin, Missouri, airport and took the plane to Mizzou Aviation for repair. Sometime between the evening of March 23 and the morning of the March 24, 1983, the plane turned up missing. Reed reported the theft to the Kansas City FBI office and to the local police then filed a claim with his insurance carrier.

Reed was eventually paid approximately $33,000, most which went to pay off a bank loan on the plane. This is a point emphasized in *Compromised* to show that money was not Reed's motive. This overlooks the fact that the payoff of the loan relieved Reed of a substantial debt.

When Reed reported the theft, the Kansas City FBI office opened an investigation and initially treated the matter as a case of interstate transportation of stolen aircraft.

In October 1987, a Little Rock private detective named Tommy Baker found a plane in a hangar at the North Little Rock, Arkansas airport. Baker's friend, Arkansas State Police Captain Raymond Young ran the serial number through the FBI's National Crime Information Center (NCIC) computer. Young had been Governor Bill Clinton's security chief.

The computer got a "hit."

The plane was Reed's missing Piper Arrow.

Further investigation by the FBI and local authorities established that the hangar where the plane was found had been rented in the names of Terry and Janis Kerr.

Kerr was the maiden name of Terry's wife.

The hangar was paid by Applied Technologies, Inc., a company the Reeds had an interest in.

Reed and his wife became logical suspects. Both were eventually indicted in Kansas for mail fraud because the US mails had been used to make the insurance claim.

This chain of events marked the beginning of an incredible government conspiracy. Reed claims the caper was all part of a CIA plot to punish and discredit him because he split from the agency.

Reed surrendered to the indictment in August 1988. He was released on bond and prepared to go to trial. He was represented by Marilyn Trubey, an attorney working in the Office of the Federal Public Defender. Reed contrived a bizarre but ultimately effective defense to the indictment. He claimed the theft and reappearance of his plane was all part of a plot hatched by the CIA and Oliver North.

Reed said that he had been an intelligence asset of the FBI and had been introduced to Oliver North by Ed Enright, who was the special agent in charge of the FBI's Oklahoma City office when the meeting occurred.

Reed alleged that Oliver North had set up a secret resupply network for the Contras and had asked Reed to donate his plane to the cause. It was dubbed Project Donation. Reed was told a CIA-controlled insurance company covered the loss. No one would suffer financially—and the Contras would benefit. Still, Reed declined to donate his plane.

As Reed tells it, Oliver North was so impressed with his expertise in intelligence matters gained as an Air Force "intelligence officer" that he sent Barry Seal to meet him. Seal ultimately hired Reed to train Contra pilots in Arkansas. Reed claimed to have trained a dozen or so Latino pilots at Seal's private airstrip at Nella, Arkansas—until North canceled the project. Reed was then hired by the CIA and sent to Mexico to set up an international trading company that was to be used as a front to smuggle weapons to the Contras, he claimed.

When he learned that the CIA was also using the front company to smuggle cocaine into the United States, he resigned in anger. His defection from the ranks of the spooks was the reason the CIA was out to get him, he claimed.

The foregoing account, though greatly condensed, is the essence of *Compromised* and it also constituted Terry Reed's defense of the federal mail fraud indictment.

In preparation for his trial, Reed through his attorney, issued subpoenas to a lengthy list of witnesses, many of whom were associated with federal law enforcement and intelligence agencies. The government responded by invoking the Classified Information Procedures Act and moved to quash most of the subpoenas.

There was a lot of maneuvering on both sides, but in the end the case never went to trial.

Terry Reed, Janis Kerr, a Stolen Plane and CIA plot

In 1990, the case was submitted to US District Judge Frank Theis for a decision based on the following list of stipulated facts:
• **The plane was left at Mizzou Aviation** at the Joplin, Missouri airport March 12, 1983 for repair.

The plane disappeared between March 23 and March 24, 1983.
• **Reed has evidence he was** in Kansas City, Missouri, March 23 and 24, 1983.
• The government has no evidence anyone acting as Reed's agent took the plane.
• A loss claim in the amount of approximately $33,000 was paid, with the majority of the insurance proceeds going to the lienholder, Lakeshore Bank of Oklahoma City, Oklahoma.
• **The hangar was owned by** Bill Canino, whose records reflect the hangar was rented in the name of Terry and Janis Kerr.
• The rent was paid by Applied Technologies, Inc., a company whose interests were held by Terry and Janis Kerr.
• Terry Reed did not sign a lease on the hangar and did not sign checks for payment of the rent.
• **There is no evidence that Terry Reed** had knowledge of the hangar lease or the rent payments.

Being tried on a set of stipulated facts was a very good deal for Reed and a no-brainer for Judge Theis. The judge is characterized in *Compromised* as sleeping with his secretary and having narcolepsy. The stipulated facts were circumstantial at best and contained scant evidence of guilt. This provided Judge Theis with little choice but to order a directed verdict of "acquittal" for Terry Reed. Following the verdict, the charges against his wife Janis were dismissed.

Reed was overjoyed with the verdict, but he was likely a bit miffed with the FBI for building a case against him when he had once been one of their assets.

Reed retaliated by filing a lawsuit against Raymond Young and Tommy Baker in Federal District Court in the Western District of Arkansas. Reed and his wife basically alleged that the two had violated their civil rights by conspiring to conduct an unconstitutional search and seizure and had deliberately given false testimony that resulted in the Reeds' federal indictment for mail fraud.

Reed stuck with the game plan that he had used to successfully defend himself and his wife against the mail fraud indictment. Reed filed a tome-length list of witnesses that contained 120 individual names or entities.

The fact that Gene Wheaton's name appears on the List of Witnesses and is footnoted in *Compromised* is significant because it indicates that Reed was aware of the RICO suit filed by Sheehan in the Southern District of Florida on May 26, 1986. The suit was a public record that included Sheehan's affidavit. It contained a summary of Wheaton's deposition concerning Seal's activities at Mena. Wheaton's tale would obviously help substantiate Reed's allegations.

The *Arkansas Gazette* had also reported and analyzed Wheaton's allegations in an article written by Michael Haddigan that was published on June 26, 1988. Therefore, there were two public sources from which Reed could have learned about Gene Wheaton and his allegations about Seal's activities at Mena.

The inclusion of Homer "Red" Hall on the list of witnesses is even more noteworthy. The only public mention of Homer "Red" Hall and his involvement with Barry Seal is found in the report of *Oversight Hearings before the Subcommittee on Crime of the Committee on the Judiciary, July 28, September 23, 29 and October 5, 1988*. A chronology of "Seal's role" contains a notation for July 7, 1984: "Homer "Red" Hall claims to have seen the C-123 on the ground at Los Brasiles"[1] The report is a public document that has been available through the Government Printing Office since 1989.

"Red" Hall said he remembered that he once received a call from a man who said he was Terry Reed and who said something about his plane being stolen by the CIA. Hall didn't know who Reed was and didn't have the slightest clue as to what he was talking about except that it had something to do with a lawsuit.

Hall is sure that neither Seal nor himself knew or met anyone named Terry Reed.

Reed's first suit against Baker and Young was dismissed on the motion of his attorney. A second suit alleging basically the same complaints was filed in September 1994. The attorneys for Young and Baker answered by filing a motion to exclude many of the allegations, assertions and the subject matter that was raised by Reed and incorporated into his first petition. In March of 1996, US District Judge George Howard, Jr., signed an order granting the motion to limit. The material ordered excluded by the judge was referred to as the "Mena evidence."

The excluded "Mena evidence" was: "Any reference to the plaintiff's participation in programs, operations or missions sponsored by the Federal Bureau of Investigation or the Central Intelligence Agency or any other agency of the United States government, covert or otherwise, as well as any organization sponsored by or aligned with the United States government specifically including but not limited to, any programs, operations or missions conducted in southwest Arkansas regarding training of Nicaraguan nationals, the funding and support for any factions involved in the Nicaraguan conflict and any contact or communications with operatives or officials of the above-named agencies or organizations, any reference to President Bill and/or Hillary Clinton and the Mena or Nella airports, any references to Barry Seal, and any alleged drug smuggling operation or other reference to the Mena and Nella airports or to a business relationship of Barry Seal and Dan Lasater, Lasater and Company and the Arkansas Development and Finance Authority (ADFA) and ADFA's former Director, Bob Nash."

The second suit was dismissed when Reed's attorney "with great reluctance" filed a motion for voluntary dismissal in May 1996. Attached to the motion was a lengthy and self-serving statement prepared by Terry Reed which basically claimed that the order protected the "scoundrels," and prevented him from going to trial and proving Young and Baker are "simply bad cops hiding behind tarnished badges and taking instructions from corrupt power-brokers and politicians who likewise should be prosecuted and forced from office to an awaiting prison cell."

The authors of *Compromised* took Judge Howard to task for the order gutting Reed's lawsuit. By doing so, they said he was exposing the "strings to which he is attached. . . strings that are obviously being pulled from Washington, and more significantly, the White House." In other words, Reed was still complaining that he was the victim of a vast government conspiracy that existed to protect the CIA, Oliver North, Bill Clinton, and the FBI and now Judge Howard was part of it.

One truth in *Compromised* is Terry Reed's claim that he was once an "asset" of the Oklahoma City division of the FBI. As he explains it, the relationship came about because he was a salesman and company pilot for Northwest Industries, Inc., a company involved in the sale of machine tools. At a Chicago trade show in 1980, he discovered a Hungarian machinery display was soliciting trading partners, and he helped establish his company as trading partner to the Hungarians. Because of his job, he was in a position to provide intelligence information and possibly "monitor" KGB "moles" within the trading company who were operating within the United States. His boss put him in touch with the FBI, and he spent sixteen months helping the FBI by monitoring the Hungarians and their interest in sophisticated machine tools.

Reed's FBI handler was special agent Wayne "Buzz" Barlow who assumed the undercover role of being Reed's copilot at Northwest Industries.

Barlow, now retired from the FBI, has a slightly different take on Terry Reed. He confirmed that Reed helped the FBI to monitor foreign government interest in sophisticated machine tools capable of multi-axis milling operations, and he recalled going on one flight with Reed. He remembers that the FBI did assist Reed in obtaining clearance from the Air Force to travel to Hungry as Reed claims in his book. Reed made one trip to Hungary after the clearance was obtained, and then left Northwest Industries to form his own business.

In Barlow's judgment, Terry Reed is a "truly brilliant guy" who basically spent three years in Mexico creating the story told in *Compromised*. He noted that there is enough truth and fact woven into the book to make it plausible—but much of it is embellished or is made up. As an example, Barlow said he did have Terry and his wife, Janis, over to his house for a cocktail party. However, he didn't throw the party to celebrate their marriage, as Reed claims. Barlow invited the president and vice president of Northwest Industries to the same party, and it was done to help Reed with his efforts on behalf of the FBI.

Reed claims he was introduced to Lt. Colonel Oliver North in the conference room of the Oklahoma City FBI office by Ed Enright, who was the special agent in charge of the office during the time he (Reed) was an asset. Reed said North was using the cover name John Cathey and told him he would be contacted by someone who was going to ask for his help with a covert government operation. When the contact was subsequently made, it was by none other than Barry Seal.

Ed Enright, now retired from the FBI, said Oliver North was never in the Oklahoma City office while he was special agent in charge and he did not introduce Oliver North to Terry Reed. He and "Buzz" Barlow are absolutely certain that Oliver North never visited the Oklahoma City office of the FBI and never met Terry Reed.

Co-author John Cummings had handwritten notes belonging to Barry Seal that contained numerous references to "JC." He viewed the notes as being proof of Seal's connection with Oliver North because

Reed said North used the code name John Cathey. Close but no cigar. Oliver North used the alias "John Clancey.[2] He was also "Wagner," "Steelhammer," "Paul," and "Mr. West." But his preferred alias, the one used on his false passport, was "William P. Goode."[3]

The "JC" in the notes Cummings has refers to John Cary, a pilot and the owner of Fort Worth Aviation, Fort Worth, Texas. He is the same John Cary that was prosecuted and convicted in 1991 in the case of *United States v. Julio Maceo, Hiram Lee Bauman, John Cary and Pedro Talamas*. In December 1982, Cary provided a Beech Baron 58 airplane to a gang of smugglers in exchange for two kilograms of cocaine. In early 1983, Cary sold a Piper Navajo with extra fuel tank capacity to the same group. Cary got a twelve-year sentence which was appealed and upheld by the Fifth Circuit. (947 F2d 1191).

Seal knew Cary and they communicated by telephone regularly. Seal made several trips to Fort Worth and in early January 1984 Cary came to Baton Rouge and stayed at Howard Johnson motel and met with Seal. Cary acted as broker on several airplanes purchased by Seal and he leased Seal a Beech King Air N1860. The handwritten notes concern the planes leased and the money that Seal owed to Cary.

Reed is characterized as having been an Air Force "intelligence officer" and that added to his credibility.

Technically he was not an officer. His rank was staff sergeant and, as such, he was a non-commissioned officer (NCO). He didn't have access to the Officer's Club or even their latrine, and he didn't rate a salute, nor did he wear bars, stars, or oak leafs. His military occupational specialty was aerial photo interpreter. He received an Air Force Commendation Medal for meritorious service as an imagery interpretation specialist. Reed was assigned to the Targets Section, Exploitation Branch of the 432nd Reconnaissance Technical Squadron at Udorn Royal Thai Air Force Base, Thailand. A copy of the citation that is included in *Compromised* indicates that he was at Udorn from February 4, 1974, to January 23, 1975, which was his second tour of duty in Southeast Asia.

Reed's first tour of duty in Southeast Asia took him to Nakhon Phanom Royal Thai Air Force Base, Thailand. A copy of a performance report found in *Compromised* indicates he was at Nakhon Phanom, at least between September 16, 1969 and March 17, 1970, the period for which his performance was being rated. At that time, he was a buck sergeant, and a photo interpreter and shift supervisor over other photo interpreters.

Reed's duties were directed toward studying aerial photographs in an effort to identify targets on the infamous Ho Chi Minh Trail.

The book, *Nam, The Vietnam Experience*, contains a detailed account of what went on at Nakhon Phanom Royal Thai Air Force Base. The Ho Chi Minh Trail was little more than a network of footpaths and US planes had difficulty finding anything of value to bomb. To find targets on the trail, the US military went high tech and began airdropping sensor devices. They were called by such names as Spikebuoy, Acoubuoy, Adsid and Acusid. The Spikebuoy employed sonar technology modified for use on land. When dropped, it hit the ground and buried most of its body and then deployed an aerial. It was battery-powered and tuned to particular sound frequencies that would pick up and broadcast to an airplane circling above. Adsid was the most widely used and was also a free-fall device that buried itself in the ground and then deployed a four-foot antenna. Adsid's battery operated radio transmitter was pre-set to transmit vibrations such as those from a passing truck.

The decision on where to drop the sensor devices was based on intelligence gleaned from observation flights of the kind once flown in his RF-4C by FBI agent O. T. Eubank, alias "Rex Eggleston."

Once the sensors were in place the data was transmitted to a Lockheed EC-121R Warning Star from the 553rd Reconnaissance Wing that circled above. The problem was that the EC-121R was vulnerable to enemy fire. The Air Force solved the vulnerability problem under the Pave Eagle program, by deploying the QU-22, an unmanned plane. This secret aircraft acted as an intermediate relay station and passed the transmissions being received from the sensors on to the EC-121 that was orbiting out of range of the North Vietnamese anti-aircraft guns and SAM missiles.

The nucleus of this operation was the top-secret Infiltration Surveillance Center (ISC) at Nakhon Phanom air base, which was run by the Air Force's Task Force Alpha. This was the unit to which Terry Reed, then a sergeant, was assigned on his first tour of duty in Southeast Asia. The Ho Chi Minh Trail surveillance operation, code name Igloo White, is what Task Force Alpha was all about. Terry Reed had a top-secret clearance because he worked in ISC as an aerial photo interpreter.

It is difficult to accept as true that Reed's job would make him an "intelligence officer" and give him access to first-hand knowledge of deep, dark government secrets and CIA "black ops" that was not directly related to his job of locating targets on the Ho Chi Minh Trail.

Need-to-know and compartmentalization are two of the principal methods of maintaining secrecy in civilian and military intelligence matters.

In the midst of the 1992 presidential primary race, Reed tried to peddle part of his then-unpublished story to *Time* magazine. The main selling point was his claim that the Democratic front-runner Bill Clinton, while governor of Arkansas, had been personally involved in the Reagan administration's scheme to arm the Contras and had worked with Oliver North. After hearing Reed's tale, the editors assigned investigative reporter Richard Behar to the story.

Behar worked most of March 1992 conducting interviews with more than thirty witnesses and sources in an attempt to verify Reed's assertions. He spoke with representatives of five companies where Reed had once been employed. Two sources told him Reed had attempted to steal money or equipment from their companies. Behar said later that he found, in the comments he collected, the common theme was that Reed was a "psychopathic liar."

Reed was interviewed in his home in Moorpark, California, by Behar, who said he gained the impression that Reed was a highly intelligent person who gave intricately detailed accounts of places he supposedly had been and conversations he purportedly had. Reed gave him an elaborate flow chart depicting the relationships between alleged participants in the Mena operation, with Clinton at the top of the chart. Reed claimed to have met with Clinton in the "mobile command post" while he was governor and watched him "do a joint." Reed claimed he was told not to be concerned about Barry Seal's death because "Barry had gotten way out of line."

Behar interviewed Marilyn Trubey, Reed's appointed public defender. She told him that during the entire time she was defending Reed in the mail fraud criminal case, he never mentioned that Bill Clinton was involved in the Mena affair and that, if Reed was now making such allegations, she would be "wary."

When Reed sued Tommy Baker and Raymond Young in federal court, he was represented by attorney John Wesley Hall. While working on his *Time* article, Behar had several phone conversations with Hall and when he interviewed Reed in person, Hall was present. While working on the defense of Reed's suit against him and *Time*, Behar obtained a sworn declaration from Hall in which he stated: "In our telephone conversations Mr. Behar several times stated that he did not believe the story that Mr. Reed told him. At one point Mr. Behar asked me whether I had generally found Mr. Reed to be credible. I responded that 'I haven't been able to corroborate him. That's the problem.'"

Behar talked to Arkansas businessman Seth Ward Sr. whom Reed said had used Park-O-Meter, a parking meter company he controlled, to make parts for M-16 rifles that were being shipped to the Contras. Ward called the allegations "preposterous" and "the most far-fetched, asinine thing I've heard in my life."

Mark McAfee, the owner of a Little Rock company named Arkansas Machine Tools, once employed Terry Reed. McAfee told Behar that when Reed arrived, he announced that if he were ever to disappear it was "because probably the CIA was trying to kill him." When McAfee asked why the CIA would do such a thing, Reed said it was because he knew that the United States had actually bombed American POWs in Vietnam.

Mark McAfee described the stories told by Reed as being "like a fantasy story. I'm not a psychiatrist, but I think he's like a kid, a little child that lies, you know. And he lies to cover up his lies."

According to McAfee, before Reed skipped town in 1986, he cheated McAfee's company out of nearly $100,000. "He's a real good con man," said McAfee.

Reporter Behar looked into Reed's involvement with a Houston company called Japan Machine Tools. The company president, Roy Yamaji, said that Reed once visited a customer and picked up a check for $85,000 payable to Japan Machine Tools. Instead of delivering the check to Houston as promised, Reed altered it by typing in the words "Terry Reed c/o" in front of "Japan Machine Tools" and then cashed it. Reed later explained that he just needed money for a short time and would repay it. Reed eventually repaid the money with funds that Yamaji speculated came from a company called Gomiya.

Yamaji explained that in 1986, Reed had brokered a deal between Gomiya and an Arkansas firm that agreed to purchase one of Gomiya's machine tools for approximately $386,000. Reed structured the transaction so that the customer would make payment to Applied Technologies, Inc., a firm controlled by Reed. Gomiya was to bill Applied Technologies which would remit to Gomiya an amount less than an agreed-upon commission. Reed followed the procedure with the customer's initial 10 percent down payment, withholding his commission and sending the balance to Gomiya. When Reed received the balance of $331,000, however, he wired it to an out-of-state bank account he controlled and skipped town. In the days that followed, Reed kept Gomiya at bay by continually moving money in and out of different banks. Gomiya went after Reed and in December 1987, the company got a default judgment against him for the full amount plus $100,000 in punitive damages.

Richard Behar is castigated by Cummings and Reed for "powder-puff" questioning of Oliver North as he attempted to verify Reed's story. Partial extracts from Behar's recorded telephone interview with North were included in *Compromised.*

North said he never met or spoke to Reed.

The authors did not include some relevant responses made by North to Behar's questions. Behar made them available to the author:

What Oliver North Said about Contras, Mena

Behar: You didn't introduce him [Terry Reed] to Barry Seal?
North: No.
Mr. Behar: And you didn't steal his airplane?
Mr. North: No. He stole his airplane, didn't he?
Mr. Behar: Well, he was acquitted.
The authors included this portion of the interview:
Behar: Was anything going on at Mena?
North: At who?
Behar: Mena, Arkansas having to do with the Contras?
North: I haven't been there. I can't imagine that anything is going on at Mena with Contras since they are all out of business.
The conversation continued:
Behar: No, I mean through the eighties, did Mena ever factor into anything to do with—
North: You're mentioning a word that is coming to my attention for the first time that I can recall.
Behar: Really, the town of Mena, Arkansas?
North: Yeah.
Behar: Wow.
North: I don't remember ever hearing the name before. I may have, but I don't remember it. What happened at Mena?

Cummings and Reed complained that Behar never asked Oliver North the "key" question of whether or not he knew Barry Seal.

From this they concluded that Behar did not want any real answers.

This writer, also looking for an answer to the "key" question, submitted it along with a few other "powder-puff" questions to Colonel North through his attorney, Nicole Seligman. He answered them on March 17, 2000:

What Oliver North Told the Author about Barry Seal

Hahn: Did you ever meet Barry Seal?
North: No.
Hahn: Did you ever meet Terry Reed?
North: No.
Hahn: Have you ever been in the Oklahoma City FBI office and been introduced to Terry Reed by Ed Enright?
North: No.
Hahn: Do you know FBI agent Barlow?
North: No.
Hahn: Have you ever heard of Project Donation?
North: No.
Hahn: Did you ever task Barry Seal to train Contra pilots at Nella, Arkansas?
North: No.
Hahn: Have you ever been to Nella or Mena?
North: No.

After completing his research, Richard Behar wrote an article entitled *"Anatomy of a Smear."* The article, which appeared in the April 20, 1992, issue of *Time*, called Reed a liar. Reed responded by filing a libel suit in the Southern District of New York in the case titled *Terry K. Reed v. Time Warner, Inc., Time Inc. Magazine Company, and Richard Behar* No. 93-Civ. 2249.

The defendants, *Time*, the parent company, and Richard Behar moved for summary judgment.

In May 1994, the judge issued an interim memorandum and order reserving decision on the motion for summary judgment. The delay was granted to allow Reed's attorneys to take the deposition of Bill Duncan, who had been interviewed several times by Behar during his investigation of Reed's story. Consequently, fortune and circumstances combined to give Bill Duncan another opportunity to present the "evidence" that he told Congress proved the Mena airport was an important hub/waypoint for transshipment of drugs and covert operations by Barry Seal, his associates, and both employees and contract operatives of the US intelligence services [CIA].

On January 5, 1995, presiding Judge Whitman Knapp granted the defendant's motion for summary judgment and dismissed the complaint, ruling that author Terry Reed had no proof that reporter Richard Behar acted either with actual malice or gross irresponsibility in researching, writing or publishing the article.

In his written memorandum and order, the judge made a noteworthy comment about Duncan's deposition, a deposition which Reed claimed would corroborate his claims. The judge wrote that Duncan "acknowledged that he had no evidence to support his belief" of Reed and that the "deposition and its accompanying documents did no such thing. Rather they reveal a witness who believes plaintiff wholeheartedly, but can, by his own admission, provide no corroboration for plaintiff's stories."

There is credible evidence that Terry Reed never met Oliver North or Barry Seal.

North said he never met Reed or Seal. Former Oklahoma City special agent in charge Ed Enright said he did not introduce Reed to North as Reed claims he did.

Two of Seal's confidants, William Bottoms and Red Hall, are both certain they never heard of Terry Reed during the entire time they were associated with Barry Seal,.

There are discrepancies in Reed's story that are difficult to believe or to explain away plausibly.

According to Reed, he spent the month of December 1983 getting better acquainted with Barry Seal through "repeated telephone conversations" and during personal visits in Little Rock.

The truth is Barry Seal was under FBI surveillance the entire month of December 1983, and the Title III wiretap was operating during the same time period. He did not talk to anybody identifiable as Terry Reed. Seal was in Baton Rouge most of that month. He made trips in his Lear jet N13SN to Miami, Panama City, Atlanta, Augusta, Ft. Worth, El Paso, and San Jose, but none to Little Rock.

Russell Welch said sometime in 1988 or 1989 he was ordered to go to the Little Rock office of the DEA to examine the contents of approximately twenty-eight boxes containing Seal's personal documents that had been seized by the IRS. Welch told his supervisor that he didn't have time to do it, but he was told to drop whatever he was doing and take as long as necessary to look at every piece of paper in those boxes. Welch said he spent two to three weeks at DEA headquarters in Little Rock looking at the material. The documents consisted of a wide assortment of Seal's personal papers — old bank statements and canceled checks going back to the 1960s.

Welch said he did not see a single piece of paper that associated Seal with Terry Reed, Oliver North, Bill Clinton, the CIA or the Contras. The only items of mild interest to him were a single "lid" of marijuana and a ticket to the Baton Rouge Police Department annual policeman's ball.

Reed crashed while flying in an ultralight plane on April 1, 1984. He said two days later, on April 3, that Seal paid him a visit in the Little Rock hospital where he was recovering. On April 3, Seal was in Miami briefing DEA agents and complaining to Bob Joura about the subpoenas being served on his associates in Baton Rouge.

From late 1982 until 1985, State Police, DEA, FBI, and US Customs agents were investigating the airport in Mena and no one heard anything about anyone named Terry Reed being at the airport or being associated with Seal.

Russell Welch spent over three years investigating Barry Seal and his associates in Mena, Arkansas and he believes that Terry Reed's story is a fabrication.

Apparently Reed didn't even know where Mena was because Welch has said that John Cummings was in his office in 1990 talking on a telephone to Reed trying to explain to him how to get to Mena.

As Welch sees it, Reed gained some information from the few files he let him review and he talked to Bill Duncan and then to Jack Blum, who was working for the Senate Foreign Relations Committee. From these conversations he learned enough to be able to "weave Barry Seal into his story."

Reed's gained some credibility with his one-time status as an FBI asset combined with a limited knowledge of specialized intelligence procedures gained while serving as an aerial photo interpreter in the Air Force. This better enabled him to convince his co-author, John Cummings, that his story was authentic.

There is enough believable evidence to conclude that Reed's story is nothing more than an imaginative and resourceful weave of rumors, half-truths, public information, stolen aircraft reports, allegations contained in a RICO suit, and information developed during Senator Kerry's hearing.

Extrusions, Inc.

Highway 69 South
Post Office Box 430
Fort Scott, Kansas 66701

316-223-1111
FAX 316-223-1139

March 30, 1994

TO WHOM IT MAY CONCERN:

In response to the statements contained in a book entitled "Compromised:
Clinton, Bush and the CIA" by Terry Reed, I would like to make the following
comments.

I noticed that, at the beginning of the book, Terry Reed stated that he
included me among the people whom he admired. Reed should not have included
me for whereas I have lived an honest, truthful life, Terry Reed, on the other
hand, is an obvious psychopathic liar.

I have known Seth Ward and his family intimately for forty years. I first
met Seth Ward in 1954 when he was employed by Delta Metals, Inc. in Dallas, Texas.
Since that time our families have become personal friends and Seth and I have been
partners in several business ventures. Seth has always conducted himself above
reproach, both personally and in business.

Terry Reed first worked for my company, Extrusions, Inc. selling shower
stall doors and he seemed to be an alert young man and a good salesman. Therefore, sometime in 1982 or 1983, when I became aware of a small ultra lite airplane
manufacturing company that was for sale, I asked Seth Ward to join me in the
venture of purchasing and manufacturing these ultra lites, and I recommended
Terry Reed to manage the operation. At first our plans were to locate the
operation in Kansas, but subsequent events required me to ask Seth if he could
locate it in Little Rock, to which he agreed. Thus the venture, known as
Command Aire Manufacturing Company, was in operation in Little Rock for
approximately one year with Terry Reed in charge. I would be the first to
agree with Seth Ward that the operation, though expensive, was a complete
failure. Toward the end of the operation, Terry Reed resigned, but he first
withdrew the money remaining in the company's bank account. He also removed
several proprietary items and Seth had to seek the assistance of the prosecuting
attorney to force Terry Reed to return these items. It is rather apparent that
Terry Reed has developed a strong, personal grudge and hatred toward Mr. Ward as
a result of being confronted with these misappropriations.

Terry Reed's statements concerning the use of Seth Ward's daughter Sally's
horse ranch as a drop point for Barry Seal's money and drugs is preposterous.
I am personally familiar with the Triple S Horse Ranch, its size, location, etc.,
and it would have been impossible for this small horse pasture to have been used
for such purposes. The method he mentioned for jettisoning the contraband would
would have been aerodynamically impossible. His description of Seth Ward and his
son is equally ridiculous. Seth Ward's son, Skeeter, has never owned or operated
a failing business. Seth is not 6' 4", but 6' 1", and his son is not 5' 6", but
5' 11". Furthermore, during the period of time, roughly a year, that Reed was
associated with Command Aire, we kept track of Reed's activities and whereabouts,
and they certainly did not include trips with Barry Seal or to the Mena Airport.

CUSTOM ALUMINUM EXTRUDER • ELECTROSTATIC PAINTING • ANODIZING • FABRICATING

Page 2

I am also very familiar with P.O.M., Inc. manufacturing company which
Skeeter Ward has operated for thirteen years, and has been the sole owner
since Mr. Ward was injured in an accident five years ago. I am personally
familiar with the company, its equipment, and its products, and the allegations
that it provided arms for the Contras are totally absurd and obviously a result
of Terry Reed's personal vendetta toward Seth Ward.

Sincerely,

J. A. Ida

Company owner Joe Ida questioned truthfulness of Terry Reed.

In *Compromised*, Reed mentioned J. A. "Joe" Ida and described him as being a person he admired who owned an aluminum extrusion company in Kansas where he once worked as a "flying salesman." According to Reed, Joe Ida immediately took note of his "industrious, disciplined work ethics" and took him under his wing.

Joe Ida's friend Seth Ward, Sr., a Little Rock businessman, owned a company named P. O. M, Inc., which was managed by his son, Seth "Skeeter" Ward, II. Reed claimed that P. O. M., Inc. was secretly manufacturing rifle parts for the CIA. Reed also alleged that Barry Seal was using Seth Ward's daughter Sally's horse ranch as a drop site for cash and drugs.

While preparing to defend Reed's lawsuit, reporter Richard Behar obtained a letter from Joe Ida. This letter contains insightful commentary on the truthfulness of parts of the story told by Terry Reed. The letter is dated March 30, 1994, and is addressed to "To Whom It May Concern."

Joe Ida was contacted by this writer in June 2003 and said that he stands by everything in the letter he wrote about Terry Reed.

When Richard Behar completed his *Time* investigation he concluded that Terry Reed was not truthful. He demolished Terry Reed's credibility while attempting to corroborate the very story he was trying to interest *Time* in publishing.

Behar's investigation was thorough and included interviews with people who knew Terry Reed and had personal experiences with him. In his written declaration prepared in defense of Terry Reed's libel suit, Richard Behar accurately and succinctly made the following assertion: "I concluded without hesitation that Terry Reed is a charlatan, and that his tales about Bill Clinton, Oliver North and the CIA were nothing but fiction. Moreover, it was clear to me that Reed had concocted his story as an alibi for the various cons he had pulled off over the years."

Reed lost his libel suit against *Time* and Richard Behar, but he bounced back and co-authored *Compromised*.

Chapter 25
"N Number" Games

This is the story about how cryptic "N numbers" on airplanes helped prove or disprove legends and rumors about Barry Seal and those who spun the legends.

Airplanes from the United States have an "N" as a first letter designator because that is the code assigned to North America. Other countries have different first letter designators. The N numbers are the publicly displayed numbers that appear on the sides of the fuselage of an airplane. They are the equivalent of license plates on cars. They are assigned by the Federal Aviation Agency. And they are public records.

Serial numbers are assigned by the manufacturer and are different numbers from the N numbers. While N numbers on a plane may change, serial numbers are permanent.

Author Terry Reed provided his co-author John Cummings with "evidence" to back up his story that he trained Contra pilots in planes provided by Barry Seal.

Reed said Seal provided him with different airplanes to use in the training program. He would use a plane for a while and then it would be replaced.

Reed said he kept track of the N numbers and the serial numbers of each plane that Seal sent to him. Reed gave Cummings an N number and a serial number for each of the seven planes he said Seal had provided for his training program.

Cummings gave the information to his friend, Jerry Bohnen, an investigative reporter for radio station WTOK in Oklahoma City. Bohnen checked the N numbers and determined they were legitimate numbers that belonged on planes of the same make and year as described by co-author Reed. The planes were scattered about the country and were not stolen.

Then the story seemed to change.

When Bohnen had the serial numbers checked by Bob Collins, manager of the International Aviation Theft Bureau, the serial numbers were all found to be from stolen aircraft of the same make and year.

By golly, Reed must be telling the truth.

Finding out that the serial numbers provided by Reed were from stolen aircraft went a long way toward corroborating Reed's story as far as Cummings was concerned. It was "evidence" that Reed was telling the truth, and it dovetailed nicely with the Project Donation story.

Project Donation is the name given to the program Reed said Oliver North wanted him to participate in — donate his plane. The plane would go to assist the Contras. Nobody would lose any dough. The CIA had created an insurance fund to take care of the losses.

All seven of the planes Reed said Seal provided to him were stolen between 1983 and 1985. They were reported stolen to various law enforcement agencies, insurance carriers and to the International Aviation Theft Bureau.

The International Aviation Theft Bureau ceased to exist in 1986. It is now called the Aviation Crime Prevention Institute (ACPI).

Bob Collins was still the manager when he was contacted by this author. He confirmed that all of the serial numbers of the seven stolen planes listed in their book *Compromised* were contained in the database maintained by ACPI. Collins has since died.

ACPI has three newsletters: the quarterly Alert Bulletin, the monthly Intel Brief, and the monthly Avionics Hot List. Theft alerts, reward offers and reports of stolen planes are regularly sent to airports in the general region of where a theft occurred. Insurance companies are known to publicize thefts in hopes of recovering the aircraft. Some owners place classified ads seeking information and offering rewards for the recovery of stolen aircraft.

Terry Reed is a pilot who had the knowledge and access to all of these sources. He could easily find seven stolen aircraft reports. The stolen reports, of necessity, contained the make, model, N number, and serial number of the aircraft.

Once he got the serial numbers of seven stolen planes from theft reports, all Reed would have to do is find seven identical planes that were not stolen and swap their N numbers. That is how he created his list of planes.

The manufacturers of the planes Reed claimed he used to train

Contra pilots were Piper, Cessna, Beechcraft, and Rockwell. Those four companies manufacture most of the airplanes sold in the US. Their planes can be found at private airports anywhere in the country.

Another source would be *Trade-A-Plane* magazine and several other aviation-related publications that regularly carry plane for-sale ads, many times accompanied by photographs with the N numbers visible. Several Web sites list planes for sale. And there is an FAA site where ownership information can be obtained by N number.

Compromised contains an explicit and laboriously detailed account of a flight Reed said he took with Seal in his Lear jet, N13SN.

The event began with a phone call from Seal on Friday evening, December 13, 1985.

We will accept this date as accurate because Reed tells us in the introduction to his book that he was a "paid intelligence professional" who was recruited, in part, because of his ability to "organize and retain facts and events."

According to the book, Seal called to invite Reed to fly with him to Panama to meet his CIA handler.

Seal gave him a coded message containing the details of the planned flight. When it was deciphered, Reed learned he was to be in his own plane flying on the 90-degree radial of the Monticello, Arkansas, VOR, at an altitude of 3,500 feet at 4:00 am Saturday, December 14, 1985. That's where and when he would intercept Seal.

Reed is using pilot lingo. VOR stands for Very High Frequency Omnidirectional Range, and VORs are the mainstay of a nationwide radio navigational system for aircraft. The United States is covered with a network of VORs and airways are defined by air routes between VORs. Visualize the VOR as a compass on the ground.

Reed was to fly at an altitude of 3,500 feet above the Monticello, Arkansas, VOR on the 90-degree arm of the compass. He did as he was told, and at exactly 0400 hours on Saturday, December 14, 1985, he made the rendezvous with Seal, who was flying a Cessna.

To avoid surveillance, Seal flew on to Love Field, Dallas. Reed flew to Greenville, Mississippi, where he landed and waited on the ground until he was sure he had "dry-cleaned" himself from surveillance. Then he took off and flew to Drake Field, Little Rock, where he landed and parked his plane. He boarded a 6:00 am Southwest Airlines flight, flew to Love Field, and found Seal was waiting for him.

Reed boarded Seal's Lear jet and at exactly 0800, they were airborne with Reed at the controls in the left-side pilot's seat.

Reed flew the jet to Brownsville, Texas, where they refueled and then he flew to Ilopango Airport in El Salvador and took on more fuel. The next stop was Howard Air Force Base in Panama where they joined up with Seal's CIA contact.

The three of them flew in a Cessna 172 some thirty miles away to a small dirt strip on the banks of the Panama Canal where they landed. They held a clandestine meeting with several other CIA operatives.

According to Reed, they spent the night at the "BOQ" at Howard Air Force Base and the following morning, they had a GI breakfast of "SOS." For the benefit of the militarily challenged, BOQ stands for bachelor officer quarters, which is self-explanatory, and SOS stands for shit-on-a-shingle. SOS is ground-beef gravy on toast. It's a military staple and, with the right seasoning, try Tabasco, it isn't too bad.

After breakfast they flew back to the United States. It was during the flight home that Seal told Reed that he had learned from people in the Medellin Cartel that former President George Bush's sons were involved in drugs. Reed is stunned and very specific about their conversation in the book.

> Seal responded, "Yup, that's what I'm tellin' ya."
> Seal explained that a "guy" in Florida had turned snitch for the DEA and "has got the goods on the Bush boys."

Seal said he had heard it earlier from a reliable Colombia source. He was just sitting on the information, waiting to use it if he ever needed it.

Seal was then supposed to have told Reed "the Republicans. . . the Bush family. . . wanted some stuff transported through Mena and into Arkansas that would end up in the noses of some very prominent Democrats."

Reed is justly flabbergasted by this news, telling Seal it was "heavy shit."

The allegation concerning former President George H. W. Bush's son, Jeb, being involved in cocaine trafficking is discussed in detail in the book, *Blue Thunder*.

The book, written by Thomas Burdick and Charlene Mitchell, was published in 1990, four years before Reed's *Compromised* was published.

Blue Thunder is an investigative report into the brutal murder in Miami of Don Aronow. On February 3, 1987, Aronow, a multi-millionaire and the world's foremost fast-boat designer, was shot dead in his car in front of his office. Aronow was the designer of the Cigarette and Donzi class go-fast boats favored by cocaine smugglers and wealthy skippers with big egos.

The drug allegation involving Jeb Bush originated from the lips of a jailhouse informant named Tommy Teagle. He was convicted in Dade County, Florida for eight counts of drug smuggling. While in prison serving a three-year sentence, Teagle contacted the DEA and claimed to have everything the feds needed to solve the Aronow murder case. He knew where the gun and the getaway car were — and he knew the reason for the Aronow murder.

According to Teagle, a man named Robert "Bobby" Young had stolen eighty kilos of cocaine from Colombian drug kingpins. The Colombians were going to execute Young but decided to give him a chance to live. They showed him a list of names and told him that, if he killed someone on the list, his debt would be erased. Don Aronow's name was on the list.

Teagle told DEA agents that Don Aronow and Jeb Bush were partners in a major cocaine-smuggling operation and they owed their Colombian suppliers $2.5 million. When Jeb and Don refused to pay, Aronow was killed.

The DEA investigated and found irreconcilable discrepancies between Teagle's story and the eyewitness accounts on the killing of Don Aronow. The DEA passed the story on to detectives of the Metro Dade Homicide Unit, who did their own investigation and found Teagle's story to be full of holes.

Teagle was undaunted and still trying for the $100,000 reward and perhaps a reduced sentence. Teagle contacted a local TV reporter and complained that he had risked his life to bring Bobby Young to the attention of investigators. He was being ignored.

Teagle claimed the Aronow case was fixed because of the Jeb Bush connection to Don Aronow and their alleged smuggling operation. The TV reporter called Metro Dade Homicide. The call resulted in more action when detectives held a photo lineup and showed a photograph of Bobby Young to witnesses. None of them could identify Bobby Young as the shooter.

In 1992, *George Bush: The Unauthorized Biography* was published. Written by Webster Griffin Tarpley and Anton Chaitkin, this book contains the same story about Jeb Bush being involved with the Colombian Cartel. The story is identical to the allegations made by Tommy Teagle and, in a footnote, the authors credit the source of the information as the book *Blue Thunder*.

Therefore, at least four years before *Compromised* was published, the story of Jeb Bush's alleged drug involvement with the Colombians was in the public domain and available to anyone ambitious enough to do some research. The fact that the allegations were already circulating because they had been written about in two books would give added "credibility" to Reed's story of his flight on the jet N13SN. This satisfied the conspiracy crowd.

Now the facts: There is documentary evidence that the December 14, 1985, flight could not and did not take place.

Ten months earlier on February 19, 1985, Intercontinental Holding Company of Dade County, Florida repossessed Seal's Lear jet. That is the one with number N13SN that Reed claims he flew on December 14, 1985.

The company had a lien on the jet in the amount of $1,010,102.47. Seal had already pleaded guilty in Miami federal court, so the lien holder feared the plane might be forfeited or seized by the federal government. Two representatives of Intercontinental Holding came to the Baton Rouge airport on February 19, 1985, repossessed the jet and flew it away.

A Federal Aviation Agency (FAA) form, Certificate of Repossession of Encumbered Aircraft, was filed for Lear jet N13SN on February 20, 1985. The date of repossession on the form is February 19, 1985.

John P. Corrigan, president of Intercontinental Holding Company, said he ordered the jet repossessed but lawyers handled the details. Corrigan could not recall much else about the matter except that he got the jet back.

Barry Seal learned of the repossession of his plane on February 20 when he went to the Baton Rouge airport. He intended to fly the jet to Mena, Arkansas. The same day he called the FBI office in New Orleans and reported the plane stolen.

William Bottoms has a vivid recollection of what happened. Seal was going to Miami and had some documents pertaining to the C-131 cargo plane he owned that was scheduled to be inspected by an FAA inspector.

When Seal got to the Baton Rouge airport, the jet was gone, so he sent Emile Camp to Mena in the Piper Seneca. Camp was to deliver the papers to the FAA representative, pick up some other papers Seal needed in Miami, then fly to Fort Smith and take a commercial flight to Miami.

Camp never made it because that afternoon he crashed at Mena. He was killed.

Seal's secretary was interviewed by a reporter and told the same story.

The *Arkansas Gazette* published an article in the June 27, 1988, edition reporting what Dandra Seale, Barry's secretary and no relation, said about the episode.

Seal and Camp were to travel in Seal's Lear jet February 20, 1985, from Baton Rouge to Mena and later to Miami. But when they arrived at the Baton Rouge airport, she said, they found that Seal's jet had been stolen. "He sent Emile in one of his other planes and caught a commercial flight to Miami," she said.

Could author Terry Reed merely be mistaken about years and dates? Not likely. Remember, he said part of the reason he was hired by the CIA was because of his ability to "organize and retain facts and events."

Flying with Seal in a Lear jet to South America to meet the CIA seems like a fairly significant event.

John Cummings, who must believe and defend his co-author, said that Barry Seal had two of everything—and was always changing N numbers on planes.

William Bottoms and "Red" Hall both disagree with Cummings. These two men spent a lot of time in Seal's company. They were pilots; they knew what planes Seal owned or had access to.

They are both certain that Seal had only one Lear jet and that was N13SN. Bottoms said N13SN was never used to run drugs. It was used for rapid transportation of people so there was no need to change the tail N number to disguise its identity.

The Baton Rouge task force did not find that Seal had two Lear jets.

Reed's description of his flight in Seal's Lear jet on December 14, 1985, seems to be a flight of the imagination.

Chapter 26
Slopping Hogs and the FBI Containment At Mena

Compromised had not been published when co-author John Cummings came to Baton Rouge to discuss his investigation of Barry Seal with this writer.

Cummings said he had an "informant" who had been personally associated with Barry Seal. The snitch had been with Seal in Mena and saw him bribe an FBI agent to obstruct the investigation. Seal described it as "slopping hogs."

His informant turned out to be author Terry Reed.

Cummings said he was not going to name the agent in his book. He pointed out that since there were only four FBI agents at Hot Springs, it would become obvious which agent it was. He theorized this would prevent a libel suit because in order to sue Cummings, the agent would have to identify himself.

The alleged "slopping of hogs" was supposed to have taken place at the Mena airport on March 15, 1985. That's when Seal tossed a "package," presumably containing cash, into a car that Reed described as having all the markings of an "undercover FBI car...black-wall tires, little hub caps, and small antennas."

The statement seems somewhat contradictory because an FBI undercover car shouldn't have distinguishing characteristics.

In an effort to prop up their story that Seal's bribe was successful, the authors of *Compromised* presented their readers with a documentary exhibit.

That document is a copy of an FBI memorandum from the Little Rock FBI office to the Records Management Division at FBI headquarters.

The purpose of the memorandum was to notify FBI headquarters that seven serials (pages) were missing from the investigative file of the Fred Hampton case. The serials had been charged out to agent Tom Ross in April and May 1986, almost five years earlier.

By implication, Cummings claims the missing documents are the evidence that FBI agent Tom Ross was the "hog" allegedly covering up for Seal by getting rid of "key" Mena files.

The FBI file system in existence during the time that Seal was being investigated required that every page removed from an investigative file be listed on a charge-out sheet. There were spaces on the charge-out sheet to record the date, the page number, and the name of the agent who removed the page. The charge-out sheet was kept in the front of the investigative file.

The missing serials are identified and listed in the Little Rock memorandum. This means the charge-out sheet must have been in the Hampton investigative file in order for Little Rock to know what was missing.

The first missing document on the list is a form FD-350. Far from being a smoking gun, this form is virtually a blank piece of paper. It is used to mount newspaper clippings so they can become pages in an investigative file. An article is clipped from the newspaper and

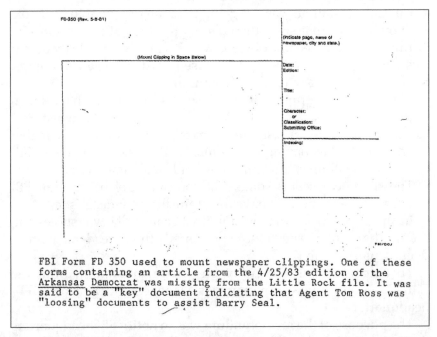

FBI Form FD 350 used to mount newspaper clippings. One of these forms containing an article from the 4/25/83 edition of the Arkansas Democrat was missing from the Little Rock file. It was said to be a "key" document indicating that Agent Tom Ross was "loosing" documents to assist Barry Seal.

This routine Form FD 350 is used to file newspaper clippings and other periodicals involved in investigative files.

mounted on the FD-350. There is a space on the form in which to enter the name and date of the publication where the article appeared.

The memo indicates that the form FD-350 contained an article from the *Arkansas Democrat* of April 25, 1983. True, one can't tell what the article is about, but all one would have to do is go to the offices of the *Democrat* and ask to see a copy of the April 25, 1983, edition. It could probably also be viewed on microfilm at the local library, online, and in archives.

Most likely, the missing document is an article about Fred Hampton or the Mena airport or something similar.

It should be apparent that the loss of a newspaper clipping from an investigative file doesn't conceal material information or cover up anything very significant. The FBI doesn't convict people with newspaper articles.

The other missing serials are six in number—pages 112 through 117. They are copies of Federal Aviation Agency (FAA) records concerning a Piper Navajo and a Cessna, and the registrations and applications of Barry Seal and someone named Jerry Harvey.

Could Jerry Harvey be the same Jerry Lee Harvey who was convicted by the feds in 1977 for leasing an airplane to persons smuggling marijuana?

Here is how he was described in a December 26, 1986, *Sun Sentinel* article by reporter Deborah Petit: a "Fort Lauderdale millionaire and convicted drug smuggler" with "prior criminal involvement and alleged ties to powerful Colombian cocaine lord Pablo Escobar Gaviria."

In any case, FAA aircraft registration and ownership records are public documents that can be obtained from the FAA on request by anyone. They came from the FAA during the course of the investigation and very likely dealt with planes observed at Rich Mountain Aviation. Maybe Jerry Harvey's plane?

None of the missing pages/serials were "key" documents. If they were lost, they would not have concealed anything significant or detrimental to the investigation of Fred Hampton. Their absence from the file doesn't prove Tom Ross was covering up anything for Barry Seal.

How could anyone with an iota of common sense conclude that Ross was destroying documents as part of a cover up when he left the charge out sheet in the file?

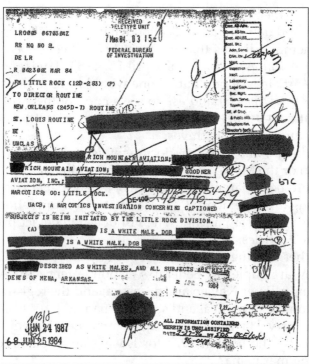

LR0005 06703042Z

RR HQ NO SL

DE LR

R 06230Z MAR 84

FM LITTLE ROCK (12D-283) (P)

TO DIRECTOR ROUTINE

NEW ORLEANS (245D-7) ROUTINE

ST. LOUIS ROUTINE

BT

UNCLAS

RICH MOUNTAIN AVIATION;

RICH MOUNTAIN AVIATION;   GOODNER

AVIATION, INC.;

NARCOTICS; OO: LITTLE ROCK.

UACB, A NARCOTICS INVESTIGATION CONCERNING CAPTIONED

SUBJECTS IS BEING INITIATED BY THE LITTLE ROCK DIVISION.

(A)   IS A WHITE MALE, DOB

               IS A WHITE MALE, DOB

        DESCRIBED AS WHITE MALES, AND ALL SUBJECTS ARE RESI-

DENTS OF MENA, ARKANSAS.

ALL INFORMATION CONTAINED
HEREIN IS UNCLASSIFIED
DATE 2-27-96 BY SDE DCE/cycl

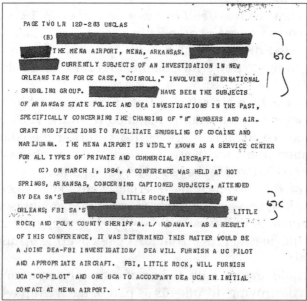

PAGE TWO LR 12D-283 UNCLAS

(B)

        THE MENA AIRPORT, MENA, ARKANSAS.

        CURRENTLY SUBJECTS OF AN INVESTIGATION IN NEW

ORLEANS TASK FORCE CASE, "COINROLL," INVOLVING INTERNATIONAL

SMUGGLING GROUP.   HAVE BEEN THE SUBJECTS

OF ARKANSAS STATE POLICE AND DEA INVESTIGATIONS IN THE PAST,

SPECIFICALLY CONCERNING THE CHANGING OF "N" NUMBERS AND AIR-

CRAFT MODIFICATIONS TO FACILITATE SMUGGLING OF COCAINE AND

MARIJUANA. THE MENA AIRPORT IS WIDELY KNOWN AS A SERVICE CENTER

FOR ALL TYPES OF PRIVATE AND COMMERCIAL AIRCRAFT.

        (C) ON MARCH 1, 1984, A CONFERENCE WAS HELD AT HOT

SPRINGS, ARKANSAS, CONCERNING CAPTIONED SUBJECTS, ATTENDED

BY DEA SA'S   LITTLE ROCK;   NEW

ORLEANS; FBI SA'S   LITTLE

ROCK; AND POLK COUNTY SHERIFF A. L/ HADAWAY. AS A RESULT

OF THIS CONFERENCE, IT WAS DETERMINED THIS MATTER WOULD BE

A JOINT DEA-FBI INVESTIGATION/ DEA WILL FURNISH A UC PILOT

AND APPROPRIATE AIRCRAFT. FBI, LITTLE ROCK, WILL FURNISH

UCA "CO-PILOT" AND ONE UCA TO ACCOMPANY DEA UCA IN INITIAL

CONTACT AT MENA AIRPORT.

FBI agent Tom Ross wrote this teletype detailing undercover operations initiated by the Little Rock office.

(D) INFORMANT EXTREMELY KNOWLEDGABLE CONCERNING THE
MENA AIRPORT OPERATIONS HAS BEEN DEVELOPED BY LITTLE ROCK.
THIS INFORMANT HAS PROVIDED POSITIVE INFORMATION AND IS IN
A POSITION TO FURNISH INTELLIGENCE DATA ON A REGULAR BASIS/
DEA AND ARKANSAS STATE POLICE (ASP) HAVE GATHERED INTELLI-
GENCE DATA FROM THE AIRPORT FOR THE PAST SEVERAL YEARS.
PHYSICAL SURVEILLANCE OF THE MENA AIRPORT HAS PROVEN SOME-
WHAT UNPRODUCTIVE DUE TO THE REMOTENESS AND SPARSE POPULA-
TION OF THE AREA. RANDOM "N" NUMBER CHECKS OF AIRCRAFT
OVER THE PAST SEVERAL WEEKS HAVE RETURNED SEVERAL KNOWN
NARCOTICS TRAFFICKERS.

(E) THROUGH UCA'S CONTACT WITH AIRPORT, RENT AIRCRAFT
HANGAR (TO UTILIZE ONE AIRCRAFT) TO BE USED AS BASE FOR
PURPORTED SMUGGLING OPERATION. UCA GROUND CREW WILL HAVE
PERIODIC CONTACT WITH CAPTIONED SUBJECTS/ AFTER INITIAL
CONTACT BY UCA'S, AIRCRAFT WILL BE UTILIZED TO SUBSTANTIATE
SMUGGLING OPERATION, INCLUDING ███████████ SUBJECTS/ - b7C
WHEN INITIAL OBJECTIVES OBTAINED, IT IS ANTICIPATED THAT
SUBJECTS WILL CONTACT UC PILOTS CONCERNING THEIR INDIVIDUAL
NARCOTICS TRAFFICKING.

UNTIL SUCH TIME AS A "SERIES OF

ELATED" MEETINGS ARE
ACCOMPLISHED WITH CAPTIONED SUBJECTS, SAC, LITTLE ROCK, WILL
NOT DESIGNATE THIS MATTER A GROUP II UCO.

(F) RENTAL OF HANGAR AND "FLY-IN" BY UC PILOTS, CONTACT
WITH SUBJECTS/

(G) INVESTIGATION IN THIS XATTER INSTITUTED THROUGH
CONTACT WITH NEW ORLEANS DIVISION CONCERNING "COINROLL" TASK
FORCE CASE AND ROUTINE CONTACT WITH DEA, ASP, AND INFORMANT
DEVELOPMENT.

BT

That's not much of a cover-up. This is clearly evidenced by the fact that five years later, the Little Rock FBI office was able to determine the paper trail. It found who removed the pages and exactly which serials were missing, described them, and admitted to FBI headquarters and eventually the rest of the world that the pages were missing.

Exhibit 13-1 in *Compromised* is a copy of a memorandum written by Tom Ross on July 19, 1984, to his supervisor, Ronald Kelly. Ross is requesting approval for an undercover operation to be directed against Fred Hampton and Rich Mountain Aviation. The authors for some incomprehensible reason concluded that it was proof that "the FBI in Louisiana, feeling that they were being stonewalled and kept in the dark by their own," decided to conduct a "sting."

This is an absurd conclusion and the proof is a teletype sent on March 6, 1984, by the Little Rock FBI office to FBI headquarters, New Orleans and St. Louis. A copy of this teletype can be found in this chapter.

Although the copy is redacted, the March 6, 1984, teletype is captioned, "Fred L. Hampton, Joseph N. Evans as well as Rich Mountain Aviation 'OO' Little Rock." In FBI parlance, "OO" means "office of origin." The office of origin starts an investigation and has control of it. Tom Ross, the author of exhibit 13-1 and the March 6 teletype, was an agent assigned to the Little Rock division, the office of origin.

It was Tom Ross who was proposing an undercover operation at Mena, not the "FBI in Louisiana."

The teletype begins "UACB," which is FBI-speak for "Unless Advised to the Contrary by the Bureau." It means just what it says: "unless someone at FBI headquarters tells me no, this is what we are going to do in Little Rock."

Ross states very clearly in the March 6 teletype that Hampton and Evans had been the subjects of Arkansas State Police and DEA investigations in the past. They concerned the changing of N numbers and aircraft modifications to facilitate cocaine smuggling.

Ross made reference to the March 1, 1984, conference at Hot Springs involving DEA and FBI agents from Little Rock and New Orleans and Polk County Sheriff A. L. Hadaway. It was decided that Hampton, Evans, and Rich Mountain Aviation would become targets of a joint FBI-DEA undercover investigation. The document disclosed that Little Rock had an informant at the Mena airport who furnished intelligence data on a regular basis. And the Arkansas

State Police and the DEA had been gathering intelligence for several years. The teletype related that random N number checks had identified several known drug traffickers.

Ross ended the March 6 teletype with a brief explanation that UCA (undercover agent) from the DEA and the FBI would be used. The DEA would provide a plane. The fact that this teletype was sent to the New Orleans FBI makes it abundantly clear that agents in Louisiana were not being stonewalled or kept in the dark about what was going on in Mena. Further proof of that fact is contained in the final paragraph (g), which states that the investigation was instituted through contacts with New Orleans concerning the Coinroll task force case.

Exhibit 13-1 in *Compromised* was also supposed to be evidence of an FBI sting directed against CIA assets operating in Mena showing that "crimes are invented to trap people."

Law enforcement officers can't be said to "trap" someone into committing illegal activity when there is evidence they are already involved in it. The illegal activity has to originate, be induced by, or be instigated by law enforcement officers before they can be accused of entrapment. In this instance, government agents already had reliable information that illegal activity was taking place at Rich Mountain Aviation before July 19, 1984, the date of the Ross memo.

The FBI, the DEA, the Arkansas State Police and the Polk County Sheriff were all aware of Seal's smuggling practices. They knew his planes were equipped with illegal fuel bladder tanks. They knew his planes were having their cargo hatches altered. They knew that some N numbers were being changed from time to time. As a matter of fact, William Earl, Jr., flew a Piper Navajo to Rich Mountain in mid-December 1983 to have an illegal fuel bladder installed. That information came to light the day it happened as a result of the Coinroll investigation that was ongoing in Baton Rouge.

The Tom Ross memo is not proof that the FBI was entrapping anybody. His memo and his March 6, 1984, teletype do prove that the FBI and the DEA were actively and aggressively investigating Rich Mountain Aviation, Fred Hampton and Joe Evans. Investigators had developed enough evidence of illegal activity to warrant the costs and risks associated with planning and carrying out an undercover operation.

Reed and Cummings accused the FBI of conspiring to "contain" Bill Duncan's investigation into money laundering and of attempting to protect Rich Mountain Aviation, a company they claim was a CIA "front." Their "evidence" is a statement alleged to have been made to Terry Reed by Oliver North, who was masquerading as "John Cathey." North was supposed to have said he would call "Revell" to see if "they can't fix it." The authors are referring to Oliver B. "Buck" Revell who, in the time frame of the author's allegation, was the FBI executive assistant director for investigations.

In a footnote, the authors claim that Revell was the person North would turn to in times of crises. In an endnote, the reader is told that Terry Reed had a document showing Revell was being briefed on Mena. The document is identified as a confidential FBI telex [sic] dated July 26, 1984, from Little Rock to Assistant Director Revell. Apparently the authors rely on the telex as evidence that there was something insidious and conspiratorial about Revell being told what was going on in Mena because he was the person North turned to in times of crises.

This is sheer speculation, and it ignores the fact that Revell was in charge of all FBI investigations. It was his job to know what was going on in the field, and he was routinely kept well-informed of what was happening in most major FBI investigations, particularly undercover operations. Nevertheless, the telex is claimed to be evidence that Oliver North was interested in Bill Duncan's investigation and had the clout to get Revell to "contain" it and the investigation of Rich Mountain Aviation.

After the details of Seal's Nicaraguan mission had become public, Fred Hampton invited Sheriff Hadaway to a meeting. The meeting was held on July 24, 1984, in the office of Hampton's attorney. A local newspaper reporter was present part of the time.

Hampton showed Hadaway a video of a CNN news report about Seal's flight in the C-123 cargo plane. Hampton told Hadaway that three aircraft then at the Mena airport belonged to the CIA. He was maintaining the planes for the CIA. One of the planes was the C-123 that Seal had used in the undercover operation.

Hadaway told Tom Ross about the meeting and that prompted Ross to send a teletype to FBI headquarters. His teletype is the confidential FBI telex [sic] dated July 26, 1984, from Little Rock to Revell. Although the authors did not include a copy of the telex in Compromised, it can be viewed in this chapter.

Ross sent the teletype to FBI headquarters to the attention of Revell and to New Orleans to the attention of special agent in charge Ed Pistey, under the case title of "Coinroll."

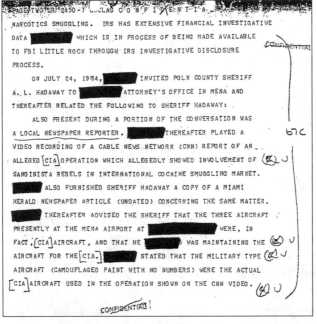

QO 001 2081709Z
QO HQ NO
DE LR
O 26 1700Z JUL 84
FM LITTLE ROCK (245D-7) (12D-283) (P)
TO DIRECTOR IMMEDIATE
    ATTENTION ASSISTANT DIRECTOR REVELL
NEW ORLEANS (245D-7) IMMEDIATE
    ATTENTION SAC PISTEY
BT
UNCLAS C O N F I D E N T I A L
        RICH MOUNTAIN AVIATION; ET AL.; NARCOTICS;
OO: LITTLE ROCK (LR 12D-283).
COINROLL; OO: NEW ORLEANS (NO 245D-7) (LR 245D-7).
    RE LITTLE ROCK TELETYPE TO FBIHQ, MARCH 6, 1984; AND
LITTLE ROCK TELCALLS TO FBIHQ AND NEW ORLEANS, JULY 25 AND
26, 1984.
    FOR INFO OF FBIHQ,   IS SUBJECT IN CAPTIONED
MATTERS WITHIN LITTLE ROCK AND NEW ORLEANS DIVISIONS.
HAS AMASSED
                AT MENA, ARKANSAS, AIRPORT ALLEGEDLY THROUGH

CLASSIFIED BY:
REASON: 1.5
DECLASSIFY ON:

CONFIDENTIAL

PAGE TWO LR 245D-7 UNCLAS C O N F I D E N T I A L
NARCOTICS SMUGGLING. IRS HAS EXTENSIVE FINANCIAL INVESTIGATIVE
DATA   WHICH IS IN PROCESS OF BEING MADE AVAILABLE
TO FBI LITTLE ROCK THROUGH IRS INVESTIGATIVE DISCLOSURE
PROCESS.
    ON JULY 24, 1984,   INVITED POLK COUNTY SHERIFF
A. L. HADAWAY TO   ATTORNEY'S OFFICE IN MENA AND
THEREAFTER RELATED THE FOLLOWING TO SHERIFF HADAWAY:
    ALSO PRESENT DURING A PORTION OF THE CONVERSATION WAS
A LOCAL NEWSPAPER REPORTER.   THEREAFTER PLAYED A
VIDEO RECORDING OF A CABLE NEWS NETWORK (CNN) REPORT OF AN
ALLEGED [CIA] OPERATION WHICH ALLEGEDLY SHOWED INVOLVEMENT OF
SANDINISTA REBELS IN INTERNATIONAL COCAINE SMUGGLING MARKET.
    ALSO FURNISHED SHERIFF HADAWAY A COPY OF A MIAMI
HERALD NEWSPAPER ARTICLE (UNDATED) CONCERNING THE SAME MATTER.
    THEREAFTER ADVISED THE SHERIFF THAT THE THREE AIRCRAFT
PRESENTLY AT THE MENA AIRPORT AT   WERE, IN
FACT, [CIA] AIRCRAFT, AND THAT HE   WAS MAINTAINING THE
AIRCRAFT FOR THE [CIA.]   STATED THAT THE MILITARY TYPE
AIRCRAFT (CAMOUFLAGED PAINT WITH NO NUMBERS) WERE THE ACTUAL
[CIA] AIRCRAFT USED IN THE OPERATION SHOWN ON THE CNN VIDEO.
                CONFIDENTIAL

FBI agent Tom Ross summarized a meeting about topics that included Mena, smuggling, the CIA, and undercover operations.

PAGE THREE LR 245D-7 UNCLAS C O N F I ̶X̶ E N T I A L

IT SHOULD BE NOTED THAT THIS AIRCRAFT WAS OBSERVED, IN CON-
NECTION WITH LITTLE ROCK'S ONGOING INVESTIGATION, AT ████ S
████ ON JULY 19, 1984, AND INDIVIDUAL EXITING THIS AIRCRAFT
WAS BELIEVED TOO BE BARRY SEAL, SUBJECT OF NEW ORLEANS "COINROLL"
INVESTIGATION.

SHERIFF HADAWAY HAS ADVISED ████████ HAS FURNISHED
HIM THIS INFORMATION SO THAT THE SHERIFF AND LAW ENFORCEMENT
OFFICIALS WILL BE AWARE OF ██████ ACTIVITIES WITH THE [CIA]
IN CONNECTION WITH NARCOTICS SMUGGLING.

FBIHQ SHOULD NOTE THAT SHERIFF HADAWAY HAS BEEN
EXTREMELY COOPERATIVE AND HAS WORKED CLOSELY WITH LITTLE
ROCK FBI AND DEA IN MANY SENSITIVE NARCOTICS CASES, SUCH AS
CAPTIONED MATTERS. SHERIFF HADAWAY HAS CONTACTED FBI LITTLE
ROCK WITH ABOVE INFO AND IS CONSIDERING SEIZURE OF AFORE-
MENTIONED THREE AIRCRAFT AS HE DOES NOT BELIEVE THE [CIA]
WOULD OPERATE WITH A PERSON SUCH AS ████ AND FURTHER
THAT IF IT WAS SOME OPERATION WITH THE [CIA] THAT ████
SHOULD NOT BE TELLING EVERYONE ABOUT IT. SHERIFF HADAWAY
OPINES THAT ████ IS ATTEMPTING TO MASQUERADE HIS OWN DRUG
SMUGGLING ACTIVITIES WITH THIS ALLEGED [CIA] CONNECTION.

CONFIDENTIAL

PAGE FOUR LR 245D-7 UNCLAS C O N F I ̶X̶ E N T I A L

LITTLE ROCK DIVISION IN REFERENCED TELCALLS TO NEW
ORLEANS HAS DETERMINED THAT DEA MIAMI MAY BE INVOLVED IN AN
OPERATION WHICH INVOLVES ████ OR INFORMATION PROVIDED BY
████ AND THAT SAC, NEW ORLEANS, HAS BEEN CONTACTED BY
AD REVELL CONCERNING A DEA OPERATION THAT MIGHT INVOLVE
████ WHICH MIGHT LEND SOME CREDENCE TO SOME OF ████
STATEMENTS.

FBIHQ IS REQUESTED TO AFFORD THE AFOREMENTIONED THE
HIGHEST EQUITABLE REVIEW AND THEREAFTER EXPEDITIOUSLY CONTACT
FBI LITTLE ROCK IF ANY OF THE ABOVE INFORMATION FURNISHED
████ IS ACCURATE NOTING SHERIFF'S HADAWAY'S CONTEMPLATED
SEIZURE. LITTLE ROCK IS ALSO DESIROUS OF ANY INFORMATION,
THAT IN THE OPINION OF FBIHQ, WOULD SEVERELY IMPEDE LITTLE
ROCK'S ALREADY EXPENDED INVESTIGATIVE EFFORTS IN THIS MATTER.
LITTLE ROCK HOLDING IN ABEYANCE ALREADY PLANNED UC SA CONTACT
████ IN CONNECTION WITH CAPTIONED LITTLE ROCK
INVESTIGATION. FBIHQ NOTE THAT REFERENCED LITTLE ROCK TELE-
TYPE TO FBIHQ ON MARCH 6, 1984, INITIATED ████ INVES-
TIGATION WHICH HAS BEEN COORDINATED WITH THE NEW ORLEANS
DIVISION WHERE APPROPRIATE.

C BY 9442, DECLY OADR.

CONFIDENTIAL

CONFIDENTIAL

The partially redacted portion of the title is "Fred Hampton dba" Rich Mountain Aviation. The teletype described the July 24 meeting between Hadaway and Hampton and made reference to Little Rock "telcals" to New Orleans July 25 and 26, 1984. This is a reference to several phone calls between Tom Ross and the author to discuss the meeting between Hampton and Hadaway and other aspects of what was unfolding.

Ross also reported that the Little Rock office had learned from telephone calls to New Orleans that the DEA in Miami was engaged in an operation which likely involved Barry Seal And, that the special agent in charge of New Orleans (Ed Pistey) had been contacted by Revell concerning the operation. That might give credence to some of Hampton's statements about the CIA involvement.

All of this information refers to Barry's Nicaragua sting operation. It had become public knowledge around July 17, 1984, and most definitely by July 26, the date the teletype was written.

Agent Ross told FBI headquarters that Little Rock was holding in abeyance a planned undercover contact by an SA (Special Agent) at [redacted name]. The redacted name is "Rich Mountain Aviation" and the undercover operation was the one involving FBI agent and pilot O. T. Eubank. Ross ended his teletype with a virtual plea to "Buck" Revell to find out if the CIA was involved.

It is illogical to contend that the July 26, 1984, teletype is evidence that Buck Revell was involved in a conspiracy with Oliver North to "contain" Duncan and protect a CIA "front" company.

The evidence of how far-fetched this theory is can be found in Buck Revell's answering teletype sent the following day, July 27, 1984. The teletype can be found at the end of this chapter. Cummings and Reed either didn't have a copy of the document—or chose to disregard it.

In his teletype, Buck Revell told New Orleans and Little Rock FBI offices that the DEA and the CIA were told about the claims made by Hampton. Both agencies had responded that neither Fred Hampton nor Rich Mountain Aviation were of any interest to their agencies, Revell wrote. Revell's teletype stated that DEA headquarters was aware that Seal was making representations to some of his associates that he had been cooperating with the government—and that consideration for his cooperation would extend to his associates as well.

CONFIDENTIAL
FEDERAL COMMUNICATIONS CENTER

DATE 7/27/84   CLASSIFICATION C O N F I D E N T I A L   PRECEDENCE PRIORITY

$F190$PP LR NO$DE HQ HO190 HYC$P 272123Z JUL 84

START HERE

FM DIRECTOR FBI

TO FBI LITTLE ROCK {245D-7} {12D-283} PRIORITY

FBI NEW ORLEANS {245D-7} ALL INFORMATION CONTAINED
HEREIN IS UNCLASSIFIED
BT   EXCEPT WHERE SHOWN
                                              OTHERWISE

C O N F I D E N T I A L

2-27-96
CLASSIFIED BY: SPS BCE/GJW
REASON: 1.5 (c)
DECLASSIFY ON: X

[redacted] RICH MOUNTAIN AVIATION; ET AL; NARCOTICS;

OO: LITTLE ROCK {LR 12D-283}

COINROLL; OO: NEW ORLEANS {NO 245D-7} {LR 245D-7}

RELRTEL TO THE BUREAU 7/26/84, AND BUTELCALLS TO

LITTLE ROCK AND NEW ORLEANS, 7/26/84.

BOTH DEA AND [CIA] HEADQUARTERS WERE APPRISED ON 7/26/84 OF

INFORMATION PROVIDED IN RETEL. DEA AND [CIA] HEADQUARTERS EACH

RESPONDED THAT NEITHER SUBJECT, [redacted]

RICH MOUNTAIN AVIATION, MENA, ARKANSAS, WERE OF ANY INTEREST

TO THEIR AGENCY.

DEAHQ RELATED THAT DEA, MIAMI HAS A HIGHLY PLACED SOURCE

ENGAGED IN A VERY SENSITIVE MATTER WHO IS ASSOCIATED WITH

DO NOT TYPE MESSAGE BELOW THIS LINE   12-16954-3

APPROVED BY	DRAFTED BY	DATE	ROOM	TELE EXT.
	JAD:DRH	7/27/84	3018/6	5709

1 - MR. [redacted] {INFO}
1 - MR. REVELL
1 - MR. CLARKE
1 - MR.   SEE NOTE PAGE 3
1 - MR.
1 - MR. [redacted] {DEAHQ}
1 - MR.

JUN 24 1987

FEDERAL BUREAU OF INVESTIGATION
COMMUNICATIONS CENTER
JUL 31 1984
CONFIDENTIAL

DO NOT FILE WITHOUT COMMUNICATIONS STAMP

This message outlines that Barry Seal had said he was cooperating with the
government.

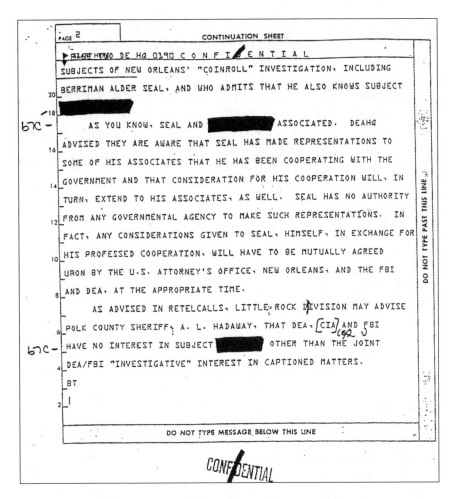

DEA stated that Seal had no authority from any government agency to make such representations. Any consideration given to Seal for his cooperation would have to be mutually agreed upon by the US Attorney, New Orleans, the FBI, and the DEA. Revell ended his teletype by telling Little Rock to tell Hadaway that the DEA, the CIA and the FBI had no interest in Fred Hampton other than the joint DEA-FBI narcotics investigation of him and Rich Mountain Aviation and the investigation as it related to the New Orleans Coinroll case.

Revell's answering teletype made it clear that the CIA had no interest in Fred Hampton or Rich Mountain Aviation. The document sent in July 1984 speaks for itself. It was prepared contemporaneously with the events. This was several years before

Mena or Fred Hampton were of much interest to the media or Congress. It was only about two months after the CIA and Oliver North had to start scrambling to find ways to keep the Contras in the fight against the Sandinistas in Nicaragua.

When the C-123 was shot down over Nicaragua, Oliver North contacted "Buck" Revell to inquire about FBI jurisdiction. Revell told him the FBI would be investigating the export of any weapons and munitions in violation of the Neutrality Act.

North did not ask Revell to stop the investigation, but he did indicate that the investigation could be a problem since it had been involved in another sensitive operation. Revell told North it didn't matter and the FBI was going forward with the investigation.

Several weeks later, North again asked Revell about the investigation and was told that it was continuing. North expressed concern that it might reveal US dealings with the Iranian government on the hostage crisis because some of the activities undertaken to support that initiative involved Southern Air Transport.

Revell figured there was some sort of CIA involvement but repeated himself. He told North that the investigation would continue. At this time, Revell had growing concerns about North's activities at the National Security Council, but he had no indications North was involved in anything illegal. Revell did initiate a limited inquiry to determine if North's dealings with former Air Force General Richard Secord and former CIA employee Glen Robinette might constitute an off-the-books plumbers-style intelligence unit. Revell found nothing at the time to confirm his suspicions. He remained concerned.

Revell's concerns about North were subsequently expressed personally and confidentially to then Marine Corps Commandant General P. X. Kelley. In October 1986, Revell told the general he thought North was in over his head at NSC and should be reassigned before he destroyed his career — or did something to damage or embarrass the Marine Corps.[1]

Revell's actions were not those of someone who was supposed to be Colonel North's "go-to" man in times of crises.

To set the record straight, Buck Revell had this to say about Reed's story: "First and foremost, I never fixed or tried to fix any case during my entire thirty-year career with the FBI. Second, Ollie North never contacted me about Barry Seal and neither I nor anyone under my authority took any action on behalf of Barry Seal.

I had frequent conversations with Ollie North in his role as counter-terrorism coordinator for the National Security Council, but he never mentioned Barry Seal to me. North did contact me on the C-123 crash in Central America and asked me what the bureau's interest was. I told him that it was being investigated by our Miami office as a Neutrality Act case. To the best of my knowledge Ed Enright did not know or have any contact with Ollie North. I was SAC [special agent in charge] in Oklahoma City from January 1978 until November 1979 and I did not know Col. North. I did not know Terry Reed and never received any request from North about him."

The authors of *Compromised* tossed in another FBI document that "clearly outlines the government's concern about pending media exposure of not only the airport [Mena] but refers to Barry Seal as a "CIA operative." The document was a "reconstructed copy" of a barely-legible secret teletype dated August 18, 1987, that was sent by the Chicago FBI office to FBI headquarters and to the Little Rock office. The document was described as a secret telex "divulging CIA activity at Mena."

The Chicago teletype passed on information received by Chicago FBI agent Francis Marrocco from a confidential source. The information he disclosed was that a TV show and the *New York Times* were preparing stories about alleged CIA activities at the Mena airport. Agent Marrocco characterized the information as being about Barry Seal, who was purported to have flown guns to South America from Mena and drugs back. Seal was a DEA informant but also working for the CIA.

In somewhat of an understatement, Marrocco wrote, "Activity at the airstrip has aroused the interest of local law enforcement." The Chicago FBI agent went on to say that attempts to investigate were blocked by the US Attorney. Agent Marrocco ended his teletype by stating it was being furnished to FBI headquarters for information and dissemination to CIA and/or DEA headquarters as deemed appropriate and asked Little Rock to provide Chicago and FBI headquarters with any information they had.

Authors Cummings and Reed apparently intend for the secret Chicago teletype to reveal and prove that the FBI in Chicago was giving a heads-up to the DEA and CIA because of a media investigation into activities at Mena. But does it do that?

Actually, the teletype is nothing more than a short summary of information furnished by a confidential informant. The information was not earth-shattering news and here is why. At the time Marrocco sent the teletype, Fred Hampton was suing the FBI in federal court, the C-123 had been shot down in Nicaragua and the story was all over the media, *20/20,* the news program, had done a thirty-minute segment about the CIA's connection to the aircraft, Barry Seal had testified before a House subcommittee and had been dead and buried for more than a year.

It should be obvious that the DEA and the CIA knew all about Barry Seal and Mena two years before the Chicago teletype was sent. Therefore, there wasn't any need to alert either agency about pending media exposure of anything involving Barry Seal and Mena.

The Little Rock office, in the person of Tom Ross, answered the Chicago teletype on September 18, 1987. The response was a document that the FBI calls an airtel. It is a message sent by regular registered mail that, upon receipt, is treated with the priority of a teletype. A copy of the airtel is included in this chapter. It should put the Chicago teletype in proper perspective.

Ross told FBI headquarters and the Chicago FBI office that the case, Fred Hampton dba Rich Mountain Aviation was placed in "pending inactive status" on March 2, 1987.

FBI cases may be *open* (under active investigation) or *closed* (no investigation is underway), or they may be *pending inactive* (investigation is complete, and the case is waiting prosecution).

The Ross airtel reported that US Attorney J. Michael Fitzhugh, was bringing three witnesses before the grand jury and that subpoenas had been served on them.

Chicago was told that the Mena airport had been under investigation by the FBI since 1983, and it was also the subject of a New Orleans task force investigation. Ross summarized the use of the C-123 by Seal. And, in a noteworthy closing comment, he wrote that Little Rock would base their investigation on activities of Hampton and Rich Mountain Aviation prior to Seal's "judicial blessing."

Ross's comment made it quite clear that the investigation of Fred Hampton and Rich Mountain Aviation would deal with illegal activities that occurred prior to the time Seal became an informant. This would prevent Hampton and Evans from claiming innocence or immunity because they were only assisting Seal in a DEA-sanctioned undercover operation.

IRS investigator Bill Duncan gave testimony to the Kerry

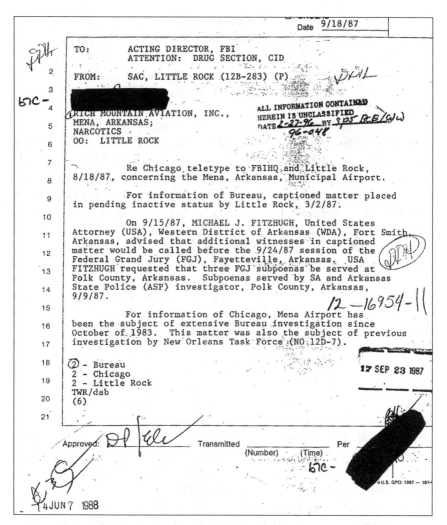

Little Rock FBI agent Tom Ross advised the Chicago FBI office September 18, 1987, that the investigation of Rich Mountain Aviation was placed on inactive status.

Committee and fully disclosed everything he discovered during his investigation. He has testified in other forums on several occasions and he has made statements to the media. In no instance did Bill Duncan claim that the FBI sabotaged his investigation. He didn't raise that complaint to any agents on the Baton Rouge drug task force, to Stan Bardwell, or to Jerry Bize, his local IRS counterpart, when he visited Baton Rouge to review the evidence in the Barry Seal case.

Duncan did complain loudly and frequently. He proved money laundering to the tune of around $300,000 — and no one was prosecuted. Something had to be amiss within the government.

The truth is there was no FBI "containment." There was no prosecution for money laundering because of the decision in the *Larson* case.

If Buck Revell was involved in a conspiracy with Oliver North to "contain" Duncan and protect a CIA "front" company, he would have stepped in when Tom Ross sent his "UACB" teletype to FBI headquarters. Revell was the man in charge of all FBI investigative matters. He had had the authority to have "advised Little Rock to the contrary." He could have brought the investigation in Mena to a screeching halt.

Revell did nothing of the kind. The FBI communications cited by Reed and Cummings do not prove that any "containment" of Duncan's investigation ever took place. What is evident from the various communications cited is that the FBI investigation was underway and in the grand jury phase. And Rich Mountain Aviation and Fred Hampton were of no interest to the CIA.

Further evidence that there was no containment was a teletype sent by Tom Ross to FBI headquarters on October 2, 1985. Ross notified headquarters that the US Attorney in the Western District of Arkansas had reviewed Barry Seal's plea agreement in the Baton Rouge Middle District of Louisiana and been in contact with the US Attorneys in Miami and New Orleans. They saw no reason not to pursue the investigation in the Western District of Arkansas. With the approval of special agent in charge of Little Rock he, Duncan, and Welch would be arriving in New Orleans October 7. They would do a detailed review of the Coinroll files and grand jury material.

It's a fact. The FBI in Little Rock and Tom Ross were going after Seal and his Mena crew for crimes committed in the Western District of Arkansas — around Mena.

Seal's agreements in Florida and Louisiana meant nothing in Arkansas.

Chapter 27
Barry and the Boys

Barry and the Boys, written by TV producer, investigator, writer and promoter Daniel Hopsicker, is another book that purports to be a true account of Barry's exploits.

Like the many-headed hydra, Hopsicker reaches out and takes bites from various rumors and half-truths and tries to stick Seal into the middle of the Kennedy assassination, which is the mother lode for conspiracy aficionados.

Hopsicker has discovered that Barry Seal was to be the getaway pilot for Lee Harvey Oswald.

Wrong.

The first chapter of his book reveals something of Hopsicker's abilities as an investigator and provides insight into what is to follow. He tells us that while he was doing personal research in the newspaper morgue of the Baton Rouge *Advocate*, he struck up a conversation with the librarian. He does not identify the lady by name but describes her as having a "throaty kind of whiskey voice." Hopsicker quotes the librarian as telling him, "My ex-husband, who was 'connected,' told me that too." Hopsicker had just let the cat out of the bag and told the woman his big news that Seal was supposed to fly Oswald's getaway plane out of Dallas after JFK was killed. This is a snippet of the "evidence" gathered by Hopsicker that is supposed to prove that Barry was part and parcel of the Kennedy assassination.

The *Advocate* librarian is Sheila Varnado, and she was not pleased when she was told of the quotes attributed to her by Hopsicker. "I was totally misquoted and I never met him," she said.

Mrs. Varnado said Hopsicker never visited the newspaper morgue. He telephoned her three times and asked her to research some names for him. She did the research and sent him the clip file without charging the usual $75 per hour search fee. "I felt sorry for him," was her reason for the gratis research.

The quotations attributed to her by Hopsicker are "lies and a bunch of baloney," said Varnado. "I never used the word 'connected' with him."

Hopsicker said that Barry Seal worked for the CIA. He named Dave Dixon, a prominent New Orleans French Quarter antique dealer, as Seal's long-time CIA handler.

Dixon said otherwise. He has never worked for the CIA and has never met Barry Seal. In fact Hopsicker never talked to him, he said.

Hopsicker wasn't even accurate when he described this writer as the "special agent in charge of the Middle District of Louisiana Organized Crime Drug Task Force investigation into the Barry Seal drug smuggling organization."

Flattering though it may be, this writer was one FBI agent assigned to the task force along with IRS agent Jerry Bize and DEA agent Charlie Bremer.

Hopsicker knows very well what the writer's role was because it was discussed fully with him during several personal meetings in 1998 in Baton Rouge. The task force was under the direction of the Department of Justice and the man in charge in Baton Rouge was US Attorney Stan Bardwell, aided by Assistant US Attorney Brad Myers. The only "special agent in charge" of anything involving the FBI in Louisiana was Edmund J. "Ed" Pistey. He was special agent in charge of the New Orleans division during the investigation of Barry Seal.

Hopsicker theorizes that Seal was associated with Lee Harvey Oswald when both were members of the Louisiana Civil Air Patrol and came under the tutelage of David Ferrie who is apparently one of "the Boys."

Barry Seal's brother, the late Ben Seal, said publicly that it was he, not Barry, who was a member of the Civil Air Patrol, and Ben was once acquainted with David Ferrie.

The plot thickens when Hopsicker ratchets it up another notch by claiming that David Ferrie was once an FBI agent who spent most of World War II working undercover in South America. This is a totally false statement.

Hopsicker has, either by design or incapacity to comprehend, confused David Ferrie with retired FBI agent Warren C. De Brueys. During his FBI career, De Brueys was assigned to the New Orleans division. He was there in 1963 and was actively involved in the investigation of the Kennedy assassination. He also spent some time working in South America during World War II. He died in December 2013.

After duty in New Orleans, De Brueys became the FBI's special agent in charge in San Juan. When he retired from the FBI in 1977, he moved back to New Orleans where, for a number of years, he headed the New Orleans Metropolitan Crime Commission.

Hopsicker contacted De Brueys while he was investigating Barry Seal, and De Brueys contacted this writer to find out who he was and what he was up to.

In an effort to give credibility to his wild fairytale about Ferrie, Hopsicker quoted this writer as "grudgingly admitting" that he saw Dave Ferrie's name on a list of "disowned agents."

This is more poppycock because no such conversation ever took place. Furthermore, the alleged "disowned agents" list is a figment of Hopsicker's imagination. There is no such list. David Ferrie was never a special agent of the FBI. This kind of nonsense, unfortunately, exemplifies Hopsicker's poor journalistic integrity.

"Trinity Is My Name Too" is the title of one chapter in *Barry and the Boys*. In this chapter, Hopsicker, "using Seal's own records," attempts to prove that his drug profits were laundered through a Louisiana company named Trinity Energy Corp.

As Hopsicker explains it, Seal's attorney and partner, Michael Roy Fugler, sold the "front" company in the spring 1995 to a Miami company named International Realty Group, Inc. for $22 million. To prove it, Hopsicker had apparently eavesdropped on a telephone conversation between "someone" and Fugler's ex-wife. She was aghast and knew nothing of the $22 million sale. The former Mrs. Fugler's lack of knowledge is quite understandable, because the sale never took place. And Roy Fugler was never Barry Seal's partner.

Roy Fugler said the Trinity story is a lie, pure and simple. There was never a sale or merger of Trinity Energy Corp. to International Realty Group, Inc. Trinity was a corporation formed by him for a client, a Baton Rouge businessman, who was attempting to organize an insurance company. To do so, he wanted to acquire a publicly-traded corporation. International Realty was trading over-the-counter and was for sale. A proposal for a merger was made, but the merger never came to fruition. There was no $22 million transaction.

Hopsicker included several other tidbits of information intended to make Roy Fugler look like the grand mogul of money laundering and financial hijinks. Hopsicker wrote of "sifting through the discarded shells of dummy corporations in the musty basement of the Louisiana Secretary of State's office" where he found a "treasure trove of conspiracy lore."

The office of the Secretary of State is located in a relatively new and modern building on Essen Lane in Baton Rouge. The state archives are boxed and stored on high shelves in this air-conditioned building. Corporation records are kept on microfilm and microfiche. One can sit at a microfilm reader in the office and view or print any corporation record that exists. As a matter of fact, the Louisiana corporation records are available on the Internet at the Louisiana Secretary of State's Web site.

Roy Fugler, like a lot of lawyers, has formed many a corporation for a client. Therefore he is frequently listed in the Secretary of State's corporation records as an incorporator or agent.

This is not to say that Fugler did not know Barry Seal—because he did. During his early years in the practice of law, Seal was a client of the law firm that employed Fugler. He occasionally did legal work for Seal. What Fugler *did not* do was put together a corporation to launder Seal's drug money.

Andrew Ezell is a Baton Rouge lawyer. He put together a corporation called Trinity Oil and Gas, Inc., for his client, Dewey Brister. Hopsicker got that right.

However, the "Trinity" associated with Brister is not the "Trinity" associated with Roy Fugler. This is a point Hopsicker grudgingly concedes before taking off on a convoluted tangent trying to link "Trinity" to "Triad" as some kind of secret code word for yet another conspiracy.

Ezell acknowledged that he met Hopsicker at the Holiday Inn in New Orleans. It was news to him that the Holiday Inn was a mob-owned hangout, as Hopsicker claims it was.

Ezell said the meeting with Hopsicker took place against his better judgment. He had a difficult time following where Hopsicker was going with his questions and his comments as well as the story he was trying to tell.

It was also a shock to learn that Andy Ezell was an LSU quarterback in earlier years. Hopsicker can't seem to get it right. Ezell's brother, Billy, was the quarterback for LSU from 1963 to 1965. Andy was the student trainer.

Hopsicker makes other errors, such as continually referring to *Partners in Power* as being written by Sally Denton and Roger

Morris. Sally Denton didn't have a thing to do with that book.

Hopsicker no doubt has the book confused with a *Penthouse* magazine article titled "The Crimes of Mena" that was co-authored by Denton and Morris.

The various conspiracy theories peddled by Hopsicker are based on rumors, insinuation, and the literary eyewink. For example, he tells of his failed efforts to interview Barry Seal's smuggling associate, William Roger Reaves. He tried to interview Reaves at the federal prison facility at Lompoc, California. After a year of trying without success to interview Reaves, he "heard" that Reaves wasn't interested in talking to him. Then he put Debbie Seal on the case, apparently figuring that Reaves would talk to his former partner's widow.

"Incredibly," when they recontacted the Lompoc prison administration, the prison denied ever having him in their facility. He re-contacted the Washington, DC federal locator who had originally given the information where Reaves could be found. He was told Reaves had *never* (emphasis Hopsicker's) been incarcerated in the federal prison system.

The implication is clearly that another government conspiracy is afoot. And Reaves has been spirited away to keep him from spilling some deep, dark government secret to our man, Daniel.

With a single call to Lompoc, this writer was told that William Roger Reaves was paroled to the Los Angeles Federal Parole District on October 9, 1998. He was sentenced to Federal Correctional Institution, Lompoc, from Los Angeles for income tax evasion, among other things.

Seal was convicted in Florida in 1984 in a case involving fake Quaaludes, normally a muscle relaxer. Calvin Briggs of Baton Rouge was working for Seal and was involved in the delivery of the drugs. Briggs was also one of the incorporators of Trinity Oil and Gas. Brister said he did not know that Briggs was involved with Seal in drug smuggling when the first drilling venture was put together and the corporation was formed. However, after he learned who Briggs was, Brister did not let him participate in any further drilling partnerships.

Hopsicker attempted to find Briggs and said he learned from Louisiana law enforcement authorities that he had committed suicide in the "mid-eighties." However, widow Debbie Seal told him she had bumped into Briggs and had lunch with him five years after his supposed demise.

Hopsicker wrote: "If Briggs *were* (emphasis Hopsicker's) dead, he'd be difficult to locate. But if he had merely 'switched' identities he'd be impossible to find, we figured. . . ." [1] Hopsicker seemingly intends to conjure up a vision of Briggs changing identities and going into hiding to protect the secrets of Trinity Oil and Gas. More claptrap.

We wondered why Hopsicker didn't just contact his "throaty-voiced" librarian friend at the Baton Rouge *Advocate* and ask her to check the obituaries. If Hopsicker had done so, he would have learned that Calvin L. Briggs didn't switch identities and disappear. He died May 7, 1995, in Ascension Parish His obituary was published in the *Advocate* on May 10, 1995.

Citing *Partners in Power* to bolster his credibility, Hopsicker said the authors referred to coded records of the Defense Intelligence Agency (DIA) that showed Barry Seal on the payroll in 1982.

Where are the documents? No one, including Roger Morris, has ever produced such documents. What Morris actually wrote on page 392 in *Partners in Power* regarding Seal working for the DIA was this: "coded records reportedly showed him on the payroll beginning in 1982." Morris doesn't name his source and doesn't further explain what the "coded records" were or who had them or how he got to view them. "Reportedly" doesn't prove anything. Show us the documents!

Hopsicker writes of Californian Gene Glick who leased a King Air, N6308F, and several other planes to Seal.

Hopsicker is correct when he wrote that this writer dismissed Glick's importance. He said my dismissal only served to fuel his suspicions. Again, he promoted this writer to special agent in charge of an inter-agency organized crime drug task force looking into Barry Seal's organization back in the middle 1980s.

The Baton Rouge Middle District task force learned about Gene Glick in early 1983 from US Customs agents. Glick came to Baton Rouge on several occasions to meet with Seal. Glick operated Continental Desert Properties and leased King Air N6308F from Ken Miller Aircraft in February 1982. Seal leased the plane from Glick. Hopsicker expressed his suspicions because of what he considered to be a "convoluted" ownership record for the plane. Glick has since died.

Maybe ownership of the King Air was once convoluted—but that was before Barry leased the plane. There wasn't any mystery after Seal leased the plane from Glick. Seal bought the insurance in his own name from a recognized insurance agency. Hopsicker included the letter as an exhibit in his book.

Seal didn't make any effort to conceal his identity as the lessee. He parked the plane at the Baton Rouge airport on many occasions.

The big deal for Hopsicker is that he traced the leased King Air through several ownerships and bankruptcies and into the clutches of the state of Texas. There it was reportedly used on occasion by then-Governor George W. Bush. Ergo! Bush must have been up to his eyeballs with Seal in the drug business — and another conspiracy has been uncovered — thanks to the Hopsicker.

The trouble is, Barry Seal was murdered in 1986. The state of Texas bought N6308F in May 1990. Bush didn't take office until 1995. If he took a ride in the plane as governor, so what?

Barry and the Boys is full of flawed logic, lies, and sensationalism. The book is dedicated to widow Debbie Seal, who provided Hopsicker with a few documents and some limited information.

Anyone who knew Barry knows that Debbie was kept very much out of the loop of her husband's dealings. Rarely, if ever, did Seal discuss his business with her. He issued standing orders to his associates never to discuss his business with her.

Further attesting to the falsehoods, errors, and libel that are found in the book is the fact that by October 2003, Chapter 35 titled "Don't Shoot I'm With Trinity Energy" was pulled in later editions. It happened after Hopsicker was sued by Del Frisco's Steak House. Hopsicker had smeared the restaurant in the missing chapter by, among other things, alleging it was a money laundering operation. In place of 35, a slip of paper has been inserted which states: "A chapter was removed from this book because of the cost of litigation. Free speech is free as long as you have the money to defend it."

In January 2004, attorneys representing Michael Roy Fugler notified Daniel Hopsicker that they were taking legal action against him because of the false, libelous, and slanderous references to Fugler that are found in *Barry and the Boys*.

Hopsicker notified the world about this suit on his *Mad Cow* Web site. The suit was settled in November 2006 when Hopsicker delivered a multi-page letter to Fugler's attorneys in which he retracted his allegations and acknowledged that they were totally fabricated and had no basis in fact.

Roy Fugler had only this to say about the matter: "After the settlement with Daniel Hopsicker, we had several one-on-one conversations, and Daniel expressed almost disbelief that what he had written about me caused such difficulty in my career and life immediately after he published his book. He admitted that he was just trying to get as much sizzle as possible to sell his book without giving much thought to who he might hurt by not having truthful facts and when he got to a dead end or the facts he had were boring just making the rest up. I forgave Daniel a long time ago and moved on. We have had several conversations since our settlement and they have all been cordial and respectful and to the best of my knowledge Daniel has kept his commitments."

According to information on Hopsicker's Mad Cow Web site, *Barry and the Boys* is once again available. "When I wrote *Barry and the Boys* almost ten years ago I had no idea that the story of America's most famous drug smuggler would shortly have relevance to the biggest event of the still-young twenty-first century — the 9/11 attack."

OMG!

Chapter 28
Closing Thoughts

When George H. W. Bush took the oath as president in 1989, he stood in front of the US Capitol and told us he would deal with the drug problem once and for all.

"Take my word," he said. "This scourge will stop." The man who had been Reagan's point man in the drug war made the pledge.

The truth is that Bush's promise to stop the scourge of drugs was no more valid than his other, more famous pronouncement: "Read my lips: no new taxes."

The drug scourge did not stop. America's defeat certainly wasn't the result of a lack of resources. During the eight years Bush was vice president and in charge of the war on drugs, the federal anti-drug budget tripled. And we as a nation had practically nothing to show for it.

The US and China first began prohibiting opium in 1880. By 1906, the federal government tried to limit cocaine, heroin, morphine, cannabis, and alcohol with the Pure Food and Drug Act. Successive administrations, Congress, and federal agencies have all tried regulations and repressive strategies. Most have failed.[1]

Bush's strategy was no different than his predecessors or his successors: more money and more federal agents. In 1983, when the Baton Rouge Middle District Task Force was organized, there were nine FBI agents and five DEA agents assigned to the Baton Rouge offices of their respective agencies. In 2015, the number of FBI agents has almost doubled.

Regardless of how many agents are working drug cases, our war on drugs grows more costly. Drug abuse by casual users and addicts has moved from cocaine to crack cocaine, from Quaaludes to pain pills.

The cost of the war on drugs in fiscal year 2013 was $23.8 billion. In fiscal year 2014, it was $25.2 billion.

And for fiscal year 2015, it is projected to be $25.4 billion, as reported in the National Drug Control Budget, March 2014.

Cocaine smugglers likely used the CIA as cover for some of their operations. As the flow of drugs, particularly cocaine from the Medellin Cartel, mushroomed in the early 1980s, there were signs that some smugglers were using the CIA's covert Contra resupply flights for guns, ammunition, military equipment, and other US aid. Smugglers wanted to protect their cocaine shipments.

DEA Assistant Administrator David Westrate told the US Senate in July 1988 that "people on both sides of the equation were drug traffickers and a couple of them were pretty significant."[2]

The CIA was actively engaged in recruiting pilots and companies to assist in supporting the Contra effort. Langley leadership had to have known or at least suspected that some of their fronts and pilots were trafficking in cocaine at the same time. The agency certainly could have confirmed their suspicions without much difficulty by asking the DEA, Customs, or the FBI to review their files.

However, there was little incentive for the CIA to want to know if cocaine was being hauled by some of their pilots who were also delivering arms and supplies to the Contras.

Such expediency could survive because the CIA could throw a cloak of secrecy around everything they did when the spotlight turned on them. They used secrecy when the agency became subject to criticism, when it circumvented the law, or when it was accused of something outright illegal. The result was a CIA Contra operation that was largely immunized from stringent and effective oversight by Congress and scrutiny from the press.

Therefore, some portion of the blame for the failure of our war on drugs in the 1980s should rest on the shoulders of the Central Intelligence Agency.

The politically-motivated Kerry Committee was characterized by Kentucky Senator Mitch McConnell as being run "like a division of the Dukakis campaign." He was the ranking Republican on the subcommittee.[3]

The committee investigated the CIA's Contra support activities.

Senators learned that a handful of pilots flew both weapons and drug flights while assisting the CIA.

Barry Seal was not one of those pilots.

One pilot was Gerardo Duran, a Costa Rican pilot. He flew for a variety of Contra organizations before US officials insisted that the Contras sever their ties with Duran because of his involvement with drugs.

Gary Wayne Betzner testified that he flew two weapons missions in 1984 from the US to northern Costa Rica. He returned to the US with loads of cocaine. Pilot and suspected drug smuggler Frank Moss flew supply missions for the largest of the Contra groups, FDN, based in Honduras.

William Bottoms provided the Kerry Committee with a complete and candid explanation of what took place at the Mena airport and Barry Seal's smuggling activity.

The Kerry Committee found no evidence that Seal worked for the CIA — or that the Mena airport was a staging base for a CIA-sponsored cocaine smuggling operation organized to generate funds to support the Contras.

Bottoms subsequently provided the same testimony to US Representative Jim Leach and his committee. They were hoping to connect Bill Clinton to the CIA and Barry Seal.

They couldn't connect them.

The idea of using illegal drug money to finance the Contras did appeal to at least one person who was involved in the secret war — Lt. Colonel Oliver North. During his testimony on July 28, 1988, Ron Caffrey said that North "asked me hypothetically" why Barry Seal couldn't just land the plane somewhere and give the Contras the $1.5 million that he was transporting to Pablo Escobar?

However, for North to express a hypothetical desire to filch a million-and-a-half bucks from the drug lords is not the same as running a cocaine smuggling operation out of Mena or the Oval Office. That is what Kerry Committee Democrats hoped to prove.

They couldn't prove it.

The war on drugs launched by President Reagan in 1982 continues in 2015.

If history is any indicator of the future, the drug war will continue and costs will increase. The DEA isn't getting any smaller.

The government and the American people are facing some tough issues.

By June 2015, twenty-three states and the District of Columbia have legalized medical marijuana, according to research group procon.org. It has yet to be determined if a state's legalization of marijuana for medical purposes will prevent the feds from enforcing the US laws.

The federal government regulates drugs through the Controlled Substances Act [21 US Code, Section 811.] The act doesn't recognize the difference between medical and recreational use of marijuana. So far these laws have generally been enforced against persons who grow, possess or distribute large quantities of marijuana.

Who gets to decide how much is a large quantity?

The Drug Policy Alliance is an organization that seeks to promote drug policies grounded in science, compassion, and human rights. Lindsey Lawson Battaglia, policy manager, makes these claims:[4]

Excessive prison sentences do nothing to deter drug crime.

Despite spending billions of dollars, the government hasn't disrupted the supply flow.

People serving mandatory minimum sentences aren't the offenders Congress intended to target.

Battaglia and her organization are advocating for a reduction in mandatory minimum sentences for drug law violations that would lead to billions of dollars in savings. She said a bipartisan coalition in the Senate agree that federal mandatory minimum laws for drug violations need to be reformed.

If she's right, Congress needs to take some action. The people who elected the politicians need to demand that they do so.

The Bureau of Prisons reported on their Web site that as of July 25, 2015, 48 percent of federal prisoners are serving time for drug offenses.

At one point it was decided that a drug czar might be the solution. Our first true drug czar was retired Army General Barry McCaffrey. He traveled to Mexico City in December 1996 to meet with Mexican Army General Jose de Jesus Gutierrez Rebollo to welcome him into the war on drugs as Mexico's new drug czar.

The drug czar generals seemed to hit it off. McCaffrey said General Gutierrez was "a guy of absolute unquestioned integrity."[5]

His integrity was challenged two months later.

In February 1997, the Mexican government arrested General Gutierrez on charges of accepting millions of dollars in bribes to protect Amado Carrillo Fuentes (1956-1997), boss of the Juarez Cocaine Cartel.[6]

In January 2000, czar McCaffrey was on the evening news fronting for then-President Clinton. The president wanted to up the ante to $1.6 billion to fight the drug war—only in Colombia. Bill Clinton's approach was the same solution that has been followed by our government for years: throw more money into the war. And apparently the strategy doesn't work.

In the same month, Jared Kotler, writing for the Associated Press, reported that then-Secretary of State Madeleine Albright was in Cartagena, Colombia. She was trying to convince Colombians that the massive US aid plan was aimed only at fighting drugs.

Something got lost in the translation.

The US aid package included funds for economic development— but the Colombian military was getting most of the dough. Valued at the requested amount of $1.6 billion, the package included attack helicopters, training, and equipment to put two new Colombian army battalions in the field. Their job would be retaking rebel-dominated southern jungle areas so that Colombian anti-narcotics operations could continue.

The plan included training of 3,000 counter-narcotic military personnel and 500 police officers. The army battalions were supposed to provide security while police arrested drug kingpins and traders and dismantled the drug processing labs.

The Colombian aid package was finally approved at $1.3 billion.

McCaffrey was again commanding troops and military hardware in a drug war that was being fought in another country.

Pablo Escobar and Barry Seal are dead.

The Ochoa brothers survived with their drug fortune largely intact. Jorge and Juan David Ochoa were interviewed in a PBS *Frontline* investigative report, *The Drug Wars, Part One.* Their comments were informative, though patently self-serving.

What Jorge Ochoa Said about Barry Seal and Smuggling

Frontline: When you turned yourself in, how much did you confess to having made in the cocaine business?

Jorge Ochoa: I never gave an exact sum. I don't know the exact sum, because you never know what you made or how much you lost.

Frontline: At that point, were you worth $50 million?

Jorge Ochoa: No. No. The big business of the cocaine is for Americans. The ones that make the money are in the United States. [They both admitted they heard of Barry Seal but said he didn't haul their cocaine.]

Frontline: Who was Barry Seal?

Jorge Ochoa: Barry Seal was an American pilot who worked for whoever offered him the most; he worked for the CIA, for the DEA, for the Sandinistas, for the traffickers, for everybody.

Frontline: What was your business with Barry Seal before he became a DEA agent and informer?

Jorge Ochoa: I surely went on some of his routes, but I didn't personally . . . talk with him or pursue. And he didn't work for me exclusively. He was one of those pilots who offered his route. . . .

Frontline: So you paid Barry Seal to run some of your cocaine?

Jorge Ochoa: No, I didn't pay him. I never personally paid him anything. I paid whoever had Barry Seal's route at that time. I don't know who was going to transport or not. I imagine it was Barry Seal. But I never paid him anything personally.

Frontline: But your group used Barry Seal to run your cocaine?

Jorge Ochoa: No. No, there was no group, as I explained. Remember, he supposedly signed with Pablo and the Mexican shipping cocaine, but not with me. I was not there. . . . He was a pilot of cocaine transportation, and I imagine that he didn't know who it belonged to at that moment. I didn't know that it would be him who would take it. One didn't know who it was.

—PBS *Frontline: The Drug Wars, Part One.*

They both blamed Pablo Escobar for the violence associated with trafficking. And they had the gall to claim Seal intimidated them.

Significantly, both of the Ochoa brothers told Americans our war on drugs is a failure. Juan David says it is a failure because as long as there is a demand for illegal drugs and great profits, there will always be a supply. He's no Adam Smith—but he may have a point.

Both advocate legalization and education as the way to end the drug wars.

Jorge said he has a very good opinion of the Americans and feels badly for having been in the drug business. Jorge thinks he has spent more than enough time in jail.

Juan David thinks the United States is a great country and he really loves it.

The cocaine business continues to thrive, notwithstanding all of the resources that have been deployed in the war on drugs. A TV special once proclaimed that the United States, with 5 percent of the world's population, consumes 50 percent of the world's cocaine production. This enormous demand allows the traffickers to generate millions of dollars every week that can be used to corrupt anyone from airline baggage handlers to jury foremen and FBI, Customs, and Homeland Security agents and judges.

Fabio Ochoa was brought to Florida in September 2001 to stand trial on his indictment for his participation in the Medellin Cartel's drug smuggling. He arrived there as a result of an extradition agreement negotiated with the Colombian government.

He faced justice in Florida but not in Louisiana.

Ochoa will never be brought to Baton Rouge to stand trial on the federal indictment brought against him in 1986. He is charged with violating Barry Seal's civil rights by ordering him killed.

The reason Fabio won't be tried in the Baton Rouge Middle District of Louisiana has to do with the Colombian law enacted in 1997 that lifted the ban on the extradition of Colombian citizens.

Fabio's sister, Marta Nieves Ochoa, once claimed that the DEA trumped up charges against her brother because he refused to work as an undercover agent after his release from a Bogota prison in 1996.

In retrospect, you'd think Fabio would have been smart enough to follow Barry Seal's lead—and cut a deal with the DEA a long time ago.

Fabio is now serving a thirty-year sentence but he is still in the news. In June 2014 the Eleventh US Circuit Court of Appeals decided that the lower court should take another look at his claim of ineffective assistance of counsel.[7]

Miguel Velez has also made the news. He's one of the shooters who murdered Seal. He painted a larger-than-life, floor-to-ceiling mural of Christ's crucifixion. The painting adorns the front of the sanctuary of Our Lady of Guadalupe Chapel located on the grounds of Angola State Penitentiary. The artwork was completed in 2014, the twenty-seventh year of the life sentence he received for his part in the murder of Barry Seal.[8]

Death shortened his life sentence at one of the toughest prisons in the US. Velez, 66, died August 25, 2015. Angola Warden Burl Cain said he died in the prison's hospice care unit.

Velez's co-defendants in Seal's murder, Luis Carlos Quintero-Cruz, 62, and Bernardo Vasquez, 61, are serving life sentences. Both are imprisoned in 2015 at the David Wade Correctional Center, located in Homer, Louisiana, in Claiborne Parish, near the Arkansas border.

The drug war has now shifted to a new theater of operations along the border with our Mexican neighbors.

In July 2012, our warriors in the DEA discovered an underground, well-lit, and ventilated drug tunnel running two hundred forty yards from Arizona into Mexico. The tunnel entrance was inside a building in San Luis, Arizona. The forty-eight-inch entrance was blocked by a water tank. The underground passage led to an ice plant in the Mexican state of Sonora.

We have no way of knowing how much cocaine and other drugs flowed through the tunnel into the United States before it was discovered.

In February 2014, dozens of Mexican soldiers and police officers nabbed one of the world's most wanted drug kingpins, Joaquín Guzmán Loera, aka "Shorty." He had dodged capture since escaping from prison in 2001.

Guzman was imprisoned in Altiplano Federal Prison, a Mexican maximum-security prison. He wasn't there for long. On July 11, 2015, the Houdini of the drug kingpins escaped once again.

On Friday, January 8, 2016, "El Chapo" was captured by Mexican Marines after a fierce gun battle that left five dead. At this writing it looks like Guzman may be extradited to the US where he faces indictments in at least seven federal courts on charges that include narcotics trafficking and murder. Too bad Burl Cain retired as warden at Louisiana's Angola Penitentiary January 1. Maybe the feds could cut a deal with Louisiana to take custody of Shorty and be guaranteed that he would not escape.

Our government continues to assist the Colombian government with their efforts to stop drug trafficking. The US—us again—offered a $5 million reward for the capture of Victor "Megateo" Navarro, a former guerrilla fighter turned cocaine trafficker. Colombian police and military forces, including an air strike—the BBC said a bombing attack—killed Navarro in early October 2015.

That's a real war on drugs.

Seal had a good job flying for TWA. He lost it because he thought he could get a nice paycheck moonlighting on a smuggling flight. The cargo wasn't drugs, but it wasn't legal either. Then he started flying drugs—marijuana first, then cocaine. He was good at it. Flying was his passion since age 15 and his profession—both legit and criminally. He loved the adventure. He calculated the risks.

Drug smuggling became his chosen occupation.

His smuggling planes were Piper Navajos equipped with a Panther conversion—four-bladed props, winglets and larger horsepower twin engines fueled by extra tanks. By his own admission, his planes smuggled 20,000 pounds of cocaine into this country.

His chief pilot, William Bottoms says Seal inflated the actual amount to impress the DEA. Bottoms puts it closer to 17,000—and he ought to know.

Whatever the accurate amount is, it was stunning. It put Seal near the top of the list of the all-time great cocaine smugglers of the 1980s.

Seal flew between five or ten trips himself. He planned another twenty-five for Bottoms. None of these drug flights were ever stopped by federal forces.

Seal testified that his smuggling organization grossed somewhere around $50 million—compare that to the billions the US spent on agents, boats, planes and grants to countries where drugs originated.

Seal, Rik Luytjes, Max Mermelstein,, and their compadres have to take part of rap for the cocaine craze that hit the US in the early 1980s.

Their narco-airlines delivered tons of cocaine into the United States. They all did it for profit. Seal loved the adventure.

Their success had to help create and feed the habits of cokeheads who claim to be recreational users and the addicts in this country.

The National Survey on Drug Use and Health estimates that in 2008 "there were 1.9 million current (past-month) cocaine users, of which approximately 359,000 were current crack users. Adults aged 18 to 25 years have a higher rate of current cocaine use than any other age group, with 1.5 percent of young adults reporting past month cocaine use. Overall, men report higher rates of current cocaine use than women," the institute said in 2015.

Barry Seal was an intelligent and talented man. He was a skilled pilot. Seal was careful. He used a pager and dozens of pay phones. His people were given code names. Drugs had code names. A paper shredder churned at his home.

He didn't talk business with wife Debbie. He usually did business by pay phone away from his home.

In one intercepted call, Seal reamed out the male party for calling his house and leaving a message for him with wife Debbie. William Bottoms confirmed that Debbie was kept completely in the dark.

Yet he got caught by DEA. It took the government years to make their case after first learning about Seal's smuggling empire. After his conviction, he turned informant to stay out of prison. Mermelstein and Luytjes did the same thing.

Seal never looked at what he was doing as a business. He didn't smoke or drink alcohol, according to William Bottoms. He didn't seem to use the drugs he smuggled by the ton. He went into drug smuggling as "a vent for a little excitement" in his life.[9]

That's a lame excuse.

As DEA agent Ernst Jacobsen later said, "Barry Seal loved living on the edge. He loved excitement. So when he began working for us, the government and DEA, he enjoyed it."[10]

Seal was a challenge for agents and prosecutors. He was resourceful—pay phones to communicate—information compartmentalized—plane avionics as good as the military. A dedicated task force was the only practical way to go after him.

He resented authority. Yet Seal wielded commanding authority over the people in his organization. He was an egotistical know-it-all. He left people either impressed or turned off by his ego. He could be friendly. He could be abrupt—especially with federal agents. The GS pukes got on his nerves.

The author's first encounter with Seal was in a January 7, 1985 debriefing with fellow task force agents after his plea agreement. Seal was cocky and uncooperative.

After retirement from the FBI, the author's two encounters with Seal were pleasant. Seal was very polite, charming and friendly.

Seal was five feet, nine inches, stocky at 240 pounds, according to his autopsy. Gray streaked his black-brown hair, thinning a bit at the top. Longish sideburns popular in the 1980s framed his portly face. He wore pilot-style sunglasses and favored polo shirts and long pants. In court he usually wore a suit and tie.

Seal lived in upper-middle class Oakbrook subdivision in south Baton Rouge. Ironically, not far from the author. Big homes, big lots, big trees. The Seal family lived in a 3,100 square foot home costing around $25,000. Present day market value is upwards of $400,000.

Oakbrook had only one entrance way in and out-a cul-de-sac. Perfect for a smuggler. Challenging for federal agents on surveillance.

Seal drove a Cadillac and a Chevrolet Monto Carlo. Sometimes his assistant Dandra Seale would drive him. He died in the Cadillac. Wife Debbie drove a yellow Mercedes 480 convertible.

Seal had an organization of aiders and abettors. They functioned in Louisiana, Arkansas, and Florida. And most nations between those states and Colombia. They recovered the airdrops of cocaine. They flew the helicopter that picked up the cocaine. They drove the carloads of cocaine to Florida. They relayed critical phone messages in code words. They bought cashier's checks to launder millions in drug money. They modified and equipped the drug planes and kept them in flying condition. All of them were paid out of the money Seal collected for smuggling. Not all of them were named in this book. Some were given fictitious names. Some were required to testify in front of the grand jury.

None of them were prosecuted.

They know who they are.

The last two years of this writer's FBI career were devoted to the war on drugs. It was new territory. It was challenging. Sometimes it was frustrating. And, as there must be in order to survive, plenty of humor.

It was a great way to end a law enforcement career. A worthy opponent. A good case to work. Good people to work with.

Two generations of FBI agents have come and gone since Operation Coinroll and the Barry Seal case ended.

The FBI's focus changed in the aftermath of 9/11 and the treachery of former FBI agent Robert Hanssen, who pleaded guilty to fifteen counts of espionage for selling US secrets to Russia. The mission and priorities of the FBI have shifted to combating terrorism, both international and domestic, and foreign intelligence threats. They can still make a good drug case.

The oath taken by an FBI agent is still the same. "I will support and defend the Constitution of the United States against all enemies, foreign and domestic; that I will bear true faith and allegiance to the same; that I take this obligation freely, without any mental reservation or purpose of evasion; and that I will well and faithfully discharge the duties of the office on which I am about to enter. So help me God."

Several weeks after Seal's murder, Louisiana Attorney General William J. Guste, Jr. wrote a letter to US Attorney General Ed Meese. It was a "formal request" to the US Department of Justice to "undertake a complete investigation with respect to the government's relationship and handling of informant, Barry Seal."

The questions raised by the government's handling of the Barry Seal case, wrote Guste, were a "cry for investigation." Guste believed an investigation could tell how the government "might better protect valuable witnesses whether they want protection nor not."

Meese never responded.

In April 1986 Louisiana State Police Captain Russell Milan, commander, and Lieutenant Robert L. Thomasson, Jr., deputy commander of narcotics, wrote a letter to David L. Westrate, assistant administrator for operations, DEA. They raised numerous questions about the DEA's handling of Seal as "cooperating defendant." They sent an eight-page letter together with a chronology of events and abstracts of Seal's testimony in two cases they made.

Seal was "cunning, calculating, deadly, and self-serving," they wrote. Seal was "the most manipulative person either of us has ever known."

"We take no pride in the fact that Mr. Seal was murdered on the streets of our capitol [sic] city," and would have preferred to see him incarcerated or under the Witness Protection Program, "which he repeatedly refused to accept," Milan and Thomasson wrote in closing.

Like Guste, Milan and Thomasson never got a response from Westrate.

If Attorney General Meese had launched the investigation requested by Guste, the facts would not have changed one iota.

The DEA, the FBI, federal judges, the US Attorney General—no one—can force a cooperating witness to enter the federal Witness Protection Program.

The US Marshals Service has protected, relocated and given new identities to more than 8,500 witnesses and 9,900 of their family members, since the program began in 1971, according to the agency's Web site reported in 2015. They could have protected Seal.

William Bottoms probably had the best insight into why Barry Seal would not ask for witness protection. Not only was it "too restrictive," he was going to continue smuggling from Costa Rica— maybe for the Mexican cartels and probably using larger and faster airplanes.

Colombian hit men stopped Seal's next career plan in the Salvation Army parking lot.

It was the smuggler's end.

If Barry Seal were alive in 2015, he would be serving time in the federal super maximum security prison known as Administrative Maximum Facility ADMAX Florence, Colorado. He would probably be in lockdown for his own protection from the Colombians.

After Seal's murder, the Baton Rouge *Advocate* published a letter written by his former wife, Barbara.

Excerpts from her letter provide another perspective on Barry

Seal. "I knew the man. I know for a fact more than anything in the world, he wanted to make up to his children, Barry, Lisa, Dean, Aaron and Christina, his mother and brothers, to all society, the great wrong he had done. Despite his seduction into the world of drugs, there was an innocent, sweet quality about him, a bigger than life quality. He had charisma, charm, and a twinkle in his eye and a quick smile for everyone. He had a loud bark but very seldom, if ever, a bite. Adler Berriman Seal, Sr., was simply a human being. He made mistakes and paid dearly for them."[11]

Seal wanted to do right by his kids, Barbara said. Seal wanted to dissuade his kids from hearing that he was a dope peddler, said his attorney Tom Sclafani.

Seal was a generous person. He bought a lot of equipment for his Boy Scout troop, according to William Bottoms. He bought several things for the Salvation Army Halfway House, including a large screen TV, while he served there. He was not religious at heart, yet he put on a show for his family.

"His worst trait was his ego. His best trait was his heart," said William Bottoms. "He loved. He was not violent. He was soft-hearted and generous to the needy. Barry befriended a lot of people and his natural charm and intrigue roused the interest of all he came into contact with — and made him more likeable. He was the most charming host ever and anyone in his presence at any given time would be captivated by him."

He loved his family. He was nice to friends and the public.

Seal valued people with shared experiences: high school, aviation, the smuggling business, even some he met in prison. He went to school with Ken Webb. Seal hired him in the smuggling business. Seal fired him twice and took him back. The gofer could not be trusted.

Seal went to Baton Rouge High with Stan Bardwell, who would become the federal prosecutor he'd face in court. Seal tried to meet Bardwell through a $50,000 intermediary. Bardwell would not meet with him. Seal overestimated his friendship from years before. That was his ego.

When Seal paid, he paid in cash. Cash for planes, boats, airplane avionics. Cash for his crew. For a Piper Seneca, $160,000 cash. Cash for his oldest son's fifteenth birthday, $10,000 in $20 bills, in a paper bag. Cash for old debts. He repaid a Baton Rouge doctor $24,000 for an old loan that helped Seal start his advertising searchlight business. He paid the doctor with cash in a paper bag in Ruby Red's restaurant. DEA agent Dick Gustafson saw the transaction.

Others said they were left holding the bag for smuggling plane work when Seal was murdered. Fred Hampton said Seal owed him $13,000.

Barry Seal did pay an enormous price—and so did society. There is no way to gauge or quantify the damage to the fabric of our society that was caused by the cocaine he and his compatriot smugglers flew into the United States.

Their legacy is one of destroyed lives and corruption.

Tom Cruise will put a new spin on Barry Seal and Mena with a new action film.

As of this writing, shooting has started on the film *Mena* but the project has run into trouble in mid-October 2015.

Lisa Seal Frigon, Seal's daughter from his marriage to Barbara, filed a lawsuit against Universal Pictures, also known as Universal Studios Inc. She claims that her father's third wife, Deborah, Aaron Seal, Christina Seal Warmack and Dean Berriman Seal sold Barry Seal's life story rights to Universal Pictures for $350,000 without court approval or the consent of Seal's estate.

The suit was filed October 14, 2015 in Baton Rouge in 19th Judicial District Court by Frigon as administratrix of the estate. The lawsuit claims *Mena* contains many factual inaccuracies. The film, still in production, has damaged Seal's persona by falsely portraying him, among other things, as a reckless pilot, and a drunkard, the suit claims. The suit seeks to stop the movie, scheduled for debut in 2017, from being released to the public.

Books, some factual, many not, may still be written about this man.

Nothing will change truth of what he did.

Barry Seal is buried in Greenoaks Memorial Park, in Baton Rouge. His father, Benjamin Curtis Seal, Sr., mother Mary Lou Seal, and his brother Benjamin Curtis Seal, Jr., are buried there. His brother Wendell Kirk Seal chose cremation and wanted his ashes scattered on the river near his home.

All grave markers are bronze plaques set flush to the ground. Vases for flowers are provided. No ornate statutes or headstones are permitted. On All Saints Day each November, the entire expanse of the cemetery is alive with color from flowers placed on graves.

Readers can decide if, as is written on his gravestone, Barry Seal was a "rebel adventurer the likes of whom, in previous days, made America great."

Where Are They Now
Key Characters in *Smuggler's End* as of October 2015

Stanford "Stan" Bardwell — Private law practice in Baton Rouge.

Wayne "Buzz" Barlow — Retired.

Jerry Bize — Retired and playing golf.

Barbara Bottoms — Barry Seal's first wife, and mother of their two children. Living in Louisiana.

William Bottoms — Living in Louisiana.

Charles Bremer — Retired.

Jim B. Brown — Retired.

Prem Burns — Retired as East Baton Rouge Parish Assistant District Attorney and serving as a special counsel.

Calvin L. Briggs — Didn't switch identities and disappear as another author suggested. He died May 7, 1995, in Ascension Parish, Louisiana.

Captain Wonderful — Barry Seal's boat sold for $40,000 by the IRS to apply against his tax debt.

Emile Camp — Killed in a plane crash near Mena airport Feb. 19, 1984.

John Camp — Living in Louisiana.

Jack Crittenden — Deceased.

Luis Carlos Quintero-Cruz — age 62, is serving life prison sentence in David Wade Correctional Center in August 2015. He was convicted of the murder of Barry Seal.

Eddie Duffard — Deceased.

Warren C. De Brueys — Deceased December 2013.

William Duncan — Retired.

Ed Enright — Retired.

Rex Eggleston — Whereabouts unknown.

Pablo Escobar — Deceased December 12, 1993.

Oscar T. Eubank — Retired.

Joseph Nevil Evans — Deceased.

Rudy Ferguson — Retired.

J. Michael Fitzhugh — Judge, Arkansas Twelfth Circuit.

Lisa Seal Frigon, Seal's daughter from his marriage to Barbara, filed a lawsuit In October 2015 against Universal Pictures disputing life story rights about Barry Seal.

Gene Glick — operated Continental Desert Properties and leased King Air N6308F from Ken Miller Aircraft in February 1982 and later to Barry Seal. Deceased.

Dick Gustafson — Retired.

Joaquin "Shorty" Guzman — Guzman was captured January 8, 2016 in a gun battle that left five dead.

A.L. Hadaway — Sheriff of Polk County, Arkansas, including Mena and the airport. Retired.

Homer "Red" Hall — Deceased.

Fred Hampton — Retired.

Clint Hebert — Deceased.

Ernst Jacobsen — Retired.

Bob Joura — Retired.

Charles S. Koon — Deceased.

John Lawn — Retired.

Lauren Lee — Barry Seal's boat was sold for $100,000 by the IRS to apply against his tax debt.

Frederik J. "Rik" Luytjes — Living, whereabouts unknown.

Bradley C. Myers — Private law practice in Baton Rouge.

Russell "Butch" Milan — Retired.

Francis "Bud" Mullen — Named administrator of the DEA by President Reagan. Retired.

Oliver North — Host of TV show *War Stories* and Fox News contributor.

Fabio Ochoa — Now serving a thirty-year sentence. In June 2014 the 11th US Circuit Court of Appeals decided that the lower court should take another look at his claim of ineffective counsel.

Juan David Ochoa — Deceased. July 25, 2013.

Jerry Phipps — Deceased.

Ed Pistey — special agent in charge FBI, New Orleans. Retired.

Frank J. Polozola — Judge. Deceased February 24, 2013. He was 71.

Terry Reed — Living in Missouri.

William Roger Reaves — joined Barry Seal in the smuggling business in 1980. In 2014 he was in prison in Australia on drug conviction.

Oliver B. "Buck" Revell — Retired.

Tom Ross — Retired.

Norman Charles Roettger, Jr. — Deceased. July 26, 2003. Was an American lawyer and judge.

Thomas D. Sclafani — Private law practice in Florida.

Barbara Seal — Living in Louisiana.

Benjamin C. Seal, Jr. — Barry Seal's brother. Deceased August 24, 2014.

Deborah Ann DuBois Seal — Married Barry Seal in November 1974 as his third wife. They had three children at the time of his death in 1986. Living in Louisiana.

Wendell K. Seal — Barry Seal's brother. Deceased Sept. 21, 2007.

Dandra Seale — Living in Louisiana.

Bob Seville. — Retired.

Mickey Tolliver — Deceased.

Lewis O. Unglesby — Private law practice in Baton Rouge with his son Lance.

Bernardo Vasquez — 61, is serving life prison sentence in David Wade Correctional Center in August 2015. He was convicted of the murder of Barry Seal.

Miguel Velez — Convicted in Barry Seal's murder. Died August 25, 2015, in Angola State Penitentiary serving a life sentence. He painted a larger-than-life, floor-to-ceiling mural of Christ's crucifixion in the sanctuary of Our Lady of Guadalupe Chapel located on the grounds of Angola State Penitentiary.

Ken Webb. Whereabouts unknown. Seal hired him in the smuggling business.

Russell Welch — Retired.

William "Rut" Whittington — Was superintendent of the Louisiana State Police. Retired.

Albert J. Winters — Deceased June 28, 2013.

Notes

Chapter 3: First Arrest
1. *US versus Kessler, Seal. et al* 530 F 2d. 1246. Diosdado's testimony is discussed.

Chapter 4: The War on Drugs
1. Shannon, Elaine. *Desperados*, (New York: Viking, 1988), 104-105.
2. Max Mermelstein as told to Robin Moore and Richard Smitten. *The Man Who Made It Snow* (New York: Simon and Schuster, 1990), 112.
3. Paul Eddy with Hugo Sabgol and Sara Walden. *The Cocaine Wars*, (New York: Bantam Books, 1989), 79.
4. Ibid., 79.
5. Ibid.
6. Ibid., 80.
7. *The Cocaine Wars*, 80.
8. Ibid., 80.
9. Ibid.
10. Ibid., 81.
11. *Desperados*, 88.
12. Rice, Berkeley. *Trafficking*, (New York: Charles Scribner's Sons, 1989) 147.
13. John Bennett writing for the Scripps Howard News Service reprinted Jan. 7, 1985 in the Baton Rouge *Advocate*.
14. *Cocaine Wars*, 81-83.
15. Porter, Bruce. *Blow*, (New York: Harper-Collins Publishers, 1993), 257.

Chapter 5: The Target and Little Rock
1. *Jack W. Crittenden versus John Camp, Louisiana Television Broadcasting Corporation dba WBRZ-TV Channel 2, et al.* Case 284,689 G, 19th Judicial Court, Parish of East Baton Rouge, Louisiana. Deposition of James Kenneth Webb, July 22, 1985, 14.

Chapter 8: Seal Cuts a Deal
1. Gugliotta, Guy and Jeff Leen. *Kings of Cocaine* (New York: Harper & Row, New York, 1989), 245.
2. Max Mermelstein as told to Robin Moore and Richard Smith, *The Man Who Made It Snow*, (New York: Simon and Schuster, 1990), 243.

Chapter 9: The Nicaragua and Las Vegas Missions

1. *The Cocaine Wars*, 296.
2. Ibid., 296.
3. *US versus Adler Berriman Seal*, Southern District of Florida, Case No. 83-6038 Motion for Reduction of Sentence, 7.
4. *The Cocaine Wars*, 197.
5. CIA Inspector General's Report, 96-0143-IG Volume II. Allegations of Connections between CIA and the Contras in Cocaine Trafficking.
6. *US versus Reyes*, testimony of Adler Berriman Seal, 23.

Chapter 10: Continuing Criminal Enterprise

1. *United States of America, Plaintiff versus James Edward Eakes, Defendant Appellant*, 783 F2d 499 (Feb.19, 1986) Paragraph 39.

Chapter 11: Counterattacks

1. *Jack W. Crittenden versus John Camp, Louisiana Television, dba WBRZ-TV Channel 2, Adler Barry Seal*. Number 284,689, Division G, 19th Judicial District Court, East Baton Rouge Parish, Louisiana. Deposition of James Kenneth Webb taken July 22, 1985, 29-30.
2. *Fred Hampton; Joe Evans and Richmountain Aviation, Inc. versus A.L. Hadaway, Polk County Sheriff, et al.* US District Court, Eastern District of Arkansas, Fort Smith Division No. 84-2368. Filed Dec. 24, 1984.

Chapter 12: The Middle District of Louisiana Plea Agreement

1. *Jack W. Crittenden versus John Camp et al.* Case 284,689 G, 19th Judicial Court, Parish of East Baton Rouge, Louisiana. Deposition of James Kenneth Webb, July 22, 1985, 14.
2. Documents. Excerpts from the interview of Barry Seal on December 27, 1985 at Baton Rouge, Louisiana by William Duncan, IRS and Russell Welch, Arkansas State Police in the presence of Lewis Unglesby, attorney for Seal. Series 2, Box 9, Arkansas Special Committee Records, Special Collections Division, University of Arkansas Libraries, Fayetteville.

Chapter 13: Air Max and Air Rik

1. Rice, Berkley. *Trafficking, The Boom and Bust of the Air America Cocaine Ring.* (New York: Charles Scribner's Sons, 1989) 26.
2. Ibid., 9.
3. Ibid., 37.
4. Ibid., 33.
5. Ibid., 52.
6. Ibid., 34.
7. Ibid., 212.
8. Ibid., 90.
9. Ibid., 69-70.

10. Ibid., 3-4.

11. Ibid., 4.

12. Ibid., 182.

13. Ibid., 181.

14. Ibid., 34.

15. Ibid., 189.

16. Ibid., 206.

17. Ibid., 229.

18. Max Mermelstein as told to Robin Moore and Richard Smitten. *The Man Who Made It Snow*. (New York: Simon and Schuster, 1990), 121.

19. Ibid., 195.

20. Ibid., 243.

21. *Trafficking*, 257.

22. Ibid., 258

Chapter 16: "Murder Most Foul"

1. Gray, Mike. *Drug Crazy*, (New York: Random House, 1998), 119.

2. Ibid., 194-195, 224.

3. Ibid., 202.

4. *Swanner versus United States*, 309 F Supp. 1183 (1970).

Chapter 17: The Crimes of Mena

1. Cate, Michael. Extracts from Mena Centennial History 1896-1996, A Photographic History of Mena, Arkansas.

2. Senate Committee Report on Drugs, Law Enforcement and Foreign Policy, Senator John F. Kerry, Chairman. The Kerry Report.

3. Investigator's Notes, Russell Welch, 11/5/85, Box 2, File 6, Arkansas Special Committee Records, Special Collections Division, University of Arkansas, Fayetteville.

4. The sworn testimony of Jim Neugent in the investigation of Freddie Lee Hampton, d/b/a Rich Mountain Aviation, Mena, AR. William C. Duncan, Special Agent, IRS. Series 2, Box 9, Arkansas Special Committee Records, Special Collections Division, University of Arkansas Libraries, Fayetteville.

5. *US versus. Larson*, 796 Fd2 244, 8th Circuit, (1986).

6. *US versus Anzalone*, 766 F2d 676 (1st Circuit July 1, 1985); *US versus Varbel*, 780 F2d 758 (9th Circuit Jan. 10, 1986); *US versus Dela Espriella* 781 F2d 1432 (9th Circuit Feb. 10, 1986) and *US versus Denemark*, 779 F2d 1559 (11th Circuit Jan 16, 1986.).

7. Joint Investigation by the Arkansas State Attorney General's Office and the United States Congress, the Oral Deposition of William C. Duncan. Appearances: William Alexander, US Congress; Winston Bryant, Attorney General, State of Arkansas. Buseman Court Reporting, Inc. Little Rock, Arkansas, 13-14.

8. Hearing before the House Subcommittee on Commerce, Consumer, and Monetary Affairs of the House Committee on Government Operations, House of Representatives, One Hundred Second Congress, First Session, July 24, 1991. 85-86.

Chapter 20: Congress Investigates

1. Cockburn, Alexander and Jeffrey St Clair. *Whiteout* (London, New York: Verso 1998), 32.
2. Peter Kornbluh and Malcolm Byrne. *The Iran-Contra Scandal: The Declassified History* (New York: The New Press, 1993), 122-123.
3, Ibid., 398.
4. Walsh, Lawrence E. *Firewall*, The Iran-Contra Conspiracy and Cover-Up (New York: W. W. Norton & Co., 1997), 76.
5. *Frontline* Series, "*Drug Wars, Part 1*" Produced by Brooke Runnette and Martin Smith. Aired Oct. 9, 2000.

Chapter 21: "I Have No Knowledge . . ."

1. *US versus Reyes*, Testimony of Adler B. Seal, 349.
2. Ibid. 351.
3. Report of Investigation. Unclassified Summary of Investigation Regarding Purported CIA Activities at or Around Mena, Arkansas and Related Topics. November 8, 1996. Frederick P. Hitz, Inspector General, CIA. Paragraph 10.

Chapter 22: The Christic Institute

1. John Semien, in the Baton Rouge *Advocate*, April 24, 1987.
2. Olson, Barbara. *Hell to Pay*, (Washington, DC: Regnery Publishing, Inc., 1999), 133.
3. Declaration of Plaintiff's Counsel, Case 86-1146, Southern District of Florida, *Tony Avirgan, Martha Honey versus John Hull, et al.* 200.
4. Sheehan, Daniel, *The People's Advocate,* (Berkeley: Counterpoint, 2013), 546.

Chapter 23: Mister Wheaton

1. Singlaub, John K. with Malcolm McConnell. *Hazardous Duty*, (New York: Simon & Schuster, New York, 1991) 515.
2. Hauck, Susan *Legal Terrorism, The Truth about the Christic Institute* (New World Publishing, Ltd., 1989), 139.
3. Bohning, Don from his article "*Distorting History*" published in *The Intelligencer*, Volume 16, Number 2, fall 2008, 73.
4. Sheehan, Daniel, *The People's Advocate, The Life and Legal History of America's Most Fearless Public Interest Lawyer.* (Berkeley: Counterpoint, 2013), 465.

Chapter 24: Terry Reed versus *Time* Magazine

1. Oversight Hearings before the Subcommittee on Crime of the Committee on the Judiciary, House of Representatives, One Hundredth Congress,

Second Session July 28, September 23, 29 and October 5,1988, US Gov. Printing Office, Document Y 4J 89/1:100/138, 249-254.

2. North, Oliver with William Novak. *Under Fire*, (New York: Harper Collins, 1991), 36.

3. Wroe, Ann. *Lives, Lies & The Iran-Contra Affair*, (New York: I.B. Tauris & Co. Ltd. London, 1991), 35

Chapter 26: Slopping the Hogs
1. Oliver "Buck" Revell and Dwight Williams. *A G-Man's Journal*, (New York: Simon & Schuster, Inc., 1998), 253-257.

Chapter 27: Barry and the Boys
1. Hopsicker, Daniel, *Barry and the Boys*, (Mad Cow Press, LLC, 2001), 378.

Chapter 28: Closing Thoughts
1. Kerry Committee Report on Drugs, Law Enforcement and Foreign Policy.

2. Ibid.

3. Fontova, Humberto, *Don't Forget The Kerry Committee*, Aug. 20, 2004, as reported by NewsMax.com October 14, 2004

4. Battaglia, Lindsey Lawson, "Will the U.S. Senate Finally Reform Harsh Mandatory Minimum Sentences for Drugs?" March 20, 2015, Drug Policy Web site.

5. Preston, Julia, "A General in Mexico's Drug War Is Dismissed," *New York Times*, February 19, 1997.

6. Wilkinson, Tracy, "Former Mexican Drug Czar Convicted of Aiding Cartel Dies at 79," *Los Angeles Times*, December 19, 2013.

7. *Fabio Ochoa versus United States*. US Court of Appeals 11th Circuit, June 24, 2014. No. 11-15620. Appeal from the US District Court from the Southern District of Florida. law.justia.com

8. *"Inmates complete prison's new Catholic chapel in 38 days,"* by Mark H. Hunter, Baton Rouge *Advocate*, February 22, 2014.

9. *United States versus Reyes, Orosco, Ravelo, et al.* US District Court, District of Nevada. Testimony of Adler B. Seal, August 19, 1985. 205, 443-444.

10. *Frontline*, WGBH Educational Foundation, *"The Godfather of Cocaine"* Produced by William Cran and Stephanie Tepper. Written and directed by William Cran. Aired March 25, 1997.

11. Baton Rouge *Advocate*, March 3, 1986, *Your Views*, 6B.

Bibliography

Albert, Steve, *The Case against the General*, Charles Scribner's Sons, New York, 1993.

Avirgan, Tony, Martha Honey and the Christic Institute as told to Joyce Barber and Thomas Yeats, *Flashpoint – The La Penca Bombing*, Eclipse Books, Forestville, California, 1989.

Baum, Dan, *Smoke and Mirrors*, Little, Brown and Company, New York, 1996.

Cockburn, Alexander, Jeffery St. Clair, *White Out*, Verso, London and New York, 1998.

Eddy, Paul, *The Cocaine Wars*, with Hugo Sabinal and Sara Walden, W.W. Norton & Company, New York, 1988.

Fonzi, Gaeton, *The Last Investigation*, Thunder's Mouth Press, New York, 1993.

Gray, Mike, *Drug Crazy*, Random House, New York, 1998.

Gugliotta, Guy and Jeff Leen, *Kings of Cocaine*, Harper & Row Publishers, New York, 1989.

Hauck, Susan Dr., *Legal Terrorism the Truth about the Christic Institute*, New World Publishing, 1989.

Peter Kornbluh and Malcolm Byrne. *The Iran-Contra Scandal: The Declassified History*, The New Press, New York, 1993.

Leveritt, Mara, *The Boys on the Tracks*, St Martin's Press, New York, 1999.

Levine, Michael with Lauram Kavanau-Levine, *The Big White Lie*, Thunder's Mouth Press, New York, 1993.

Mallard Press, *NAM, The Vietnam Experience*, New York, 1990.

McClintick, David, *Swordfish*, Pantheon Books, New York, 1993.

McCoy, Alfred W., *The Politics of Heroin*, Lawrence Hill Books, New York, 1991.

Mermelstein, Max as told to Robin Moore and Richard Smith *The Man Who Made It Snow*, Simon and Schuster, New York, 1990.

North, Oliver L. with William Novak, *Under Fire*, Harper Collins, New York, 1991.

Olson, Barbara, *Hell To Pay*, Regnery Publishing, Inc., Washington, DC, 1999.

Oversight Hearings before the Subcommittee on Crime of the Committee on the Judiciary, House of Representatives, One Hundredth Congress, Second Session, July 28, September 23, 29 and October 5, 1988. US Government Printing Office, Superintendent of Documents, Doc. Y4J89/1:100/138

Porter, Bruce, *Blow*, Harper-Collins Publishers, New York, 1993.

Revell, Oliver "Buck" and Dwight Williams, *A G-Man's Journal*, Pocket Books, a division of Simon & Schuster, New York, 1998.

Rice, Berkeley, *Trafficking, The Boom and Bust of the Air America Cocaine Ring*. Charles Scribner's Sons, New York, 1989.

Scott, Peter Dale and Jonathan Marshal, *Cocaine Politics*, University of California Press, Berkeley, California, 1991.

Shannon, Elaine, *Desperados*, Viking, New York, 1988.

Strong, Arturo Carrillo, *Corrido de Cocaine*, Harbinger House. Tucson, Arizona, 1990.

Walsh, Lawrence E. *Firewall, The Iran-Contra Conspiracy and Cover-Up*. W.W. Norton & Co., New York, London, 1997.

Webb, Gary, *Dark Alliance*, Seven Stories Press, New York, 1998.

Wroe, Ann, *Lives, Lies & The Iran-Contra Affair*, I. B. Tauris & Co., Ltd., London-New York, 1991.

Index